Two Ways Out of Whitman

I hear America singing, the varied carols I hear
— Walt Whitman

Also by Donald Davie from Carcanet

POETRY

Selected Poems

To Scorch or Freeze

Collected Poems

Poems & Melodramas

CRITICISM

*Under Briggflatts: a history of
poetry in Great Britain 1960–1985*

*Slavic Excursions: essays on
Polish and Russian literature*

Studies in Ezra Pound

*Older Masters: essays and reflections on
English and American literature*

Essays in Dissent

*With the Grain: essays on Thomas Hardy
and modern British poetry*

AUTOBIOGRAPHY

These the Companions

Two Ways Out of Whitman

DONALD DAVIE

CARCANET

First published in Great Britain in 2000 by
Carcanet Press Limited
4th Floor, Conavon Court
12–16 Blackfriars Street
Manchester M3 5BQ

Essays copyright © The Estate of Donald Davie 2000
Introduction and selection copyright © Doreen Davie 2000

ISBN 1 85754 460 9

The publisher acknowledges financial assistance
from the Arts Council of England.

Funded by
THE
ARTS
COUNCIL
OF ENGLAND

Set in 10pt Bembo by XL Publishing Services, Tiverton
Printed and bound in England by SRP Ltd, Exeter

To the grandchildren
Peter, Jonathan, Joseph,
Christopher, Beth, Emma

Acknowledgements

I am most grateful to Vincent Giroud, Curator of the Beinecke Rare Book and Manuscript Library, Yale University, and to his staff. Their helpfulness during my weeks working through the Davie archive made it a pleasant task. Also, to Marice Wolfe, Head of Special Collections of The Jean and Alexander Heard Library, Vanderbilt University, whose anticipation of my visit greatly helped speed my search through the Davie archive deposited there.

I wish to express my warmest thanks to my son, Mark Davie, for his interest and guidance throughout this undertaking, and to Birgit de Gennaro for her friendship and generous hospitality during my stay in New Haven.

Contents

Introduction

Donald Davie's lifelong interest in American writing, and especially in American poetry, began soon after his return to Cambridge, after service in the Royal Navy during the Second World War. He has recounted how he discovered a copy of Winters's *In Defense of Reason* in the library of the Cambridge Union, and wrote to Winters with admiring enthusiasm. Winters,

> with characteristic generosity, then maintained a correspondence with this unknown neophyte from the other side of the world. I learned much from Winters – about how to live, as well as how to read and write. For present purposes I shall isolate one debt that I have to him: he alone, through his printed writings as well as his letters, educated me as regards poetic rhythm and poetic metre, and the relations between them. This will be thought a narrowly technical matter; but it is one of the peculiarities of poetry, as of the other fine arts, that what seem to be considerations merely of technique turn out to have far-reaching implications stretching even to one's sense of the cosmos, of its unity and its rationality. The numbering of syllables – on the fingers if necessary – witnesses ultimately to a conviction that the mathematician's account of the cosmos, and the poet's, are not at odds.[1]

In 'The Canon', the first essay in this Collection, Davie discusses the difference between English and American poetry. United by their common language, when did poetry in the United States become not English but *American* poetry; did Cultural Independence coincide with Political Independence, in 1776? He notes that in the mid-nineteenth century Ralph Waldo Emerson regretted that his country was still striving towards such cultural independence, though he could praise Walt Whitman for having achieved just that. It is true that most American writers were slow to break free from British models but Walt Whitman casts a long shadow, and in this volume Davie considers the works of American poets who come after the nineteenth-century poet and how their poetry has moved away from British influence. William Carlos

Williams has been a dominant influence in this, for his declared intention was to break free of British precedents. His lively correspondence with his friend Ezra Pound continued throughout his life, and from that correspondence there emerged a style of poetry that might be described as a combination of Williams's speech-as-verse and Pound's imagism. It attracted many followers, leading towards just such a tradition as sought by Williams. Nevertheless, his influence was not without controversy, as any reader of these pages will observe – witness Davie's startling attack in 'A Demurral', an essay written as late as 1987.

In the essay that follows 'The Canon', however, Davie is concerned to bring the work of William Carlos Williams to the attention of a wider readership. 'My purpose is straightforward: to get known and read in England two American books which are, as far as I can see, little known and little read' is his opening sentence. The two books are *In the American Grain* by William Carlos Williams, and *The Invasion* by Janet Lewis. He goes on to discuss the differences between the two cultures, British and American, and to explore the reasons for this. Though *The Invasion* and *In The American Grain* are prose-pieces, both authors are esteemed poets, and, beyond the subject-matter, Davie gives the writing the same scrupulous attention that he would give to the reading of their poems.

Winters's influence can be discerned in many of the essays collected here. In 'Arthur Yvor Winters', Davie looks back over the life of Winters-as-critic, his assessments and discriminating judgements. It was Robert Lowell who testified that for his generation it was Winters's praise of Williams that at a crucial time tipped the balance of critical opinion in Williams's favour. Together with Williams, Lowell has been a prominent figure in American poetry since Whitman. He is the acclaimed trend-setter for 'confessional' poetry, drawing many followers, as did Williams. In the essays in this volume, however, he is perceived as restlessly questing, constantly finding a new style only to discard it, endlessly revising the *Notebooks* until, with *The Dolphin*, so Davie claims, there is evidence that 'his new life is a new life of his art also, a shucking off at last of the self-contradictions that snarled him in *Notebook* and the collections that came out of *Notebook*'.

In 'The Black Mountain Poets' (Charles Olson and Edward Dorn) Davie traces their lineage back to Whitman thus: 'these poets, as Americans, use Pound (to bypass Eliot) so as to re-establish contact with the great American poet of the last century, Walt Whitman. (The line of descent from Pound to Olson can be traced in more detail through two other American poets – William Carlos Williams and Louis Zukofsky.)' And he quotes Williams, writing in a manifesto in 1930: 'To what shall the mind turn for that with which to rehabilitate our thought and our lives? To the word, a meaning hardly distinguishable from that of place, in whose great virtuous and at present little realized potency we hereby manifest our belief.' This is by no means a new idea, as Davie observes, whilst agreeing that it is indeed important for a poet to know his *locality*, to know where he belongs. Olson's *Maximus Poems* are about *place* – his place, Gloucester, and its geography. But that is not all. Geography encompasses history; geography and history encompass tradition, and therein a poet can fix his *locality,* take his stand, before moving out and moving on (as Dorn's poems notably do).

From his reading of Olson, Davie was led to the geographer Carl Sauer. In his Journal (12 July 1980) he wrote that since coming to live in the western USA, he had

> a wholly non-European sense of how in forbidding and sparsely peopled landscapes the human being has no special privileged status, but must compete for living room and security with non-human creatures like scorpions and bodies of water. The proportion that I had taken for granted, between the human and the non-human creation, was knocked from under me. And this was frightening, but the fright was salutary: the human race's purchase on the earth's surface and the earth's resources was more precarious than Western Europe was aware of. I had discovered in fact the abiding relevance and imaginative richness of geography … What enlightened me was, first, non-European land-scapes themselves, but secondly a poet: the six-foot-something massive Swedish-American, Charles Olson, for instance in his pamphlet, *A Bibliography on America for Ed Dorn*. It was there I read of, and duly noted and followed up … the name of the great geographer Carl Sauer.

One of the many ideas which intrigued Davie, from his reading of Sauer, was the idea that we are not confined to man's measurement of time as linear, but that we also live in topographical time. In a poem he wrote at the time he sets this concept of vast space in an English landscape, though surely the East Anglian Fens must be one of the few places in England offering such imaginative scope.

A Winter Landscape near Ely

It is not life being short,
Death certain, that is making
Those faintly coffee-coloured
Gridiron marks on the snow
Or that row of trees heart-breaking.

What stirs us when a curtain
Of ice-hail dashes the window?
It is the wasteness of space
That a man drives wagons into
Or plants his windbreak in.

> Spaces stop time from hurting.
> Over verst on verst of Russia
> Are lime-tree avenues.

I have pointed to essays in this volume which trace the beginning of a distinct American tradition, but not all poets followed William Carlos Williams and Ezra Pound along that road. Others held to Winters's example of rhyme and metre. It is a serendipitous collection, each new poem and poet approached with a fresh eye and open mind. The earliest essay was written in 1954, a reading of Wallace Stevens' *Auroras of Autumn*. It is a study in how to read a poem, and as stimulating for today's reader as when it was first written. The latest is dated 1991, an essay on Postmodernism, as lively and provocative as any Donald Davie wrote. Let him have the last word:

> I have at all times suffered from being thought of as Critic first, Poet second. I have spent much energy repudiating this, asserting that I wrote my criticism not to work out what poems I should write, but in order to understand what I had been about in poems I had already written. What bedevils this issue is the very common assumption that the critical intelligence and the poetic intelligence are at odds. Like Yvor Winters, who is my master in these matters, I refuse this because to believe it is an offence against rationality. Now I've got to the point where I hardly care any more. Ford Madox Ford described himself as 'an old man mad about writing'. I am an old man mad about writing in verse – whether in verse I have written myself, or in verse written by others, hardly seems to matter.[2]

These words were written in 1986. He died in 1995. His passionate love of poetry, writing about it, writing it, reading it, stayed with him to the end of his life.

DOREEN DAVIE
Silverton, 2000

2   Ibid.

1 American Literature: the Canon

I come before you asking what I hope are patient questions, as pretty much an ignoramus, certainly an amateur. This has not much to do with my being a subject of Her Majesty Queen Elizabeth II, but it has something to do with that. And I should like to begin by spending a few minutes on the rather peculiar difficulties that a British reader feels when he approaches American literature. These difficulties will not be unfamiliar to you because they are a mirror image of what you as Americans encounter when you consider modern British literature. You know that modern British literature is a foreign literature to you, and yet quite plainly it is not foreign in the same way as French literature is, or Italian, or German, or Spanish. And the Englishman regards American literature in the same way: it is somehow a foreign literature, and yet it isn't, it is not foreign in the way other literatures are. As a matter of fact, of course, there are people on both sides of the Atlantic (though they are more prominent and numerous in the United Kingdom than in the United States), who would deny even this much, who would deny that the other English-speaking literature is a foreign literature at all. This is an attitude which was very common, particularly among the English, up to a couple of generations ago, and the people who still hold this view in England are, for the most part, in their declining years. They would say that 'English literature' is a term applied to literature in English wherever it is written, whether in North America, in Australasia, Polynesia, Asia, emergent Africa, anywhere. And in fact, there are quite strong arguments which can be brought to support this nowadays very unfashionable, and I think dying, attitude. In particular, people of this way of thinking can ask: If I as an English reader am to regard the literature of the United States as a foreign literature, am I not to regard the literature of Australia as foreign likewise? Indeed, am I not as an Englishman to regard Scottish literature written in English as a foreign literature, Anglo-Irish literature as foreign, Anglo-Welsh literature as foreign? These are difficult and ticklish questions to answer because what is involved in them is a sense of national identity on the part of various peoples. If we are to say that the literature of the United States exists as a literature foreign to English, but we refuse to recognize, let us say, New Zealand literature as having the same sort of status, patriotic New Zealanders are likely to be annoyed, for it seems we are denying to New Zealand a cultural independence and identity which we are allowing to the United States. Particularly, here in the state of Montana, how can we fail to reflect upon the vast nation to the north of us? Is Canadian literature an independent literature foreign both to the British Isles and to the United States, or is it not? Is Canadian culture still in a colonial and dependent relation, and if it is, which nation is it culturally a colonial dependency of? Of the United Kingdom, or of the United States?

If I have any Canadians in this audience, they are undoubtedly feeling already outraged and affronted. What's certain is that the very phrase, 'American literature', as enshrined in our curricula, is anything but helpful, for one thing we have to say of such 'American literature' is that it isn't the literature of America. The literature of America is written in Spanish, Portuguese, French, Quechua, Nahuatl, and various other Indian languages, as well as in English. Even if we take American literature to mean the literature of *North* America, we still, if we are to be logical, must recognize that much of that literature is written in languages other than English, since much Canadian literature, for instance, is in French. British and American alike, we stand convicted, I fear, of overweening presumption in supposing that literature in English is for most practical purposes shared between the United Kingdom and the United States. Of course this is not true. On the contrary, one of the most remarkable things about the language which we speak and write in common is that it is more likely than any other language to become a *world* language. A great number of the most significant and beautiful poems and stories and plays of newly independent Africa are in fact written in our language, and we pay all too little attention to that fact. If we paid more attention to such facts, our imperialistic presumptions, American and British alike, would be cut down to size in a way which would be very salutary for both nations. The old and now discredited idea that English literature was literature written in English wherever written, and hence that American literature as an independent and autonomous phenomenon did not and could not exist, had at least this to recommend it: that it took account, as *we* find it very difficult to do, of the literature in the English language that is being produced in regions of the world quite remote both from the United Kingdom and from the United States.

However, it is clear that that old view has been discredited and cannot long survive among us, whether in the British Isles or the United States. It smacks too much of the presumptuousness of the metropolitan culture centred upon London, regarding all the other English-speaking cultures as colonial dependencies. And I think there are stronger arguments against it. For we cannot believe that literature exists, or is produced, in a 'pure' realm, quite unaffected by the political and social and physical dimensions of the region where it is produced and responded to. Accordingly, the sheerly physical, geographical scale of regions of the world like Canada, the United States, and Australia, so different from the small-scale physical landscape of the British Isles, is enough in my view to ensure that the English-language literature produced in those regions either is now, or in due course will be, autonomous and independent of British literature. Accordingly, I have no difficulty in conceding that the literature of the United States is, from my point of view as a British reader, a foreign literature (in some sense).

But the question now presents itself: At what stage did the literature of the United States *become* a literature foreign to the Englishman? And when I consult authorities, I find a bewildering variety of answers to this crucial question. At one extreme I find people claiming that the devotional poet Edward Taylor (1642?–1729), who wrote his poems as a Calvinist minister in New England, is already an ornament of an American literature conceived of as distinct from British – this despite the fact that Taylor spent his first twenty-five years in his native England! At the other extreme, I find William Carlos Williams in our own time still castigating his contemporaries, Eliot and Ezra Pound, for having lived abroad and having seemed to conceive of themselves as contributing to a European or a world culture, thus delaying the achievement of genuine independence and autonomy for the literature of the United States. In between these extremes is to be found the figure of Ralph Waldo Emerson, asserting that in the middle of the nineteenth century the United States had still not achieved a cultural independence from Britain to match the political independence which had been claimed in 1776 and won by 1783. Emerson exhorted his fellow Americans to achieve that cultural independence, and he saluted that one of his fellow Americans who, in his view, had achieved this for himself and for his countrymen – that is to say, Walt Whitman. Groping for guidance in the fog of my imperfect knowledge, I find this attitude of Emerson's the most plausible on offer. Nevertheless, it does not solve all my problems, for if Walt Whitman had indeed liberated the American writer from dependence upon British models and precedents, there were plenty of American writers in the next two generations who did not realize they had been liberated, who did not thank Whitman for the release he had brought them. Well into the present century there appear to have been American writers who still looked for ultimate approval to London rather than Boston or New York, who were to this extent psychologically still 'colonials'. Moreover, in those generations after Whitman, there are the two massive figures of Henry James and T.S. Eliot, American by birth but British by adoption. Am I to regard Henry James's *Portrait of a Lady* and T.S. Eliot's *Four Quartets* as works belonging to a literature foreign to me as an Englishman? At this point it may well be felt that the whole discussion is getting silly; it cannot be right for these intriguing and important questions of national tradition in literature to be reduced to the accident of what sort of passport a given writer flashes at the international frontier. You will see, however, that I have already arrived at what I advertised as the principal concern of this talk; that is to say, which writers belong in American literature, and which others don't. Is Henry James yours, or mine? Is T.S. Eliot mine, or yours? Is W.H. Auden mine until 1939, yours after 1940? And does it matter?

As it happens, however, I am less interested in the twentieth-century writers as to whom this question can be raised, than I am in certain writers of the seventeenth and eighteenth centuries. I had the experience not long ago in a graduate seminar of having an American student protest that for her Chaucer, Shakespeare, and Milton were foreign authors. She contended that she ought to be able to study her own literature, American, without have to 'carry' some English also. I responded by saying that these great writers were as much hers as mine, since they were great writers in the English language at a time when the two branches of the English-speaking people on either side of the Atlantic had not yet split apart into two distinct national identities. As it happens, though, the student who made this comment was black, and I could not fail to realize that if indeed her ancestors were already in the continental United States at the time when the Declaration of Independence was signed, they were here through no choice of their own, and in a disfranchised, deliberately unprivileged condition, when for instance they were almost certainly denied the chance of becoming literate. Accordingly, there were certainly considerations on her side of the question which made her attitude under-standable, which made my retort to it somewhat uncomfortable and apologetic.

All the same, I believe that the retort which I made is the only right and possible one: Chaucer and Shakespeare and Milton, Edmund Spenser and Ben Jonson and John Donne, John Dryden and Alexander Pope are as much yours as they are mine – *if you want them*. Whatever we may think of the literature produced in the United States in the hundred years after the Declaration of Independence, it is surely nonsensical to speak of an American literature, as distinct from and foreign to English literature, at any period before 1776. And yet I get the strong impression that this, as it seems to me, self-evident truth is not one that is generally recognized. There come into my hands anthologies of American literature, designed for classroom use, which start with a section called 'The Colonial Period', in which appear selections from Ann Bradstreet, Edward Taylor, Jonathan Edwards, Phyllis Wheatley, to go no further. Yet it must surely be the case that if before 1776 Milton and Shakespeare and Donne are yours as much as they are mine, so Anne Bradstreet and Edward Taylor and Jonathan Edwards are as much mine as they are yours. My students stare at me in surprise when I point out that in the one hundred and fifty years between the landing of the Pilgrim Fathers and the Declaration of Independence very few people of Caucasian race, born and living in the territory of what is now the continental United States, conceived of themselves as anything but Englishmen who happened to live on the opposite side of the Atlantic from most of their compatriots. Yet so far as I can see (I stand ready to be corrected) this was indeed the case. Indeed, those very Americans who themselves created the American nation as a political identity distinct from the British, the very fathers of the Republic themselves – Ben Franklin, John Adams, Thomas Jefferson – conceived of themselves, at least up to 1776, as Englishmen who happened to live overseas. How could they have thought otherwise?

So far as I can see, however, the colonial period is passed over rather rapidly in most surveys of American literature. I seem to detect a general consensus that American literature proper begins in the post-revolutionary period, with Philip Freneau or Washington Irving or Fenimore Cooper, and that it gathers speed and impetus only with Emerson, Emily Dickinson, Herman Melville, Walt Whitman. But this surely has the alarming effect of drastically foreshortening the cultural and historical experience of mankind in North America. Leaving aside the admittedly special case of the native Americans (the Amerindians), we can say that mankind in North America did in fact experience in some sort those two phases of European culture to which we give the names of the Age of the Baroque and the Age of the Enlightenment. But there is, I sometimes think, a general conspiracy to ignore these experiences, and to act as if the cultural memory of North American man reached back no further than to the romantic movement of the end of the eighteenth and the beginning of the nineteenth centuries. And this is, in at least one sense, flagrantly and demonstrably untrue. No man has, it may be thought, a firmer claim to be a true American than John Adams, who helped draft the Declaration of Independence and lived to become second president of the United States; and if one consults the diaries which the young John Adams kept, while he was still a country lawyer in New England, long before he attained international reputation as a diplomat and revolutionary, one finds him recording in his diary his impressions (very intelligent and perceptive ones) of the poetry of Donne, of Pope, of Shakespeare – all of whom he takes to be, naturally enough, the poets of his nation. Indeed, the Declaration of Independence itself, and still more the Constitution of the United States, are self-evidently documents of that historical phase of Western culture which is defined as 'the Enlightenment'. Among the inci-dental advantages which just might be derived from the interminable Watergate investigations, there might emerge a necessity for every American to understand that, insofar as he is safeguarded by and depends upon the Constitution, he is an heir to the eighteenth century neoclassic Enlightenment at least as much as to the romantic movement.

But then, I ask with some diffidence, is there any anthology of

American literature for classroom use which reproduces, among the monuments of literature produced in the United States, the Declaration of Independence or any part of the Constitution of the United States, or John Adams's *Discourses on Davila,* or even Thomas Jefferson's *Notes on Virginia*? There may be such anthologies, but I have not come across them. And this strikes me as odd. After all, nobody denies that in the canon of English literature there figure, as of right, the political pamphlets of Jonathan Swift, the political polemics and parliamentary orations of Edmund Burke. But so far as I can see, 'American literature' is very seldom taken to include, as a distinct and ancient literary genre, political speculation and commentary and political oratory. Do any of the political writings or orations of Henry Clay, for instance, deserve inclusion in any respectably comprehensive and representative anthology of American literature? So far as I know, not only has the question never been answered, it has perhaps never been asked.

I have reached the point where, in my impertinent temerity, I am suggesting that, despite the man–hours now devoted over several decades to 'American literature', rather few scholars have brought themselves to question highly questionable assumptions, both as to period and (still more momentously) as to genre or literary kind. Is it not the case that, through the now several decades since American literature was recognized as a respectable academic discipline, both in the United States and abroad, never a year has passed without new books and articles on Herman Melville, Nathaniel Hawthorne, Stephen Crane, Ernest Hemingway, Emily Dickinson, Thoreau, Walt Whitman; but that, on the other hand, years and years go by without anyone's ever offering a new candidate for inclusion in the canon of what American literature is taken to consist of? It was Ezra Pound, that expatriate and maverick American, who insisted through year upon year that the letters exchanged between Thomas Jefferson and John Adams as old men were a monument of American literature as well as of American history; and what college text in American literature shows that its author has even considered Pound's contention, let alone acted upon it? The letters of Horace Walpole, Thomas Gray, William Cowper, John Keats (to go no further) are accepted classics of English literature, as the letters by Mme. de Sevigné are of French. Where are their American counterparts? Do they not exist? Or do they indeed exist, but have never been looked at, or never from this point of view? Even if we restrict ourselves to the arbitrarily accredited genres of poem, story, and drama, how long is it since any scholar of American literature put forward a candidate, a practitioner of any one of these genres, as meriting inclusion in the canon? So far as my admittedly imperfect information goes, I find I have to track back thirty or forty years, to find the late Yvor Winters proposing for inclusion in the canon of American poets Jones Very and Frederick Goddard Tuckerman – a contention which seems to have been neither straightforwardly denied nor gratefully acceded to, but rather considered, at least in some quarters, as a gratuitously annoying qualification of what was already a profitably going concern. (For, if Frederick Goddard Tuckerman was, as Yvor Winters contended, a remarkably serious and accomplished poet, this was for some scholars a confounded nuisance, since Tuckerman could be shown to have been in constant contact with, and emulation of, the British poet Alfred Lord Tennyson, whereas the accepted orthodoxy required it to be believed that in the mid-nineteenth century no American poet *could* attain to first-rate stature except by denying the validity of British models and British precedent, as Walt Whitman did.)

You will see in any case that I am trying to register my confused impression that we have, in what is commonly accepted as American literature, a literature in which the canon of classic works has never yet been established. I have no time to do more than glance at one more category of works as to which this question of classic status seems never to have been raised: bearing in mind how travel narratives so different as Kinglake's *Eothen* and Cobbett's *Rural Rides* have been accepted as classic in the canon of English literature, how can we fail to be surprised that scholars of American literature seem never to have looked from this point of view at books like Alexander Ross's *Adventures of the First Settlers on the Oregon or Columbia River* (1849), or William L. Manly's *Death Valley in '49. The Autobiography of a Pioneer* (1894)? The journals of Lewis and Clark, Ross's narrative, and Manly's, must serve as representative of a vast number of books along the same lines, of which some (it may be surmised) still exist only in manuscript. Who has looked at them all? And if some scholars have reviewed them all – including those published by the Hudson's Bay Company (for in relation to these works the distinction between Canadian and United States literature seems to be more than ever impracticable and fatuous) – who has looked at them with a view to their status *as literature*? This does not mean asking: Do they contain purple patches of self-consciously 'fine' writing? The question is rather, I'd suggest: Were the writer's feelings and imagination engaged, no less than his solid good sense and scrupulous concern for accuracy? I will dare to go even a little further, and ask: Who, except for a few honourable eccentrics like Yvor Winters, and David Levin in his *History as Romantic Art* (1959), has considered *historiography* as a genre of literature magnificently practiced and adorned in North America by Washington Irving in his *History of Astoria*, by Bancroft and Prescott, by Motley and Parkman, and (I would add) Walter Prescott Webb? I can only report that in the first *Anthology of American Literature* which I take down from my shelves (by Thomas M. Davis and Willoughby Johnson, 1966), the only one of these authors who appears is Irving, and he is represented by – you guessed it – 'Rip Van Winkle'. If Gibbon and Macaulay are glories of English literature, are not Prescott and Parkman among the glories of American? For all practical purposes, apparently not, despite the lip service that is hastily paid them when their names are guiltily remembered.

I should like to offer very tentatively my guess as to why and how it is that 'American literature' has flourished as an academic discipline for so long, without the canon of classic works in that literature ever being established or indeed enquired about. To do so I must revert to one of my earlier observations, when I proposed that caucasian man in North America had experienced both the Age of the Baroque and the Age of the Enlightenment, yet stubbornly denied having experienced any phase of Western culture earlier than the Romantic. I think it is true to say that the Romantic movement, as in the early nineteenth century the tide of it engulfed one Western literature after another, had the effect of blurring and ultimately destroying one after another of the distinctions on which rested the doctrine of genres, of literary kinds, as that doctrine had been elaborated and ambitiously systematized by the neoclassic theorists of the Renaissance. The distinctions between idyll and eclogue, between elegy and complaint, between satire and lampoon – these distinctions, and the many more that might be cited, soon gave way in the early nineteenth century, under the interrelated and typically Romantic convictions (1) that artistic form was self-generating and 'organic', and (2) that artistic style was above all distinctive and personal. Moreover, the Romantic and post-Romantic generations were, and have been up to our own day, particularly suspicious of those genres of literature which most manifestly called upon predetermined design and calculation as to overall structure, and on discursive reason as to method. It seems to me we may not need to look any further for the reason why the nineteenth century, not just in America but in Europe also (and certainly in England), could regard historiography and political oratory as being literature only 'after a fashion', only, as it were, by special licence. It is because the American insists on regarding *his* literature as wholly Romantic and post-Romantic, that he is unable even to contemplate the possibility that that literature includes the letters of Adams and Jefferson, the histories of Francis Parkman, or the political oratory of Daniel Webster or Henry Clay.

What is so baffling about this for the Englishman is that, if I may reiterate, eighteenth-century habits of thought and language persist in American public life as they do not in the public life of England. The Constitution of the United States was framed according to eighteenth-century pre-Romantic ideals, and is couched in eighteenth-century Enlightenment language. By contrast, the English system of government, the English ideas of how society is ordered, though they were given an eighteenth-century face-lift by John Locke, in fact derive by slow incremental process from medieval times, and found their most impassioned apologist in Edmund Burke, who extolled them on grounds that most people would agree to describe as Romantic-reactionary. Thus it ought to be the case that it is the Englishman who finds it hard to sympathize with the Enlightenment frame of mind, whereas the American has ready access to it. But this is far from being the case. It would be wrong to say the very opposite is true, for in fact most Englishmen *do* find it hard to sympathize, except very shallowly, with the eighteenth century and what it stands for in the history of Western man. Yet that the American should refuse to sympathize with his own pre-Romantic past, to the extent of denying (unless he is a constitutional lawyer or a professional historian) that he has any eighteenth-century past at all – this cannot fail to astonish us. Pope and Dryden, Fielding and Goldsmith, ought to be *more* your authors than they are mine, simply because the institutionalized public life of your nation has kept open avenues of access to their imaginative and intellectual world, in a way that the public life of England has not.

What reasons there can be for such an extravagant cover-up, for denying that colonial North America ever had an Enlightenment culture, whereas in fact the polity of the United States is a product of that culture – this is a question which I cannot answer, and must leave aside. But that the cover-up exists I think cannot be doubted. The most astonishing proof of it came into my hands a short time ago, in the shape of a book lately published in New York, *America: A Prophecy*, edited by George Quasha and Jerome Rothenberg. This is an anthology which advertises itself with justice as 'A New Reading of American Poetry from Pre-Columbian Times to the Present'. It makes for fascinating reading, and is obviously the product of much curious learning. Perhaps the most immediately striking feature of it is what might be expected from the collaboration of Mr Rothenberg: the inclusion of many pieces (few of them strictly 'poems' in the perhaps too narrow sense we usually give to that word), which are translated from Iroquois, Sioux, Navajo, and other Native American languages, including languages from south of the border, such as Maya, Toltec, and Aztec (nothing, on the other hand, from the Spanish of Central America – which may seem odd). However, for my present purposes the most striking fact is that, of the more than three hundred items in this anthology, just six were written in English in North America before 1800. Six, out of more than three hundred! And of these six the four most substantial and interesting pieces – by John Fiske, Cotton Mather, and Edward Taylor – in fact represent what I have called, perhaps unhelpfully, the *baroque* rather than the Enlightenment; that is to say, they are clearly products of seventeenth-century habits of thought, not of those eighteenth-century ways of thinking which impelled Adams and Jefferson and Washington, James Madison and John Jay and Alexander Hamilton. This slanting of the evidence is too marked to be accidental. It must have been intended, and indeed so it was. For Quasha and Rothenberg take not just their title but, as they explain very lucidly, all the assumptions on which they structure their book from the writings of William Blake, that English poet who pronounced a relentless anathema on the thought and art of the century to which he was born, with its Enlightenment culture. William Blake, I should say, nowadays provokes more enthusiasm in North America than any other British poet whatever. And we begin to see why: Blake it is who tells the American that he not only may but must ignore the Enlightenment culture which informed and shaped the American Republic. It is an odd state of affairs, to say the least of it.

However that may be, I should like now to suggest that the theory of American literature which I have been hesitantly sketching explains also another very striking feature of that literature as it is customarily presented to us: its being much of the time a parade of giants, a star show with hardly any supporting cast. Please notice that I speak only of American literature *as it tends to be presented to us*. It is not the case that American literature lacks figures in, as it were, the middle distance, writers who are estimable and memorable, even irreplaceable, though of something less than giant stature. A host of names comes to mind, across the generations: William Cullen Bryant and Frederick Goddard Tuckerman, Edith Wharton and Willa Cather, Hamlin Garland and Sarah Orne Jewett, Glenway Wescott and Wallace Stegner... and how many more? (I name only those to whom I'm immediately aware of feeling grateful.) All these writers, I believe, have secured a place in what may one day be acknowledged as the canon of American literature. But I think it is not writers like these, writers of this stature, whom we think of first when we say 'American literature'. The writers we think of first are the titanic figures that march, one after another, across the foreground. Emerson and Thoreau, Hawthorne and Melville, Whitman, even in her own way Emily Dickinson, even in his own way Poe – these are indeed gigantesque figures, larger than life. I think we have difficulty, though, in remembering that each of them had contemporaries, writers who deserve to be honoured though they are very different from these Prometheans, certainly not giants and yet not dwarves either. And I use the word 'Promethean' advisedly, and the word 'titanic' also; for the difficulty we have in placing and justly esteeming the minor American classics, the minor masters who set themselves and secured limited but valuable objectives, can be rather easily related to the characteristically Romantic view of the agonized and untamable artist as Prometheus – with its implication that one 'goes for broke' or not at all; that a modest or limited achievement is almost worse than no achievement whatever; that the only honourable ambition is to be a *great* writer, not just a good one. What bears this out, I suggest, is that we experience a similar difficulty in the Romantic and post-Romantic phases of other literatures besides American; in English literature, for instance, Walter Savage Landor and Robert Bridges and Mrs Gaskell are writers of less than giant stature whom we are continually forgetting about, whom we cannot find a place for when we are reminded of them. In both literatures we are really much happier with, and more confident about, writers of another sort again – those who rather plainly aimed at gigantesque or titanic structure, as we see from the copiousness and variety of their 'output', but who failed, more or less narrowly, to 'make the grade'. A James Fenimore Cooper, a Henry Wadsworth Longfellow, a Theodore Dreiser – those who scored a near miss, the failed or imperfect titans, giants brought low (more or less honourably) by Jacks who climbed the beanstalk after them . . . we find it easier to admire the flawed achievements of such writers than the relatively flawless but more limited achievement of a minor master such as (to name one from our own day) Janet Lewis. And this is because, whether we know it or not, we approach literature with Romantic assumptions and Romantic expectations.

As I draw to the end of these remarks, I cannot dispel from my mind something that perhaps has been growing in your minds as you have listened: the possibility that I have been on the wrong track from the first and all along; that by making play with such ideas as 'the canon' and 'the classic' I have only convicted myself of approaching a non-European literature with European assumptions and concepts that just don't apply as soon as the critic or literary historian crosses the Atlantic to the New World. After all, I cannot but reflect that the only notable occasion on which the word 'classic' was applied to American literature was when it was used by a *British* writer, D.H. Lawrence, in his *Studies in Classic American Literature*. I have, however, come across the term being used by an American writer. This writer was William Carlos Williams, who wrote: 'The future American poetry has to arise from speech – American, not English . . . from what we *hear* in America. Not, that is, from a study of the classics, not even the American "classics" – the dead classics . . . which we have *never heard* as living speech. No one has ever heard them as they were written any more than we can hear Greek.' In this American voice, as I hear it speak to me off the page, the word 'classic' plainly is uttered with a contemptuous ring to it, such as it does not have in the English voice of D.H. Lawrence, taunting and sardonic as that voice often was. To opt for the spoken language so uncompromisingly as Williams does here, and in similar passages, is to deny that past generations of writing have any relevance at all to American writing today. (Williams's own writing now belongs to the American past; so presumably on his own showing his writings might as well be, and perhaps ought to be, forgotten.) This is to deny any continuity between one generation and the next; it is to make the history of American poetry a disconnected series of ever new starts, and I will readily confess that I am too European in grain to be able to come to terms with such a possibility. Of such a literature one could not write a history, only a chronicle. If that were the sort of literature that

American literature is, I should be much less interested in it than in fact I am. I have to believe, and I think I begin to discern, that there is a continuity in American literature, as in any European literature that I know of; that there can be discerned, running throughout, a tradition, or else several traditions alternating and sometimes conflicting. If so, then a history of that literature – as distinct from a mere chronicle – becomes a possibility. What I have been suggesting in the last few minutes is that the present climate of opinion about American literature seems to be such that the literary history I've been envisaging won't be written at all soon, if only because at present the *dis*continuities seem to be emphasized more than the continuities. ('Recurrence' is another matter: recurrent *patterns* in American literature can be, and often are, discerned – but such recurrences and repetitions in fact testify to discontinuity, not to a continuous and evolving *tradition*.)

I will end by expressing two hunches: (1) that the sort of continuity I have in mind may be in fact carried by minor writers rather than major ones; and (2) that it may be carried, not just by prose writers rather than poets, but by discursive and analytical and expository prose rather than by narrative prose, especially when that narrative prose is as 'poetic' as the prose of Herman Melville on the one hand, Ernest Hemingway on the other. You will notice how each of these propositions has to do with the points that I made earlier in these remarks. And neither of them, surely, is at all novel or startling. The first rests upon the obvious fact that genius is often idiosyncratic. A major writer, therefore, by the very fact of his genius, is likely to be 'off centre'. A Milton or a Melville does not merely rise above the tradition which he adorns; he pushes it askew under the force of the highly personal vision which he compels it to incorporate. The tradition therefore may be carried more securely by writers with less talent and less urgency. And my second proposition is likewise far from new. It was expressed with memorable force more than sixty years ago, by J. S. Phillimore:

> Poetry is a wind that bloweth where it listeth; a barbarous people may have great poetry, they cannot have great prose. Prose is an institution, part of the equipment of a civilization, part of its heritable wealth, like its laws, or its system of schooling, or its tradition of skilled craftsmanship.

Phillimore wrote thus in an essay, in the *Dublin Review* of 1913, on 'Blessed Thomas More and the Arrest of Humanism in England'. And the sentences were quoted by R.W. Chambers in *The Continuity of English Prose from Alfred to More and his School*, where I found them. This makes it plain that Phillimore, and Chambers after him, had in mind not the prose of novelists, not narrative prose at all unless it were the prose of travellers and historians, but rather discursive and expository prose. And this is my warrant for suggesting that if the time ever comes when students of American literature are more interested in its continuities than its discontinuities, they will do well to look for them in literary genres other than those of poem, story, or drama – precisely, in fact, in those genres which American literature, as commonly taught, appears not to possess. I do not need to underline the fact that, if Phillimore is right, such an investigation would be a study not just of North American literature but of North American *civilization*.

This was originally a lecture delivered at the University of Montana. First published in *Trying to Explain* (Carcanet Press, 1980).

2 The Legacy of Fenimore Cooper

My purpose is straigthtforward: to get known and read in England two American books which are, as far as I can see, little known and little read. *In the American Grain*, by William Carlos Williams, had a *succès d'estime* when it first appeared in 1925, but in common with Williams's poetry attracted few readers until after the last war; in the last few years the concerted effort in America to do belated justice to Williams has resulted in this book getting the classic status of a paperback edition. (This is quite unironical; the discrimination shown by the paperback publishers is extraordinary and impressive.) It cannot be long before the current American vogue for Williams produces British reverberations; and already, in fact, there has been a laudatory essay in *The Twentieth Century* by Denis Donoghue. Better late than never; and a British edition of *In the American Grain* cannot be deferred much longer. *The Invasion* by Janet Lewis is rather a different case; it is still almost entirely unknown even in America, and the second edition (University of Denver Press, 1932) is unexhausted to this day. A British edition of this book, as of the same author's historical novels, *The Wife of Martin Guerre* and *The Trial of Soren Quist*, is greatly to be hoped for, but at the moment unlikely.

Both books are, to quote Williams himself in quite another connection, 'very subtly made as far as the phrasing, the words, the godliness of words is concerned'. And it would not be hard to get the reader's sympathy by quoting from both of them passages of prose which he would be prepared to call distinguished whatever their contexts. But it is perhaps not hard, either, to dig out of many undistinguished books certain pages of distinction which can then be presented as, in the betraying phrase, 'key-passages'. Moreover, what is likely to give the British reader most trouble with both these books is precisely the contexts which they create, the *genre* to which they belong. It's necessary to define the *genre* and establish the contexts first.

The *genre* may be defined as 'impressionistic history'; a bastard kind, of which the only examples we are likely to recall belong to sub-literature. The reader may be forgiven for fearing, on the one hand, self-consciously 'fine writing', on the other, as in the historical novel, fact eked out by fiction, and imagination in difficulties sinking groggily to rest on antiquarian fact. As for the first charge, self-consciously poetical writing can be found in Williams, in for instance the section 'De Soto and the New World', where the personification of the American earth as a woman seems to be, here as in Hart Crane's *The Bridge*, an irresistible temptation to roseate muddles of both thought and language (like the Irish Cathleen-na-Houlihan); but this is only a temporary lapse by Williams, and in Janet Lewis there is no 'fine writing' at all. The second question, as to a muddle not just of literary kinds but of intellectual disciplines (the historian's and the poet's), is more interesting and reaches further.

Anyone who asks suspiciously how much of Williams and of Janet Lewis is historical fact, how much is interpretative fiction, will come up with the unexpected answer that far more is fact than he had supposed, and fact of the irrefragable kind; unacknowledged wholesale quotation or minimal adaptation from sources. Williams says exultantly of his chapter given to John Paul Jones, 'Battle Between the Bon Homme Richard and the Serapis', 'no word is my own'. This whole section, in fact, is a scissors-and-paste job on Jones's own dispatches; and the same is true in only slightly less degree of many of the other sections, for instance those on Cotton Mather and Benjamin Franklin. (See *Selected Letters* of Williams, p. 187.) Similarly, even those who know of Ross Cox's *Adventures on the Columbia* will hardly expect that when Janet Lewis introduces him into her narrative, she is not just appropriating his name, or building upon the virtual certainty that he must have been a visitor to the fur-trading post she deals with, but reproducing faithfully an episode for which she has his specific authority. One is reminded of those American history *Cantos* of Pound which are similarly a catena of snippets from Jefferson, Benton, and the Adamses; and of Williams and Miss Lewis, as of Pound, it is more rational to complain that the historical fact is reproduced unlicked and unmodulated than that it is 'fictionalised' out of usefulness. This is particularly the case with *The Invasion*, which is so close to the documents that it could without much trouble or loss have been framed as orthodox historiography. In such a case to settle deliberately for the unclassifiable and therefore disconcerting form (with the foreseeable result that, falling between specialities, the book was neglected) is an act of faith in this *genre* of writing, which ought to give us pause.

In Williams's case, the closeness to authentic documents immediately determines the quality of the style. As Williams says of *In the American Grain* (*Selected Letters*, p. 187), 'The book is as much a study in styles of writing as anything else. I tried to write each chapter in the style most germane to its sources, or at least the style which seemed to me appropriate to the material. To this end, where possible, I copied and used the original writings … I did this with malice aforethought to prove the truth of the book, since the originals fitted into it without effort on my part, perfectly, leaving not a seam.' In other words, the governing principle of the style is delicate *pastiche*; and here once again is an instructive parallel with Pound's *Cantos*, where the medley of styles and the pervasiveness of pastiche as stylistic principle – so far from proving, as they are taken to prove, Pound's dilettantism – prove his determination to hew to the contours of his subject, to 'prove the truth' of his book. For Janet Lewis the case is rather different, since most of her quotations from sources (unlike her borrowings from Ross Cox) are acknowledged and printed as such. Still, in order to sustain the slow but unfaltering pace of her narrative, she does need a style of her own into which quotations in a past style can be inserted without a retarding change of gear. Her principal source was the papers of the Irish gentleman John Johnston, who in 1791 established a trading post at Sault Ste. Marie, married the daughter of an Ojibway chief, and founded a family whose last generation was known to Miss Lewis in her own youth. What follows is an example of how she uses her source, a paragraph skilfully interlarded with quotations:

> Of the Sault he wrote in a fine legible hand: 'The situation of the village is pleasing and romantic. The ground rises gently from the edge of the river.' He wrote that the houses were scattered over a slight ridge, four hundred yards from the river, and there was a great deal of sweet clover; that the soil was a light mould mixed with sand, twelve to eighteen inches deep over a bed of cold clay; that the whitefish season was from May to November, that the largest fish caught in the past season weighed fifteen pounds. He wrote that the rapids were one mile wide and half a mile long, descending over a bed of red freestone interspersed with white rocks, and that the Northwest Company had a fine sawmill on the north side. He wrote, 'The south-west channel of the rapids takes its course south-west for five leagues to the rapid called Nibith, the whole extent of the shore covered with maple and is one continued meadow of the richest soil I ever saw.' He mentioned the Northwest Company's shipyard at Point aux Pins, reported the finding of pure silver ore at Point Iroquois, of cinnabar at Vermilion Point, compared Gros Cap and Point Iroquois to the Pillars of Hercules, and called for a poet to immortalise them. He then proceeded, with many moral and geological reflections, to a minute description of the southern shore, cove by cove, indentation by rocky indentation, exactly as it was revealed to him in all its beauty and danger on that slow, shore-tracing journey. It was a record for a voyageur, with warnings about winds, currents, reefs, good and bad camping places. He had a theory that the water of Lake Superior was exceedingly pure and light, giving for its support the fact that it ruffles very easily. He said, 'At the Falls I have often seen the water rise from two to three feet in as many minutes, the rising followed shortly by a north-west breeze.'

Even if we cannot place Point Iroquois on a map or are undecided about what cinnabar is, there is not an item here which fails to make its effect.

Each exact observation is the natural expression of the grateful eagerness in the face of plenitude which is embodied in the rhythms, rapid yet carrying such weight, of the prose both in its cadences to the ear and in its syntax. In 'He wrote … He wrote … He wrote' (that this was so, that that was so) the prose itself persuades us that this quality in Johnston was admirable, that his life was admirable in so far as this was its dominating tone. Accordingly there is no use for condescension towards him, for any detachment, however affectionately ironic, for any 'placing' of him that will be in the slightest degree limiting or invidious. The phrase 'pleasing and romantic', which the amateur of periods would lovingly savour on his palate, is set down dead-pan and rapidly left behind; Johnston's comparison with the Pillars of Hercules (again, to the amateur, so charmingly 'dated') is given the same syntactical form and so the same degree of respectful seriousness as his reporting on silver ore; his calling for a poet to immortalize Point Iroquois is made neither more nor less quaint than his reference to the shipyard; and the obsolete science behind his theory about the lake's water is bound up with his far from obsolete, immediately useful observation on the rapid rising of the waters and the breeze which comes thereafter. Useful and useless, all alike express the only proper and admirable response to the Canadian wilderness as he knew it. Miss Lewis's writing preserves the same difficult and necessary equilibrium as Johnston's – 'beauty and danger on that slow, shore-tracing journey'; the ungainly snag of 'shore-tracing' holding back the surge through 'beauty and danger' – the voyage though beautiful had its purpose, the danger though beautiful was real. Similarly, 'moral and geological reflections' – the two have equal validity. If there is irony in the phrase, it appears only in the context of the whole book, when we know that the mineral riches of the geological reflections drew in 'the invasion' which, destroying the wilderness and wilderness life, made obsolete the moral reflections which were the proper response now made impossible.

Such a passage should be compared with places where Williams too is overtly interlarding quotations, as in 'The Discovery of Kentucky', where he uses John Filson's so-called Autobiography of Daniel Boone, or in his treatment of Champlain in 'The Founding of Quebec':

> 'I was in a garden that I was having prepared,' he writes. In a garden! that's wonderful to me. He was in this garden when the pilot of the second barque came to him with a story – for his private ear …
>
> But now he is awakened, what does he do? What? It is too amusing! Mind you, his life is threatened. He gets the pilot, his informer, to send the four chief felons two bottles of wine from the second barque, a gift, we'll say, from their friends, the Basques, and will they come to dinner at the barque that night?
>
> They come, of course, …

Williams has more verve and charm. Almost certainly, I suppose, he learned this from Lawrence's *Studies in Classic American Literature*, which similarly works on American history by interlarding quotations from the documents. (And there is more to be said of that. Lawrence reviewed Williams's book and liked it – 'the unvarnished *local* America still waits vast and virgin as ever …'.) But Janet Lewis's method, in keeping with her less free-ranging plan, is as effective and less coarse.

Her most difficult assignment in this direction, one supposes, is one which, surmounted, proves her greatest local triumph – the necessity to incorporate Johnston's poem on the death of his father-in-law, the Ojibway chieftain, Waubojeeg, or the White Fisher. For Johnston's verse, as one might expect, is more dated than his prose. The whole section about the chief's death (Section IX of Part I) is composed very carefully and intricately indeed. Mrs Johnston hears of her father's death by word of mouth through the winter forests – 'Waub-ojeeg-e-bun. The White Fisher *was*'. The Indian who brings the message asks about their infant, the dead man's grandson. Then the Indian wife of the white man is left alone to take in the news, to visualize the corpse of her father hoisted in a stiff shroud and cedar mats to swing in the treetops, then to recall (as her husband enters again and presently begins to write – 'an occupation which she understood, but which interested her little') tales now 'solidified into legend' about her father's life. In particular, she recalls his encounter with a moose:

> Waub-ojeeg, clad in his hunting shirt and leggins, a short knife at his belt and a small hatchet in his hand, cutting spruce boughs and twisting them to his uses, set forty marten traps, establishing a line for the season, and, having set the last, turned towards home. He had travelled perhaps half the distance between the last trap and the place where his lodge was, when, rounding a small ice-shagged evergreen, he came suddenly upon a moose, which confronted him with its head lowered, and barred his way. A great beast, gray and sulphurous, with curious long lips and intelligent eyes, it stood there, taller than the man, balancing the broad palmate horns before him, and regarded him with a determination and hostility rare to its species, as if it had set itself up challenger and defender for its race. Waub-ojeeg retreated slowly one step, and the moose attacked, lunging heavily in a straight line. The man dodged, circling the evergreen, and found the moose again confronting him. Having no suitable weapon and not being in any great need of meat at the time, he would have been glad to go his way without molesting the beast, but the moose would not permit it. For half an hour the pursuit continued, the moose lunging, the man dodging, until, as he ran, the Indian picked up a long stick, undid the fastenings of one of his moccasins, and with the moccasin string bound

his knife to the end of the stick. He then stationed himself behind the trunk of a tree, his lance in his hand, and the moose flung itself upon the knifehead. The blood streamed from its throat, smoking, but the moose, undismayed, reared and plunged again. Again the Indian met him with the lance, and again the blood gushed from the gray shagged body. The sky clouded, as if to snow, and cleared again, and a wind rose, shaking the withered leaves and lifting the loose snow in feathers, and still the moose, though staggering, pursued the Indian and met the lance, and still Waub-ojeeg, bespattered with blood, his breath tasting bitter upon his tongue, his forehead damp with sweat in spite of the cold air, dodged from tree trunk to tree trunk, avoided the skilful colossal horns, and held steady his lance. Finally the moose dropped. Waub-ojeeg approached it, and kneeling before the solemn head, cut out the tongue. He unbound the knife from the stick, put it back in his belt, fastened his moccasin again, and taking the tongue only, set off for home. The women, following his directions, found the place of the fight easily, for the snow was trampled down in a great circle, and trees and snow and bushes were besprinkled with blood as if thirty men had been fighting there. The moose, they said, was the largest ever killed within the memory of any living Ojibway.

Now that the moose was dead the woods were quiet. The room was quiet, also. Johnston had finished his writing, but the Woman of the Glade still looked into the fire. She presently felt his hand on her shoulder. 'Come,' he said, 'it is very late.'

What he had written he hesitated to show her then, but left it folded in his portfolio.

The hint about 'solidified into legend' permits the introduction here of an effect almost of hallucination − 'A great beast, gray and sulphurous, with curious long lips and intelligent eyes' ('sulphurous' is marvellous); and the hallucination becomes fully legendary with the rendering of the passage of time − 'The sky clouded, as if to snow, and cleared again, and a wind rose, shaking the withered leaves and lifting the loose snow in feathers, and still the moose ...' Without ever leaving the bounds of the possible (for what came and went, we may suppose, was no more than a squall), the story has moved into the legendary time of folklore; 'All day they fought, and the sun sank and rose again, and when ...'. Accordingly, here is a point where the irony can afford to become local, or where a local irony can be allowed to figure forth the total irony of history; the moose fighting the Indian 'as if it had set itself up challenger and defender for its race' becomes the Indian fighting with equal hopelessness the advance of the white man. The identification of Waub-ojeeg with his moose is effected tacitly, with marvellous discretion, in the simple shift of a sentence from the end of one paragraph to the beginning of the next −

'Now that the moose was dead the woods were quiet. The room was quiet, also.' The room and the woods come together of course for Mrs Johnston, the Woman of the Glade, as she concludes her reverie; but also they come together for the reader – and to different effect. And only after the solemnity of the event is thus powerfully established (Miss Lewis risks placing that very word, and beautifully – 'the solemn head'), only after the event has been established as peculiarly hers, not her husband's, only then can we see what he was writing, and his poem can be introduced with the effect of a cracked gesture, of anti-climax not bathos:

> My friends, when my spirit is fled – is fled,
>> My friends, when my spirit is fled,
> Ah, put me not bound in the dark and cold ground,
>> Where light shall no longer be shed – be shed,
>> Where daylight no more shall be shed …

And so on.

II

As for *genre*, if the historical romance has come down in the world since *Waverley*, we need not suppose that this represents any scruples on the part of the public about a confounding of the roles of poet and historiographer. In fact, at a time when the layman seems to see the academic historiographer leaving less and less margin for imaginative interpretation of the material he presents, it may well seem that the historical romance and the historical novel are due for a revival. But in any case novels are not what we are confronted with; and if the *genre* of impressionistic history appears to be a peculiarly American form, there are interesting reasons why this should be so. It makes some sense to say that if Williams and Janet Lewis confound the roles of poet and historian, they do so in the interest of the larger synthesis of *myth*. That too of course is a word of ill-omen; where 'the American myth' doesn't mean bluntly 'the American self-deception', it may seem to promise nothing better than yeasty heavings from the Jungian unconscious. But some fears may be allayed if we take 'myth' to mean, for present purposes, no more than what Lawrence sought to uncover in his *Studies in Classic American Literature*. What Lawrence seems to have recognized is that, just because American history begins after the invention of print, printed literature has played a part in the forming of the national self-consciousness such as in older cultures has been played by folklore and legend. It is not hard to see that this is so. It isn't necessary, for instance, to share the Lawrencian mystique, or to adopt the Lawrencian rhetoric (of racial blood-flows, and the rest of it), in order to agree with and make use of his perception, in his essay on Cooper, that the fate of the red man is an unhealed and perhaps unhealable wound in the white-American psyche. Even this language may be thought too figurative for comfort. If so, consider merely Albert Keiser's *The Indian in American Literature*, a 'standard work' of painstaking diligence but strikingly inept in whatever approaches critical judgement. Keiser lists painstakingly all the even minimally serious treatments of the Indian question in American literature from Captain John Smith to Edna Ferber; and nothing is so remarkable as the all but unanimity with which writers before and after Cooper have taken the part of the red man. Of one of the books that Keiser considers, Helen Hunt Jackson's *Ramona* (1884), Carey McWilliams remarks in his *Southern California Country* (1946, p.70): 'What is astonishing is the presence in the legend of an element of masochism, with the Americans, who manufactured the legend, taking upon themselves full responsibility for the criminal mistreatment of the Indian and completely exonerating the Franciscans.' What is here said in relation to the California mission Indians seems equally true, in the light of Keiser's book, of the white man's attitude to all Indians elsewhere, at least as represented in the white man's literature. 'Masochism' is probably inaccurate, certainly over-emphatic; what there is, however, is a sense of guilt, or a need to have such a sense. And the evidence for this is so overwhelming that, so far as literature is concerned, the question doesn't arise whether the guilt is justified; justified or not, the feeling apparently exists, and so persistently that one can only suppose it satisfies a profound imaginative demand. The myth exists, and is infinitely more powerful than the reality (which anyway there is now no way of knowing, and perhaps there never was – for how could a white man know the reality of the red man's life before the white man knew him?); therefore any writer on the Indians, which is to say any writer on American history, has to come to terms with Fenimore Cooper's Indian, has to take him on Cooper's terms. It is too late to try to explode the myth – at least in imaginative writing. The American imagination has invested too much in Chingachgook; and its need to do so can never be allayed or met by a writer who refuses to acknowledge the investment. We need mean no more than this when we speak of the myth of the Indian, and applaud Lawrence as the first to decipher it.

There is no better index of the sophistication of American criticism, and of the worth of that sophistication at its best, than the ability of American critics to incorporate and utilise Lawrence's insights, so 'prophetic', so intransigent as they are. One suspects that British criticism, placed in the same or an analogous situation, would not have coped so well. I take almost at random a formulation from the Preface to the thoroughly hard-headed *Virgin Land* of Henry Nash Smith, which has the sub-title, 'The American West as Symbol and Myth':

The terms 'myth' and 'symbol' occur so often in the following pages that the reader deserves some warning about them. I use the words to designate larger or smaller units of the same kind of thing, namely, an intellectual construction that fuses concept and emotion into an image. The myths and symbols with which I deal have the further characteristic of being collective representations rather than the work of a single mind. I do not mean to raise the question whether such products of the imagination accurately reflect empirical fact. They exist on a different plane. But ... they sometimes exert a decided influence on practical affairs.

Smith's work is one of several examples that could be cited to justify Richard Chase in his recent book, *The American Novel and its Tradition* (itself a distinguished example of the usefulness of the 'mythic' attitude), when he writes:

Lawrence's approach to American literature, which may be described variously as historical, cultural, or mythic, has been congenial to those modern critics who have not devoted themselves merely to textual analysis. The recent critical effort has responded to the tone of the times, and the times have been all in favour of the reassessment of the American past and a consolidation of knowledge and opinions about it ... History has fully justified the critics involved in this first period of reassessment and consolidation.

This is pertinent to any consideration of *In the American Grain* and/or *The Invasion*, because they can equally well be regarded as works of critical 'reassessment and consolidation'; and as themselves supplements to the myth of American history. In particular Williams in part, and Janet Lewis almost entirely, are concerned with that part of the myth which has to do with the fate of the Redskin.

Williams's debt to Lawrence is obvious, though I don't know that it has ever been acknowledged. It extends much further than the similarity of style illustrated from 'The Founding of Quebec'. The long section, 'Père Sebastian Rasles', which begins with magnificent gusto and audacity among the expatriates of Paris of the 'twenties and then proceeds, through a conversation with Valéry Larbaud, into a comparison between the French Catholic missions in Acadia and the Protestants in New England in the seventeenth century, is the place where the Lawrencian note is struck and sustained in content as well as in manner:

He would not suffer the contrite Indians to lay their hands upon him, as the Catholic fathers in the north had done, but drew back and told them to address themselves to God alone. Ah, very fine, you say. But it is very ugly – and it is *that* which has persisted: afraid to touch! But being forced to it every day by passion, by necessity – a devil of duplicity has taken possession of us.

It is hard to think of another instance in which the Lawrencian vocabulary, along with a centrally Lawrencian idea, has been taken over to other than calamitous effect. The 'touching', the readiness to risk that intimacy, is made the basis of all that Williams claims for Rasles:

> He was a great MAN. Reading his letters, it is a river that brings sweet water to us. THIS is a moral source not reckoned with, peculiarly sensitive and daring in its close embrace of native things. His sensitive mind. For everything his fine sense, blossoming, thriving, opening, reviving – not shutting out – was tuned. He speaks of his struggles with their language, its peculiar beauties, *'je ne sais quoi d'energique'*, he cited its tempo, the form of its genius with gusto, with admiration, with generosity. Already the flower is turning up its petals. It is *this* to be *moral*: to be *positive*, to be peculiar, to be sure, generous, brave – TO MARRY, to *touch* – to *give* because one HAS, not because one has nothing. And to give to him who HAS, who will join, who will make, who will fertilize, who will be like you yourself: to create, to hybridize, to crosspollenize – not to sterilize, to draw back, to fear, to dry up, to rot. It is the sun. In Rasles one feels THE INDIAN emerging from within the pod of his isolation from eastern understanding he is released AN INDIAN. He exists, he is – it is an AFFIRMATION, it is alive. Père Rasles, often suffering the tortures of the damned as a result of an early accident – fracture of both thighs, badly mended – lived with his village – alone, absorbed in them, LOST in them, swallowed, a hard yeast –

English prose has never got nearer than this to approximating to the rhythms and contours of excited speech. Lawrence, I think, even in *Studies in Classic American Literature*, never went so far. And it may be thought that the recourse to italics and capitalizations betrays that already this is to go too far, that the style fails of its effect because we feel it to be not excited but excitable, that it protests too much. In context, as the climax of a train of thought itself arising from a dramatic situation, I think the manner is justified, and a remarkable if eccentric achievement. Certainly Janet Lewis, however, if we may judge from internal evidence, might well protest that the rhetoric is coarse and brow-beating, too anxious to persuade. For that matter, she may also be restive at having her book connected with a figure so inflammatory as Lawrence, and a concept so dubious as myth. For her own manner is scrupulously self-effacing, and if her book has the explosiveness of myth (as I think it has), the fuse burns discreetly and slowly from the first page through to the last. Her style is anything but flashy; and if in this discussion I have found the right context for *The Invasion*, the achievement of that book is precisely in its so subduing local excitements as to reveal how inflammatory it is only when the last page has been read and it is held in the mind as a whole. *The Invasion* is one continuous, even pedestrian, narrative, where *In the American Grain* is a sequence of rhetorical exhibitions.

To be sure, Miss Lewis does not always refuse to pass judgement, at least to the extent that she is prepared sometimes to 'place' people in the way she scrupulously refused to place John Johnston. Longfellow is 'placed'. So, but with affection (in a tone as of eyebrows raised in perpetual mild astonishment) is the English best-seller Mrs Anna Jameson, who visited the Johnston ladies and wrote about them, there on the frontier in the 1830s. Or the judgement can even be so nearly overt as this:

> The next summer occurred the Treaty of Fond du Lac, in which the northern tribes agreed to the lines settled upon at Prairie du Chien, ceded the mineral rights of the Lake Superior region to the United States, and asked that an Ojibway mission school be established at the Sault. The Senate, in ratifying the treaty, struck out the school, but retained the magnificent gift of copper, silver, and iron.

But these are untypical. What is characteristic is the unremitting pressure to *realize* every item recorded. As one perceptive critic remarked on the book's first appearance, 'even the characteristic step of an Indian is presented as it were directly to the reader's leg muscles'. It is not only the justness and vividness of these compact images that is impressive, but also the assumption, conveyed by the scrupulously impersonal style, that this is the only way in which history can or should be contemplated, as a past pressed hard up against the present, conditioning it, and therefore to the imagination continuously present. There is no acknowledgement of exceptional imaginative effort involved, no 'Let us imagine if we can', nothing of 'How remote it all seems' or 'How clearly one envisages the scene', nothing even of Williams's 'But you shall see' or 'Is it not clarity itself?' The images are clear, but not diminished as seen down the wrong end of history's telescope, nor with the glowing colours of nostalgia, nor with the laborious heightening of the pageant's set scene. Simply, we are carried *there*. A fine example is this description of the Sault in the present century, when 'the unfinished Sabin Lock, a deep pit enclosed yet by the great coffer dam, had absorbed Oshawanoe's Island, had moved the bed of the actual rapids farther to the north, had rearranged the whole scene in a new and rigid pattern':

> Cold and green, translucent but not transparent, heavy with a vast chill inertia, the water lay in the canal of the Weitzel Lock, held in a wall eighteen feet above the level of the river. If the slow, barely percep-tible motion of the water in the long vat had not been sufficient to

indicate its heaviness, the bars and counterbars, and bolts and steel plates of the ponderous mitered gates, mitered towards the west, and locked shut, were another image of this innocent, terrific force, which, if loosed, would toss the *Douglass Houghton* against the farther gates and smash freighter and barrier as if they were the stuff of shingles. Deep in the lock chamber the *Douglass Houghton,* made fast by twisted steel hawsers to the blunt metal posts, waited while the water bubbled up about her, trickled down from the intricately barred inner side of the gates, seethed and eddied upward from invisible vents, and lifted her slowly, very slowly, between the sheer walls. Stains of iron rust, water stains, the faint lines of the stone seaming, were all that broke the monotony of the long, mathematically straight cliff-sides of the lock. Standing on the cement walk beside the lock, passers-by could look down upon the red steel decks of the freighter, upon the long double rows of slightly raised hatch covers, the little swinging railing that ran the four hundred and fifty feet of the vessel's middle section, upon the winches, the capstans, could look into the open galley door. Gradually she rose, her name appeared above the wall's edge, and her anchor. Among the grassy lawns, the gravelled and cemented walks, the plumy autumn trees, she stood, appearing, from a little distance, as if she had no business there. Her weathered sides, a grayed red-oxide from the prow to the stern, hung there eighteen feet above the river ...; her prow and stern a darker red, having been freshly painted at the beginning of the season. The bolts and plates of her shell were plain to behold. Bells sounded from the tower in the midst of the canals, a man ran out along the gate bridge to unlock the wings, the great flanges, that folded back against the walls, moving slowly, ponderously, hardly daring to stir the water, moving against liquid weight as one moves in a dream against an unnamable impeding substance. The water from Superior, lying quietly in the long canal, mingled with the lock water, and the freighter, convoyed by her tug, went westward, free. From the locks one could see Superior, a larkspur blue, beyond the black web of the railroad bridge, beneath the amethystine blue of the cold Laurentians.

The essential point to make – and it is too seldom made by the Americans themselves – is that myth and allegory are essentially distinct. Essentially; yet, in one distinguished instance after another through American literature, the two are blurred together. Hawthorne is the stock example, and the telling one. One reason, perhaps, for the neglect of *The Invasion,* and one way in which it differs very markedly from *In the American Grain,* is that if Janet Lewis's book is mythopoeic at all, the myth it creates at all points resists the exegete's breaking of it down into the schematic one-for-one correspondences of allegory. In this example, for instance, to take the freighter, the *Douglass Houghton*, as 'standing for' the forces which invade and rearrange in rigid patterns – this would do violence to the immediately exact and copiously vivid image which it makes simply as observable fact. If, when the lockwater rising brings her into view over the lawns and gravel walks, 'she stood, appearing, from a little distance, as if she had no business there', this appearance is first and foremost just that – an appearance exactly rendered. If she *and all she stands for* has no business there in another more spiritual sense (and she is, after all, named after a geologist), this reality exists only as a resonance from her appearance; and the appearance, rendered so abundantly and with such scruple, cannot be 'read into' as by the allegorist, only to be thereafter discarded. The *Douglass Houghton* might be described as a symbol; it is much better to take her, afresh in every situation where she appears, as a metaphor.

If I read aright Marius Bewley's admirable essay on Cooper (*Scrutiny*, Winter, 1952–3), it would be possible to credit Cooper, as against Hawthorne, with providing the model for narrative action and situation presented in this way as verging on myth while having no truck with allegory. At any rate, by 'myth' in this context we mean what Mr Bewley means by it, 'the incarnation of racial aspiration and memory'; and no one will dispute that Cooper is the father of myth in this sense as it appears in American literature. To dissolve it away into terms of the history of ideas, murmuring out of superior knowingness a ritual exorcism like 'noble savage' or 'Rousseau-istic', is an exercise of the same sort as the rendering down into schematic allegory. It is a stock reaction which will obscure for us, which has already obscured for us, some of the greatly imaginative works of our time.

3 Arthur Yvor Winters (1900–1968)

In 1983 Donald E. Stanford, the justly esteemed editor of Edward Taylor's poems, published *Revolution and Convention in Modern Poetry*. Subtitled 'Studies in Ezra Pound, T.S. Eliot, Wallace Stevens, Edwin Arlington Robinson, and Yvor Winters', Stanford's book rates the five poets in this sequence on a rising scale of merit from first to last. The book went largely unnoticed, as was customary with critics of Stanford's persuasion: the judgements that he arrived at were so far from those commonly accepted, that the majority seemingly could not find any common ground that would make dispute profitable. Yet Stanford reached those judgements out of a coherent understanding of the poetic tradition in English over the centuries. As he declared elsewhere:

> The 'meditative short poem', written from a fixed mental point of view but not necessarily from a fixed point in the landscape, that achieves coherence and unity of thought and feeling by means of rhythms derived from traditional metres (in English usually the iambic), that speaks in a single, not a multiple voice, is I believe the finest instrument available for examining and evaluating human experience, simple or complex. It has been employed by such poets as Donne, Herbert, Vaughan, Valéry, Wallace Stevens, Winters, and Cunningham. I think they are better role models for the future than Jeffers, Whitman, Pound.[1]

Winters would have named Ben Jonson along with Herbert, and would have reversed the rankings of Pound and Eliot in Stanford's hierarchy. Yet we hear in these comments Yvor Winters still speaking twenty years after his death. Before dismissing such views as merely crotchety, it must be noticed that they come to terms with certain figures that the current consensus is uncertain about. One such is Edwin Arlington Robinson. Another is J.V. Cunningham. And a third is Paul Valéry. More generally the consensus is uneasy with the assumption that poetry is an instrument for *evaluating* experience; and it is reluctant to legislate for the future, as Stanford does with his concern for 'better role models'.

1   *Southern Review*, Summer 1987.

All these emphases are characteristic of Winters: he devoted a book to Robinson (1949); he never ceased to applaud his own younger contemporary, Cunningham; he was sure that a good poem evaluates (morally) the experience that it deals with; and the readers that he had in mind were always, in the first instance, beginning poets. The French name, Valéry, is particularly significant. Though Winters refused to travel outside the USA, he was sure that an understanding of poetry derived only from poems in English must be deficient. Not only did he in his youth study Renaissance poetry in some Romance languages before he turned to English, but in the first issue of his magazine *Gyroscope* (August 1929) he cited as required reading, along with Allen Tate, I.A. Richards, Irving Babitt and (surprisingly) T.S. Eliot, René Lalou (*Défense de l'homme*, 2nd edn, 1926) and Ramon Fernandez (*Messages*, tr. Montgomery Belgion, New York 1927). Winters after his college days in Chicago hardly ever moved far from the Pacific Coast, but he was neither provincial nor chauvinist. On the contrary, when he embarked in the 1930s on a sustained examination of his American cultural heritage (*Maule's Curse*, 1938, dealing with prose fiction and historiography more than poetry), provincialism was what he convicted his inheritance of, in its undue reliance on what he thought the baleful bequest of Emerson. And among the neglected twentieth-century poets whom he campaigned for, there figure the non-American names of T. Sturge Moore, Robert Bridges, and Bridges's daughter Elizabeth Daryush. Because the case to be made for Bridges and Daryush, for Robinson and Cunningham, for Fulke Greville and Frederick Goddard Tuckerman, nowadays mostly goes by default, the Wintersian strain in criticism, still alive and vigorous, cannot be weeded out of the garden as a querulous and eccentric off-shoot, but must be seen as in many ways more generous than the accepted wisdom it seeks to supplant.

Winters in his lifetime was not at once, nor for several years, relegated to that outsider status which a successor like Donald Stanford has learned to endure with hard-earned equanimity. On the contrary, in the 1920s Winters wrote for what were recognized as the mainstream periodicals of the *avant-garde*: *The Dial*, *Transition*, and especially *Poetry*. And he was corresponding with Marianne Moore, Allen Tate and Hart Crane. True, from the first there was a characteristic fearlessness in passing judgement; and Francis Murphy, who collected this early criticism, was surely right to remark, of these pieces as of later ones, that 'Evaluation is so infrequent in criticism that any act of judgement seems to most readers harsh and surprising.' But in this early criticism because we cannot detect what principled position the judgements are delivered from, the judgements often seem perky or cocky, the licensed extravagances of a recognized *enfant terrible,* as it might be Richard Aldington. What was new on the other hand, and would always characterize Winters's procedure, was a determination to discriminate inside a writer's *oeuvre* between pieces where he was at the top of his bent and others where he wasn't – Winters was always at pains to point to the weaker performances of a writer whom on the whole he fervently admired, notably at this period Robinson. In other words, from the first he was more interested in poems than in poets. However, his youthful animadversions at their most caustic were still delivered from a position undefined indeed but securely within a set of assumptions that may be called 'modernist', even 'Poundian'. And this is in line with the poems that Winters was writing in those years, which he thought of, not implausibly, as 'imagist'. Robinson, he thought in 1922, was one founder of 'a tradition of culture and clean workmanship that such poets as Messrs. Stevens, Eliot, and Pound, as H.D. and Marianne Moore, are carrying on'; and though by 1928, reviewing the anthology *Fugitives*, he declared 'the poetry of Mr Eliot is a catastrophe', the alternative that he recommended was still 'modernist': 'the tremendously energetic forms of such writers as Williams, Pound, and Miss Moore'. As Eliot in poems like *Ash-Wednesday* began to struggle mournfully with questions of religious belief and unbelief, he alienated many more unbelievers than Winters; but Winters, at this time still vowed to 'perceptions' and distrustful of 'generalities, concepts', remained within the world of that Eliot who praised Henry James for having a sensibility too fine to be violated by ideas. The Winters of 1928 was very far from the critic whose precepts Donald Stanford was still swearing by in 1983.

That later Winters first emerged in several contributions to *The Hound and Horn*: 'Traditional Mastery' (about Bridges, 1932); 'The Objectivists' (1932–3); and 'T. Sturge Moore' (1933) – to which may be added his short story, 'The Brink of Darkness' (1932). The essay on Sturge Moore is often cited to show how perversely wrong-headed Winters could be. And certainly the verses by Moore chosen for approbation by Winters reveal how deaf he could be to diction, especially British diction. Moreover Winters here exposes a sort of racism that would always colour his comments on W.B. Yeats, applauding Moore in his dramas for choosing Greek or Hebrew themes, whereas Yeats 'has chosen most of his subjects from the formless and sentimental myths of Celtic tradition'. The essay on Bridges stands up much better. But the sting of these pieces is in the Anglo-American comparisons, as when Winters says that 'the diction of Dr Bridges is as fresh and living as that of Dr Williams; his metres allow him greater freedom, or rather greater range; he is in general a more civilized man'. Again, having detected in J.M. Synge 'a vast excess of mannerism', he remarks that 'the verse and prose of writers so varied in talents and aims as Carl Sandburg, Ezra Pound, Marianne Moore, and Elizabeth Madox Roberts, suffer rather seriously from the same vice'. Sturge Moore and Bridges provide a smoke-screen behind which Winters can launch an attack on American modernism in poetry, an attack which

thenceforward he never flinched from, but pressed home with special
acerbity because he judged he had himself been deluded by it through ten
years or more. He discerns, first, that despite coat-trailing gibes at romanticism by Eliot and others, American modernism was deeply romantic.
(This, others have noticed since, but equally, quite without Winters's
sense of betrayal.) Secondly – and in this he is original and still disconcerting – he diagnoses romantic *irony* as a manoeuvre in writers since Jules
Laforgue which enables them 'to correct the stylistic defects of looseness
and turgidity tolerated by the Romantics, *without understanding the concep-
tual confusion which had debauched Romantic style and Romantic character alike*'
(italics added). This reveals first that Winters's condemnation of what he
calls 'romanticism' is an ethical judgement, but secondly it shows how
seriously by 1933 he was taking those 'concepts' which ten years before,
writing of Robinson, he had airily dismissed as 'generalities'.

His review of *An 'Objectivists' Anthology* shows how incapable Winters
was at this stage of showing any sympathy for the Poundian cause in which
he had soldiered himself not many years before. His story, 'The Brink of
Darkness' has been made much of by his admirers, as showing that Winters
had personally experienced those gulfs and gusts of irrationalism which
thereafter he never ceased to warn against. But who ever doubted this?
Those who most strenuously urge us to be reasonable are those with most
cause to fear the irrational. Samuel Johnson is one case in point; and
Winters shared with Johnson more than an admirably lucid and trenchant
prose-style. Johnson however, it may be thought, was clearer than
Winters about the difference between rationality and rationalism.

In this momentous turn-around Winters was impelled by considerations partly practical, partly theoretical, but also in part religious. Affronted
by how Eliot, in poems like *Ash-Wednesday* and 'Marina', recorded with
a curious passivity the processes which might, and again might not, lead
him into the Christian Church, Winters adumbrated a morality, 'stoic',
which left to the individual will far more margin to decide its own destiny.
The crucial document here is an essay, first published in *The New American
Caravan* III (1929), which, drastically revised, became 'The Experimental
School in American Poetry'.[2] The hero of this essay in its first version was
Charles Baudelaire. And though Winters cannot have been unaware of
the argument that Baudelaire cannot be understood except as a believing
Roman Catholic, Winters presents him, as he does also that hymn-writer
and hymn-translator, the Anglican Robert Bridges, as a *stoic:*

> The man who, through a dynamic and unified grasp on life, lives fully
> and to the point of being able to renounce life with dignity, having

---

2   *Primitivism and Decadence* (1937). Temperate and judicious, this essay was reprinted in *In
    Defense of Reason* (1947)

known it, achieves something vastly more difficult and more noble than the immediate evasion and denial of the mystic or the whimper of the nihilist. It is in the consideration of this fact that we find the true function of the poet...

Though in subsequent years this message would be cloaked in the vocabulary of the literary historian or literary critic, this is the strenuous and heroic version of man that Winters would henceforward promulgate alike in his verse and his prose.

It was the strenuousness that set him at odds with John Crowe Ransom. Ransom it was who coined the slogan-label, 'The New Criticism'. And Winters's none too civil arguments with Ransom – notably in *The Anatomy of Nonsense* (1943; later comprised in *In Defense of Reason*) – explode the still common misconception that Winters was himself a 'New Critic'. Ransom's distinction between 'structure' and 'texture' in poems affronted Winters's conviction that a genuine poem was, or came out of, a unitary act of the mind. That conviction he arrived at not theoretically but out of painfully personal experience: the suicide of Hart Crane in 1932. Winters along with Tate had been at great pains to keep Crane on an even keel and productive. And Terry Comito is surely right to say that there is no passage in modern criticism more moving (or more flagrantly in breach of academic convention) than the pages in which Winters contrasts Professor X, who toys with irrationalist theories of literature, to Crane who took such notions seriously enough to live them out to their logical conclusion. For, he declared in *In Defense of Reason,* 'the doctrine of Emerson and Whitman, if really put into practice, should naturally lead to suicide'. Winters's bad manners in *The Anatomy of Nonsense* towards Eliot and Ransom, less noticeably towards Henry Adams (a 'nominalist') and Wallace Stevens (a 'hedonist'), should be seen in the light of the grief and indignation he felt at the wasteful extinction of Crane's genius. Wrong ideas, he thought (and thought he had seen) could *kill*; hence his vehemence in exposing them.

Though Winters's ear for diction was faulty – like his friend and contemporary Tate, he was oddly susceptible to high-flown archaisms – his ear for rhythm and cadence was incomparably fine. And it is the niceties of his discriminations about metre which make him irreplaceable. The distinctions that he made in 'The Experimental School in American Poetry' between syllabic, accentual, and accentual-syllabic metres ought to constitute (though it's plain that they don't) a rudimentary primer for every reader. They are plain and commonsensical, in an area where common sense is hard to come by. His attempt to scan the short-lined unmetred verse of William Carlos Williams must be judged a failure; it represents one stage in a dogged but ultimately hopeless rearguard action on behalf of the author of *Sour Grapes* (1921), who in every collection after that early one disappointed Winters more than he found it, until the very end, possible to acknowledge. The essential supplement to Winters's prosody is 'The Audible Reading of Poetry' which, originally a lecture to the Kenyon School of English in 1949, was reprinted with four other essays (one on Hopkins, one on Frost) in *The Function of Criticism* (1957). The fine discriminations that Winters could make in metred verse – in unmetred also, though there he never found a terminology for registering his perceptions faithfully – was possible only to a reader who acted on the principle, idly subscribed to by many, that the rhythmical character of a poem is near to the heart of it; who thought moreover that that 'character', perceptible to us as deviations from a norm of expectation, could emerge only when that norm was firmly established and not trangressed lightly. One sees clearly why Winters was outraged by Ransom's supposition that at a late stage in composition a poet might choose to 'roughen' the metre of a poem so as to make it more 'interesting'.

Winters's last book, *Forms of Discovery* (1967), has been thought by intemperate admirers to crown appropriately his solitary and embattled career as a critic. But it is hard to agree: leaving aside the justified resentments at ill-treament which colour its pages to those in the know, it seems to represent a sadly instructive instance of how *not* to combine literary history with the history of ideas. In *Maule's Curse* and elsewhere Winters had powerfully called on intellectual history to buttress his strictly literary judgements. But, dealing with American writers, he could safely assume in himself and his readers (it might not be a safe assumption today) sufficient knowledge in the broadest terms of other dimensions of American history – political, social, economic, demographic. Winters had no such inwardness with these dimensions of the history of the British Isles, and reading that history through the single lens of the history of ideas brings about such anomalies – alike in *Forms of Discovery* and the associated anthology *Quest for Reality* (1969, completed by Kenneth Fields) – as finding no British poet of merit between Charles Churchill (1731–64) and Thomas Hardy (b.1840). One may sympathize with Winters's distrust of 'romanticism', whether in its British or its American versions, and yet doubt whether it was a misconception dreamed up in poets' and philosophers' studies without some pressure from extra-intellectual developments like the Industrial Revolution. The strength of *Forms of Discovery* is all in its first chapter, where Winters showed all over again his sensitivity to what he first isolated as 'the plain style' in Elizabethan poetry; but that style and the principles that inform it, were not, as Winters would have us believe, lost to sight between the seventeenth century and the twentieth.

From a signed typescript, not dated.

4 The Poetry of Yvor Winters

The fundamental distinction among English-language poets – the one of the coarsest mesh, but the one that the working poet daily lives with and operates by – is not any distinction between Romantic and Classicist, between rationalist and irrationalist, between a strict kind of formalist and the loose or 'organic' kind. The fundamental, the radical split is between those who think that a poem is a considered utterance, and those who think it is unconsidered.

Nobody, one might think, has ever seriously advanced a theory of poetry as unconsidered utterance. But on the contrary such a position has been, and is, defended repeatedly. And the defences available range from some that are self-evidently fatuous to others that are sophisticated and superficially plausible. Among the more sophisticated, for instance, are those theories that start from the proposition that over by far the greater range of his daily activities modern man is required to be all too 'considering', that at every point man and woman in our technologically advanced societies are required to calculate, to anticipate consequences, to reckon up the odds. This necessity (so the argument develops) thwarts and chokes our capacities for spontaneous behaviour, so that for instance even our sexual behaviour becomes calculated, all too monstrously 'considered'. On this showing poetry has a duty to be 'unconsidered', at least in some respects and to some notable degree, because only by being so can it discharge its therapeutic and social duty to defend such threatened areas of experience as our sexuality.

Yvor Winters was always sure – whether he was writing his unparaphrasable lyrics in the 1920s, or the later partly paraphrasable poems by which he is better known – that a poem is a considered utterance, indeed that some great poems may well be the most considered utterances that mankind has yet shown itself capable of. But we mustn't suppose that Winters didn't know the arguments on the other side, or that he thought they had no weight. He might have pointed out that language, the medium poets work in, is far from being a product of consideration; that on the contrary it is the product of quite exuberant spontaneity, continuous and continuing. This is more conspicuously true of English, the language of Shakespeare, than of the Romance languages. (And Winters, it is not often realized, when he began his study of Renaissance poetry, began with poems in Spanish, not English.) Thus the poet who seeks to make of his poems considered utterances is in fruitful tension with his medium, because that medium, his language, will always be budding out in multivalences, double meanings and ambiguities under his very hands. It might even be true to say that in this conflict the language of Shakespeare always in the end defeats the poet; the finished poem, because it is the product of the language as much as of the poet, will *never* be as clear, as exact and conclusive, as the poet dreamed it might be. And if so, the attempt to make considered utterances can never do damage, precisely because in the last analysis the attempt must always to some degree fail. Which doesn't mean however that the attempt, since it is foredoomed, was by that token misconceived. On the contrary, from poems that attempt only to *go along* with language, happily accepting the patterns that language throws up of its own accord (for instance the intriguing verbal doodles and sometimes intricate jingles that come into one's head between sleeping and waking), there will always be missing precisely the tension that comes of the artificer bending his will against his medium, going against the grain of it. And nothing can make up for that lack. Moreover, what is true of the semantics of English is true also of its other dimension as patterned sound and sequences of sound; and here the argument makes for meter against free verse.

These reflections are all mine, my impressions from remembering Winters the man as I knew him, and from pondering the poems which he wrote. I am not paraphrasing any page of his criticism, for as critic Winters approached these questions in a very different way – though that way led him, I believe, to very similar conclusions. In any case it is advisable – I might even say, it is absolutely necessary – to suppress whatever one may know of Winters's criticism, when approaching his poems. That is the only way for those poems to get a fair hearing. And because on both sides of the Atlantic nearly every one of the few who have read Winters's poetry, have done so only after first reading in his criticism, it is almost true to say that Winters's poems have never yet had a fair hearing. It is not the case of course that Winters's criticism points one way, his poetry another. The poems and the criticism can be matched up, right enough; and the one can be made to validate the other. But what an eccentric and impoverished and mean-spirited way that is, of reading poetry! Winters's poems are considered utterances, to be sure; but what they have considered, and now utter, is not such or such a contested and challenging position in poetic theory or literary history, but the matter of what it is like to be human, the pains and the pleasures of it – of being a man acting in history, acting in society (a highly specific and sharply specified society), acting in landscapes (some landscapes rather than others, and those exactly described), and acting in a web of human relationships and the responsibilities which those impose. Winters's poems were not written for class-room use or for polemical purposes; they were composed and made public not as models or *exempla* or illustrations of 'how to write', but as considered statements of how to *live*, or of how the business of living had been experienced by one thoughtful and feelingful man. That awkward amphibian the poet–critic runs the danger, which Winters certainly has not escaped, of having the poet in him immolated for the sake of the critic. And whether the immolation is for the purpose of exalting the critic or decrying him, hardly matters; in either case the poet has been denied the sort of attention which we readily give to poets who either aren't critics at all, or else self-evidently foolish and careless ones. We may go further, and ask: what is the poet inside the poet–critic doing, if not outwitting the critic in him? There are things happening in Winters's poetry that were not dreamed of in his criticism; if it were not so, why should he have bothered writing the poems at all?

Winters had a proper contempt for the parochialism which, lacking historical perspective and historical knowledge, regards the particular span of years that we are living through as unprecedented – for no better reason than because we, such specially interesting people as we are, happen to be living in it. For that sort of know-nothing 'modernism' he had nothing but impatient scorn. But that does not mean that, as he wrote his poems, he thought of himself as anything but the creature of a particular geographical place at a particular historical time. His 'View of Pasadena from the Hills' is every inch a twentieth-century Californian poem, as its title indicates. But it is not therefore *provincial;* for the depletion which the poem mourns, of one particular Californian landscape, is only an instance of a depletion – rather, a rape – that other landscapes have suffered in the present century. I remember his making the point quietly but firmly, with reference to this particular poem of his, when in the last months of his life he and I were reading Hardy's poems together, and I had reflected mournfully on what had transformed the landscapes of Hardy's Wessex since Hardy died. Because Winters never travelled outside the United States, and through the latter part of his life could only with difficulty be prevailed upon to leave the environs of San Francisco, it is assumed that his knowledge of other parts of the earth's surface – particularly of the mediterranean Europe from which (so he maintained, very unfashionably) American culture derived – could only have been, in a damaging and emasculating sense, 'literary'. Thus, when he writes in his 'Anacreontic',

> Peace! there is peace at last.
> Deep in the Tuscan shade,
> Swathed in the Grecian past,
> Old Landor's bones are laid ...

it is easy to come up with the glib and canting objection: since he'd never been to either Tuscany or Greece, how could the words, 'Tuscan and

'Grecian', have for him anything but a merely *verbal* significance? Even as I say that it is easy to raise the objection, I cudgel my memory in vain for any one who has raised it. Which is a pity; because the objection forces us to find an answer which is surprising and touching, and therefore illuminating. By way of answer I read from 'In Praise of California Wines':

> With pale bright leaf and shadowy stem,
> Pellucid amid nervous dust,
> By pre-Socratic stratagem,
> Yet sagging with its weight of must,
>
> The vineyard spreads beside the road
> In repetition, point and line.
> I sing, in this dry bright abode,
> The praises of the native wine.
>
> It yields the pleasure of the eye,
> It charms the skin, it warms the heart;
> When nights are cold and thoughts crowd high,
> Then 'tis the solvent for our art.
>
> When worn for sleep the head is dull,
> When art has failed us, far behind,
> Its sweet corruption fills the skull
> Till we are happy to be blind.
>
> So may I yet, as poets use,
> My time being spent, and more to pay,
> In this quick warmth the will diffuse,
> In sunlight vanish quite away.

'As poets use' ... the very usage of 'use' is archaic. But what has the poem been saying, if not that it has a right to such archaisms, as also to ''tis', and numerous inversions of the order of spoken American? Every one knows that California has a mediterranean climate; not everyone knows that the climate has produced, insofar as California has produced any indigenous culture or 'life-style' at all, a mediterranean style of life – in which for instance the culture of the grape plays a central role. Winters has a right to the words 'Tuscan' and 'Grecian', and to the time-honoured locutions which those words summon up as their appropriate accompaniments, because the landscape and the climate which Landor encountered as soon as he stepped outside his door in Florence are identical with the climate and landscape that Winters walked into as soon as he stepped towards his little orchard in Los Altos. What I am saying is that one of the strongest impulsions behind Winters's poetry is Virgilian *pietas* – towards a native or adopted (in Winters's case, adopted) terrain. And if we ask what place there is, in Winters's critical theory, for such an irrationally powerful

sentiment and impulsion, the answer has to be, so far as I can see: no place
at all – which is just one example of how the poetry traffics in realities that
the criticism knows nothing of. As myself an adopted Californian I put it
on record that the California I move about in is more redolently and
vividly present in Winters's poems – and in their way of saying, as much
as in what they say – than in any of the much-touted urban poets of San
Francisco and Los Angeles, or in the self-consciously rural and 'opting out'
poems of Gary Snyder.

Before this archaic yet so lately fabricated backdrop, there are enacted
dramas which are similarly archaic and urgently topical – the drama, for
instance, of David Lamson, accused of murdering his wife. Or there is
'Before Disaster', dated Winter, 1932–3 ;

> Evening traffic homeward burns,
> Swift and even on the turns,
> Drifting weight in triple rows,
> Fixed relation and repose.
> This one edges out and by,
> Inch by inch with steady eye.
> But should error be increased,
> Mass and moment are released;
> Matter loosens, flooding blind,
> Levels drivers to its kind.
>
>   Ranks of nations thus descend,
> Watchful to a stormy end.
> By a moment's calm beguiled,
> I have got a wife and child.
> Fool and scoundrel guide the State.
> Peace is whore to Greed and Hate.
> Nowhere may I turn to flee:
> Action is security.
> Treading change with savage heel,
> We must live or die by steel.

Wherever I have read this poem in the English-speaking world, I have
heard objections raised to what is called the 'stilted rhetoric' of the second
half – particularly, so some of my listeners have said, when it comes on
the heel of Winters's early but conclusive treatment of what it feels like to
drive on a multi-lane freeway. Such objections, it seems to me, come not
out of any perception of the poem as a rhetorically consistent because
considered statement, but out of a prejudgement about the English-
speaking societies of our time or of the 1930s. The poet assumes that those
societies are worthy to be judged, and of course castigated, in a vocabulary and by standards not wholly out of touch with those by and in which
Juvenal judged Domitian's Rome, and Dryden judged William III's

London. He pays his society that compliment. But such a compliment is harder to forgive than any insult. Because we are (we suppose) unprecedented, or in unprecedented situations, we demand to be judged by standards peculiar to – which is to say, more lenient than – the standards by which societies of the past were judged and castigated by *their* poets. I will not pretend that all Winters's archaisms of diction and rhetoric can be justified in this way; but certainly sometimes we jib at them because we are not prepared to be called for judgement at the bar of the centuries and the millennia.

Winters, I would say, is not a good model for young poets of today to emulate. He cannot be such a model precisely because he is so much a poet of his nation, his region, and his time – a conjunction which, in the nature of things, can never recur. Yet this does not mean that he is 'dated'. On the contrary his achievement is, through his style, to have enforced the generally acknowledged but in particular cases always unacceptable paradox that the more rootedly particular poems are – think of Thomas Hardy! – the more universal their significance.

Introduction to *The Collected Poems of Yvor Winters* (Carcanet Press, 1978).

5 An Alternative to Pound?

Edgar Bowers, *The Form of Loss* (Denver: Alan Swallow, 1956)

The Stanford school of poets, grouped around and schooled by Yvor Winters, seems to me perhaps the most interesting feature of the poetic scene in the US. Where other masters – British as well as American – have tried to come to terms with the challenge of the Poundian-Eliotic poetic mostly by diluting, muffling, taking what they want and evading the harder truths, Winters has met the challenge by offering a considered and coherent alternative, an alternative poetic theory grounded in an alternative morality driving through to an alternative practice. And so, while most talent can and does spring up in other quarters of the poetic scene, it is only from the Poundian wing (and by that I mean rather Charles Tomlinson, say, than Louis Zukofsky) or else from this other extreme at Stanford, that one can expect talent, when it appears, not to have to save itself by *ad hoc* improvisations, hairsbreadth escapes from eleventh-hour expedients. It is especially good, if also ironical, that this most traditional and forbiddingly 'classical' of current schools should be, at Palo Alto, within the orbit of that San Francisco bohemianism which, in its naïve reliance on the generous impulse, spells death to any poetic whatever.

Edgar Bowers has been hailed by Winters and others as exemplifying at last the Stanford poetic in the service of a major talent. In fact, he is not so good as that – hardly so good as Winters himself, certainly less good than an older hand, Howard Baker. All the same, his first collection is impressive – impressive, and also puzzling, in a way that is characteristic, more or less, of the whole school. The puzzle is how so much licence can exist along with so much discipline. On the one hand Alan Swallow, in an unusually educated blurb, is right to invoke the name (unexpectedly recondite) of Fulke Greville:

> O sages,
> Of whom we are the merest shades, you are
> The undemanding whom indifference
> Has least defiled, those few whose innocence
> Is earned by long distraction with minute
> And slow corruption proving all they know,
> Till patience, young in what may come to pass,

> Is reconciled to what its love permits,
> And is not proud that knowledge must be so.

It is quite true that if we look for precedents for this close and abstract ratiocination in verse, the grotesquely neglected Fulke Greville is one of the few names that can be invoked. (A less remote and therefore perhaps more tactful precedent is in some unfashionable poems by Edwin Arlington Robinson.) And the whole of the poem from which these lines are taken – it is called 'The Prince', and is a dramatic monologue analysing human evil in the shape of intellectual perversity – manifests the same virtues of close and scrupulous thought in verse, virtues for so long out of fashion that they strike with all the shock of absolute novelty. It is always possible to argue of course (though I wouldn't) that these are not virtues at all, at any rate not in poetry, which has its own and quite different ways of thinking – as we say, 'through images'. That would make the poem a perverse achievement, but an achievement none the less.

Not an unflawed one, however. Alongside the forbiddingly strict discipline of ratiocination and the no less strict (though perhaps equally perverse) discipline of metre still bound to the iambic, both diction and syntax are permitted unusual freedoms. Diction for instance is free to indulge an occasional melancholy blast on the Tennysonian organ: 'Austere old lonely grandeur's complete pride' (where the dryness of 'complete' can't mop up the sogginess of 'austere' and 'old' and 'lonely' – three words very long on suggestion but short on sense). More generally, Bower's diction is at all points very far from the usages (i.e., the word-order) of either modern prose or modern conversation; its lean compactness cannot disguise the fact that it is very *poetical* diction, and sounds a muffled note in consequence.

Syntax goes along with, and is part of, diction:

> Despite erratic fires which chance
> In self-consuming, bright array
> Hurls from our gaze, let us advance
> Desire that puts despair away.
>
> In loving keeps the hope for love,
> And, though inconstant and perverse,
> Conform to law in how we move
> Like lucid stars: let love coerce.

This is really very bad, especially from a poet whom Winters names with six others as signalizing a formal recovery to set against 'the decay of form… in men such as Pound and Eliot.'[1] The poeticisms ('Desire that puts despair away') are part and parcel of the one inefficiency that, for instance, invites

---

1   Yvor Winters, *The Function of Criticism: Problems and Exercises* (Denver: Alan Swallow, 1957)

us to take 'chance', isolated at the line-ending, as a verb – a misapprehension corrected with extreme discomfort only when we reach line 3. But there is worse though similar discomfort inherent in the syntax: 'puts' and 'keeps' are both governed by 'desire'; since there is no 'and' at the start of the second stanza, we inevitably expect that the 'And' at the start of the next line will introduce yet a third verb governed by 'desire'; when the next verb arrives, however, it is 'conform', and the unexpected plural form jolts us right back to 'let us', in order to find its antecedent. The only possible explanation of this is the sheer inability, within the exigencies of rigid metre, to find room, between 'puts' and 'keeps', for the 'and' that would make all clear. Admittedly this is as bad as Bowers gets. And yet the same looseness shows up elsewhere, in more distinguished contexts:

> His nerves have left his figure loose, as mine
> Must let it go, and with it memories
> So violent they dominate the sense,
> Lest mind should settle like soft dust in trees...

Is it memories that should dominate, or nerves that must 'let it go', lest mind should settle? There is no way of deciding, except by the logic of the poem's argument as a whole; and though this reveals that the second alternative is the right one, we understand this only when we study the poem, not as we read it, however many times we do so. This syntactical uncertainty (cf. lines 32–7 of 'The Prince') is especially important of course, and especially betraying, in poetry like this which offers a surface of close discursive reading.

No, it's no good. The alternative to a Poundian poetic – it exists in theory (though the theory too needs trimming and extending – notably into a rationale of poetic diction); it does not exist as a proven alternative in practice. At least, Bowers's poems have not supplied that proof. It's a pity they have been asked to carry that responsibility; for considered simply as a first collection of poems, *The Form of Loss* is a very distinguished performance. After all, what Pound and Winters have in common is an unremitting moral concern, driving through their poems to acts of judgement which nourish programmes of right action. And it is this urgency and seriousness which lift Bowers out of the ruck. His poems are never merely accomplished. Not one, for instance, of his poems about Europe is a glossy picture-postcard in verse, such as the Guggenheim Fellows so incessantly dispatch to the folks back home; his poems are written out of genuine inwardness with the European (mostly German) mind and destiny, a true commitment of intelligent sympathy. In fact he is that rarest bird, a new poet more interested in what he has to say than in himself saying it.

First published in *Spectrum* I: 3 (Fall 1957). Reprinted in *The Poet in the Imaginary Museum* (Carcanet Press, 1977).

6 Poetry's Imaginary Museum

The Faber Book of American Verse, edited by W.H. Auden (Faber & Faber, 1956)

The American reader has doubtless never questioned, what the Briton finds comically hard to believe, that when Auden left Britain for the United States, what counted with him was what he was escaping to, not what he was escaping *from*. This anthology ought to reveal what he was hoping to find, and how far he has found it. And certainly the volume deserves respect – at all events Auden has looked, quite hard, in places off the beaten track; and what he has found isn't what other anthologists have found. The short prefatory essay ought to give us some clues. In fact it's tantalizing. Doubtless the only way to deal with the imponderables in such a theme as 'the American poetic genius', is by being tentative and graceful. But several of the ideas that Auden throws out are novel enough, and manageable enough, to be pursued a good deal farther. One of these, itself far from novel, is the point that the American poet, if he looks towards Europe at all, sees it as a whole. At the simplest level this produces the lines from Robinson Jeffers, very thrilling to a European:

> The Atlantic is a stormy moat, and the Mediterranean,
> The blue pool in the old garden,
> More than five thousand years has drunk sacrifice
> Of ships and blood and shines in the sun; ...

It produces also what is as evident in Longfellow as in Pound and Eliot:

> Longfellow had a curiosity about the whole of European literature compared with which Tennyson, concerned only with the poetry of his own land and the classical authors on whom he was educated, seems provincial.

Since the day of Longfellow and Tennyson, the British poet has got more provincial (as a rule 'the classical authors' are no longer part of his education), while the American has grown ever more polyglot and knowledgeable. There are plenty of exceptions no doubt – Dr Williams, for one – but the generalization holds good. And it is not hard to see why: the advent of 'the modern movement' aggravated the obstinate provincialism of the British even as it endorsed and encouraged the cosmopolitanism of the American:

> When a revolutionary break with the past is necessary it is an advantage not to be too closely identified with any one particular literature or any particular cultural group. Americans like Eliot and Pound, for example, could be as curious about French or Italian poetry as about English ... in a way that for an Englishman ... would have been difficult.

The American poet, in other words, was a natural for Malraux's *musée imaginaire*.

All the same, however much one has to indict the British of complacency and sheer lethargy, the British poet (if he chose to think of it – in fact he doesn't) has some right on his side, when he refuses to flock into the imaginary museum along with the painters and sculptors, the musicians and architects. A language, he might maintain (and Dr Williams might endorse him), is necessarily a provincial matter; words are words in some one language, and the poet's medium can never be international as is the painter's or the musician's. Hence the whole of the poetic past, even of Europe, can never be available to the poet as a repertoire of styles, as the whole of the world's painting is nowadays, with the perfection of techniques of reproduction, available to the painter.

For proof of what happens when a poet forgets or will not tolerate this provincialism in his medium, the Englishman might point to the two poems here by Allen Tate. This is a good example of editorial boldness, for Auden ignores all the earlier Tate to give 'Seasons of the Soul', and a long extract, headed 'The Buried Lake' from the poet's work in progress, which seemed to promise rather well, from what one had seen of it previously. All of this is very Dantesque:

> As in a moonlit street
> Men meeting are too shy
> To check their hurried feet
> But raise their eyes and squint
> As through a needle's eye
> Into the faceless gloom, –
> My father in a grey shawl
> Gave me an unseeing glint
> And entered another room!

This is very like a famous passage of Dante; the question is whether it is much like anything else, whether when men meet by moonlight they behave as Tate says, whether indeed we have any clear idea of the behaviour he means. If we haven't, the lines have an exclusively *literary* distinction. The Yeatsian Dantesque (in 'Supernatural Songs'), and the

Eliotic (in 'Little Gidding') are much more tentative; but this may be because being Dantesque wasn't their sole or main objective, because for them the Dantesque was a means, not an end. To put it another way, the extraordinary preciosity and pedantry of diction ('Small dancing girl who gave the smell of dill / In pelts of mordents on a minor third') are symptoms of the malaise infecting language when twentieth-century American straining after fourteenth-century Italian, is so exhausted by that struggle that it cannot register twentieth-century reality. The imaginary museum becomes a whispering gallery.

This of course is precisely the sort of thing that is said about Pound, to whom it does not apply. One should look not at the subjects of poems, but at what happens to the language. After its dealings with Arnaut Daniel and Propertius, Pound's language comes out not at all exhausted but invigorated and clean. The same can be said of Robert Lowell's dealings with Virgil, in 'Falling Asleep over the Aeneid'. So long as the struggle is there on the page, as in Lowell's savage enjambements, the language is still healthy; but in Tate, as in Ransom and Léonie Adams, the struggle is over before the poem begins, and the language issues from it already exhausted into literature, words pulled loose from their referents and from the pegs of syntax, florid and precious, violent sometimes but with a violence that attacks the nerves. In Ransom and Léonie Adams, who are much less ambitious than Tate, this language achieves its own overblown distinction – an achievement not different in kind from the late Tennysonian music of a Trumbull Stickney. Stevens's 'Sunday Morning' is infected in this way, though mildly; the language is much cleaner and more vigorous in 'The Snow Man' and 'Disillusionment of Ten O'Clock', or even in 'Be thou me, said Sparrow', a lyric which Auden salvages from 'Notes toward a Supreme Fiction'.

To do Auden justice, it appears that this is not what he was looking for. (If it had been, he might have done better by Hart Crane.) And if he is indulgent at all (as he surely is – eighty poets is a lot), it is towards those poets who most defiantly stay outside the Museum. In his Introduction, he speaks of what he calls 'the fingering', meaning by that the differences – especially of pace and pitch – which American speech introduces into standard English metres. His examples, from Robinson and Frost, are sufficiently convincing; but once let loose on the poems, the English reader is at a loss to know whether, for instance, Vachel Lindsay's 'Bryan, Bryan, Bryan, Bryan' would sound less lamely from American lips, or whether an American voice no less than an American mind can make sense of John Berryman's 'Homage to Mistress Bradstreeet', or of José Garcia Villa or Horace Gregory. Apart from Robinson and Frost (Robinson's poems are particularly impressive), the fingering was for me most notable and delightful in the selection from Jeffers, who denies to the ear the cadence it expects, only to force upon it another, unexpected.

To conclude with some random notes – the anthology confirmed me in my admiration for Robert Penn Warren (not to mention more usually honoured names, like Marianne Moore and Cummings); it left me unpersuaded as to Dr Williams; it disappointed me with its selections from Yvor Winters and Theodore Roethke; it shamed me in my past indifference to Elizabeth Bishop; and it wrung from me a reluctant respect from Richard Eberhart. There are good poems, also, by John Holmes, Stanley Kunitz, and Robert Fitzgerald.

Manuscript, dated December 1956.

7 The Auroras of Autumn

The Auroras of Autumn is a cycle of ten poems, each of twenty-four lines arranged in groups of three. It first appeared in book form in 1950, in a volume to which this poem gave a title. It can be taken as a typical example of the poet's recent style and of his current preoccupations.

When I first read the poem a couple of years ago it struck me as delightful and impressive, but difficult to understand. I therefore made notes on it to elucidate it for my own sake, and this is at bottom what I offer here – no more than a painstaking, deliberate, even leaden-footed elucidation of the poem from first to last. But, as often happens, the process of elucidating, of trying to understand, turned to evaluation as I proceeded with it. And I now find that the poem is not the completely assured masterpiece I thought it at first. In fact it now seems to me that the sequence breaks down just after the halfway mark. I was led to this conclusion when I found that my efforts at interpretation broke down at just this point, and suspicious readers may make of this admission what they please – may decide that the critic's inability to understand is no reflection on the poet. However, I find sufficient evidence of a loss of touch in the last few poems in the sequence to make me stick to my guns. And in what remains of the poem after all my objections have been made, there is sufficient splendour to justify the close attention that I have given and that I ask for.

The title prepares us: Aurora = dawn = beginning; Autumn = eve = ending. 'In the end is my beginning,' the cyclical pattern – this is the theme of the work. The first poem exhibits this clearly. Here the autumn is said to be a snake, because the snake sloughs his skin; and is he then the beginning of a new thing or the end of an old thing? Of course he is both; and this is the paradox to be explored. But the snake is also inevitably the serpent of the Garden of Eden, who tempts to the knowledge of good and evil; and this, as we see later, looks forward to what is unique in this treatment of what is otherwise almost a poetic commonplace. The cyclical human knowledge, what it is, how it comes, how reliable it is. The verse strikes me in this first poem as not yet strung up to the pitch it is soon to reach. It is difficult in places to make expressive sense out of the rhythms, and there is also what seems to me the solecism:

> His meditations in the ferns,
> When he moved so slightly to make sure of sun,
>
> Made us *no less as sure.* (my italics)

This is important however to the meaning. Sure of what? Of some constant principle behind the elusive metamorphoses of the natural world as proffered to us by our senses? Or of there being no such underlying constancy to look for? Elsewhere in the poem we seem to learn that the changeability of that snake, the world, when it leads us to accept the second alternative, leads us astray – 'This is his poison'. Nevertheless, the poem ends in a cluster of images which are thoroughly and (I take it) deliberately ambiguous. We cannot tell from them whether we ought to believe that there is no principle governing the world except the principle of continual change, or that, in some way as yet unexplored, the metamorphoses of the world prove the existence of some more constant principle underlying them.

The next poem is splendid and delicate. It begins, 'Farewell to an idea ...'; but the rest of the poem is concerned with a concretely presented scene, a whitewashed cabin on a beach. The quality of its whiteness changes with changes in the light and changes in the seasons. In this context, 'Farewell to an idea' can mean (1) farewell to the idea of whiteness, because 'whiteness', we realize, is not the name of one idea, but a name conveniently attached to many different ideas ('idea' in this case being used, as by Berkeley, to mean 'sense-impression'); or it can mean (2) farewell to the idea of summer, now that autumn has come; or it can mean (3) farewell to an idea in the more conversational sense of something that has been a governing principle in one's thought. In the last case, one may say farewell to the idea, not when it is proved unsound, but as soon as it comes to seem less important, to move out of the centre of one's mind; and if so, then the changes in the landscape drawn in the poem are metaphors for a mental process:

> The wind is blowing the sand across the floor.
>
> Here, being visible is being white,
> Is being of the solid of white, the accomplishment
> Of an extremist in an exercise ...
>
> The season changes. A cold wind chills the beach.
> The long lines of it grow longer, emptier,
> A darkness gathers though it does not fall
>
> And the whiteness grows less vivid on the wall.
> The man who is walking turns blankly on the sand.
> He observes how the north is always enlarging the change,

> With its frigid brilliances, its blue-red sweeps
> And gusts of great enkindlings, its polar green,
> The color of ice and fire and solitude.

I sympathize with any reader who insists on taking this for what it so beautifully is on the surface, an astonishingly felicitous description, offered for
its own sake. But the more one looks at the poem, the more one is forced
to see that every item so lovingly and precisely offered has a function
beyond the merely descriptive. Thus, 'The wind is blowing the sand across
the floor' is a piece of information interrupting the detailed charting of the
changing play of colour in the scene, and it says in effect that the change
of colour seems just as aimless as the blowing of the sand, or the move-
ments of the walker who turns 'blankly' (how else, in this context?) on
the beach. And the question whether these changes are in fact as aimless
as they seem is, as we have seen, precisely the question that is being
discussed throughout.

The last stanza, that seems at first merely decorative, though beautiful,
in fact links up with the images of the next poem in the sequence, and not
just with its images but with its themes (e.g., solitude). This third poem is
again very beautiful indeed. This too begins, 'Farewell to an idea'. It paints
the picture of a family gathering at home in a tranquillity and security that
centres on the mother and is in contrast to the bitter weather outside,
which seems to invade the members of the family as they say 'Goodnight'
to the mother and separate to their beds. The simplist reading of this is:
summer gives way to autumn as a mother leaves her family when they all
retire to rest. It is a beautiful simile, but it is not the whole of the poem.
For as we are concerned not with summer but with the idea of summer,
so we are concerned not with the mother but with the idea of the mother.
This epistemological element is much more prominent here, so much so
that one may read the poem as an account, not of an actual domestic occasion, but of how the poet writes a poem about such an occasion, present
only in his imagination. The point is indeed that the actual occasion is no
more 'real' than the imagined occasion. In either case:

> The necklace is a carving not a kiss.
>
> The soft hands are a motion not a touch.
> The house will crumble and the books will burn.
> They are at ease in a shelter of the mind
>
> And the house is of the mind and they and time,
> Together, all together.

So, throughout, 'their present peace' is presented as precarious and partial.
The theme once again is the hackneyed but permanent one of transience,
seen alike in the autumn poised on the change to winter, in the poem that

slides out of the mind once it is written, in the mother who grows older and more remote as her family grows up. In this last connection, a possible reading would be: Children accept the mother as a presence; adults necessarily see in the presence the *idea* of a mother and so they possess her less completely. The meaning is clinched in the consummate wit and beauty of:

> Upstairs
> The windows will be lighted, not the rooms.
>
> A wind will spread its windy grandeurs round
> And knock like a rifle-butt against the door.
> The wind will command them with invincible sound.

That is, the watchers are inevitably *outside* the thing they watch, watching not a home but the idea of a home. How scrupulous this poet is through all his brilliance may be seen from the audacious and difficult image, 'The necklace is a carving not a kiss.' The necklace, one of the mother's charms, being a carving, is cold. Our idea of a mother's charm, just because it *is* an idea, is an artifact, something we have constructed for ourselves; and to that extent it is inevitably cold, colder than the warm presence itself as the child understands it. Moreover, this strikes off against the images that follow – being a congealing where these others express dissolution. The change, that is, may be from fluid to rigid as well as the other way round.

The fourth poem is difficult. As the third poem was concerned with the mother, this concerns the father; as that was elegiac, this is affirmative; as that dealt with the world of feeling, this deals with the world of intellect. The father, of course, is the idea of the father or, if you like, Father principle, among other things God the Father. The poem affirms His constancy beneath and despite the cycles of change; hence it affirms in particular the existence of a body of reality set over against us, not the projection of our own feelings. Here is a new note, which can best be defined by using an unfashionable word and calling it the sublime. I quote the poem in full:

> Farewell to an idea … The cancellings,
> The negations are never final. The father sits
> In space, wherever he sits, of bleak regard,
>
> As one that is strong in the bushes of his eyes.
> He says no to no and yes to yes. He says yes
> To no; and in saying yes he says farewell.
>
> He measures the velocities of change.
> He leaps from heaven to heaven more rapidly
> Than bad angels leap from heaven to hell in flames.

> But now he sits in quiet and green-a-day.
> He assumes the great speeds of space and flutters them
> From cloud to cloudless, cloudless to keen clear
>
> In flights of eye and ear, the highest eye
> And the lowest ear, the deep ear that discerns,
> At evening, things that attend it until it hears
>
> The supernatural preludes of its own,
> At the moment when the angelic eye defines
> Its actors approaching, in company, in their masks.
>
> Master O master seated by the fire
> And yet in space and motionless and yet
> Of motion the ever-brightening origin,
>
> Profound, and yet the king and yet the crown,
> Look at this present throne. What company,
> In masks, can choir it with the naked wind?

Seeing it laid before us like that, we are naturally tempted to try the fatal and impossible task of appreciating it in full, word by word and line by line. Instead, one can only comment on one or two points, taken almost at random. First, 'As one that is strong in the bushes of his eyes.' This gives a flavour at once exotic and primitive, almost as of the Old Testament. The primitive idea that eyes exert power ('he has the evil eye') is being vindicated after a fashion in this poem, as in many others by this poet. If, as Berkeley believed, nothing exists except as it is perceived, or if, as Berkeley did not believe, the eye created the things it sees, then the eye obviously has all the power in the world. 'Bush' suggests, given the biblical flavour, the burning bush – so that the eyes are fiery. But there may be a hint of that other kind of bush that is a piece of machinery. 'Masks,' in line 18 and also in line 24, looks forward to the theatrical metaphors of the next poem. But again, to know Wallace Stevens' work as a whole is to know that he bears very heavily on the old idea of life as a stage whereon we play our parts; and that he means by it something very precise which rejuvenates the old commonplace. All men have parts to play; the eminent person is he who elects to play his part with a vengeance, with panache – but this is to digress. 'The fire', of course, in line 19, reminds us of the domestic scene drawn in the previous poem. In the last stanza, 'this throne', together with 'wind', seems to refer back to the terms in which the question was first posed, of autumn poised on the brink of winter. Finally, a carping comment, on the lines, 'From cloud to cloudless, cloudless to keen clear / In flights of eye and ear, the highest eye …' The alliteration in the first of these lines, and the play on the 'i' sound in the other, are obvious, rather vulgar effects. It is worth making this point here because, if I am right, when the poet's touch fails him, this is one of the ways in which it shows itself and this sort of thing is found, later in the sequence, in places where it does more damage.

It occurs, for that matter, in the very next poem. But here it is fully under control, and, judiciously exaggerated, is used very successfully for a specific purpose. For, following up the hint at the end of the preceding poem, the poet now introduces the human being called to play his part in the universe thus constituted of female and male principles, which have been defined in poems III and IV respectively. Much is made of the abundant provision made for him by the father. But what *is* his part? What is the play? What is the plot?

> What festival? This loud, disordered mooch?
> These hospitaliers? These brute-like guests?
> These musicians dubbing at a tragedy,
>
> A-dub, a-dub, which is made up of this:
> That there are no lines to speak? There is no play.
> Or, the persons act one merely by being here.

To convey this idea of the human actor as bewildered, out of his element, unbriefed, the effect of a lumpish vulgarity in the diction is of course splendidly appropriate.

Instead of answering these questions just posed, the next poem (VI) tells us of the theatre in which the play, whatever it is, takes place. It is Shakespeare's 'insubstantial pageant', massive and evanescent at once, impermanent because continually changing, out of nothing else it seems but a splendid abundance for ever expressing itself. This is still a hymn to the glory of God the Father, but in the last two stanzas there is a sudden return on man, and therefore (by implication) on the mother. All this sublimity is as nothing until it is perceived, and the perceiving of it is man's role, or part of it. Very aptly, the images of III (the home, the winter night) make a memorable reappearance in these last lines:

> This is nothing until in a single man contained,
> Nothing until this named thing nameless is
> And is destroyed. He opens the door of his house
>
> On flames. The scholar of one candle sees
> An Arctic effulgence flaring on the frame
> Of everything he is. And he feels afraid.

'This is nothing until in a single man contained'. In Berkeleyan terms, there is no *esse* where there is no *percipi*. Nothing *is* until it enters some consciousness. But now comes the twist, for having perceived a thing one gives it a name. Yet to name is, as W.R. Rodgers says, in some way to numb. The thing once labelled can be put away or at a distance, shelved. It is then no longer 'in a single man contained'. It must be 'felt upon the pulses', and cannot be so felt until it is nameless, all the accredited names discarded as inadequate. In the last splendid stanza, the 'one candle' seems to stand for the individual consciousness, which has to acknowledge that every star is an intelligence, that everywhere there are modes of consciousness – by no means only human ones – foreign to its own.

We now approach the crux, for the next poem (VII) seems to me the turning point in the sequence – at least in the sense that the three poems which follow fall far short of the brilliant assurance of what has gone before. On this showing, it is significant that the poem should be, as it appears to me, the most obscure of the whole group. The piece pursues in more splendid and metaphysical terms the same arc of thought as the preceding poem – the ultimate reality may be a Divine Imagination which barely needs, and yet does just need, the collaboration of a human mind to perceive its workings. But there is rather suddenly a much narrower range of feeling expressed and appealed to. The fear invoked in the last line of the previous poem ('And he feels afraid') seemed, in the context of that piece, equivalent to awe, a sort of *frisson* in the face of abundant glory, including fear certainly, but also worship, even a kind of rapture. But in this, the next poem, the mood darkens to a sort of resentful terror at a universe ruled by a transcience considered as predetermined law. And this is not only a darkening but also a narrowing of mood. The Father here becomes almost exclusively the 'bad angel' which in IV was seen as only one of his aspects or his roles. The last two stanzas move up and out of this trough of dejection (this pattern, incidentally, is to be found in other poems of the sequence, with a change of direction before the last six lines, rather as before the sextet of a sonnet):

> But it dare not leap by chance in its own dark.
> It must change from destiny to slight caprice.
> And thus its jetted tragedy, its stele
>
> And shape and mournful making move to find
> What must unmake it and, at last, what can,
> Say, a flippant communication under the moon.

The argument here is difficult but seems to be something like this: an iron law of continual change *does* govern nature, but the presiding genius, the Father, has to make exceptions to this – 'must change from destiny to slight caprice' – just so as not to be ruled by his own law. The obvious fallacy in this argument (for if the Father *has* to introduce caprice, he is thereby constrained just as much as if he never acted capriciously) would not matter if the poetry were powerful enough to carry us over it and make us content with paradox. But I doubt if it is so. Such a locution as 'jetted tragedy' surely gives it away. To call 'tragedy' dark or black would be lame enough, but 'jetted' is worse since it adds nothing to the idea of 'black' except the taint of the precious and the poetical; and on top of that seems dishonestly to be trying to cover up the poverty of an idea that 'black' would reveal altogether too nakedly.

The eighth poem appears, again, to go off at a tangent, in a discussion of 'innocence', which (the poet affirms excitedly) *exists*; whether in actual time and space or only as idea, makes no difference. The link with what has gone before appears if we remember the title of a book by Sir Herbert Read, *The Innocent Eye*. One mode of innocence is the child's capacity for seeing immediately – seeing a white thing without needing an idea of whiteness. To say that innocence *exists* means, in this connection and among other things, that adults can achieve the ability to see with this childlike eye. And at the end of the poem this is asserted all but explicitly. Randall Jarrell has objected to the 'philosophizing' in some of the recent poetry of Wallace Stevens, and this poem is open to attack on those grounds. But we need to be clear what we are objecting to, and why. I think we should not object to a certain amount of quite unashamedly lean and dry 'philosophizing' in verse, so long as it makes no pretense to be anything else. (If the New Critics are forced to object to it even then, so much the worse, I would say, for their doctrine.) One objects to it, surely, when it is ashamed of itself and pretends to be the poetic concrete thinking which it is not. This sort of thing has impaired for me some of Mr Stevens' earlier work, notably the frequently magnificent early poem, 'Le Monocle de Mon Oncle'. It occurs in this poem in conjunction with the too-obvious play on sounds, which I have already objected to as 'vulgarity'. The specious concreteness is to be seen here, along with the facile alliter-ation, in 'pinches the pity of the pitiful man', where I suspect we have 'pinches' rather than 'touches', partly because it contributed to a jingle of sound too obvious to be interesting, but partly because it gives the illu-sion of a greater 'concreteness'. In fact, to consider this phrase in its context is to see that some part of the meaning of 'pinch' – as when we say, 'pinched with the cold' – works against the meaning apparently aimed for, by introducing a pointless ambiguity.

Next comes a difficult rather wayward piece. The imagery already established, of warm home (the mother) and the winter night (the father), is crossed with another image, of two brothers. The reason for the entry of brothers is not far to seek – the examination of man's role toward God the Father is to be supplemented now with an account of his role toward his neighbour; and, as in the Gospels, the one is a corollary of the other. The first four stanzas create the impression of 'taking other people for granted'; the remainder assert the far from novel truth that we cease to do so under the stress of a common calamity. On the level of epistemology, calamity is change – and (this is the point) the pain of change, for example, from summer to autumn, bringing the message of our own frailty, sharpens our innocence and makes us draw closer to our neighbour. It is when the beauty is about to depart that we see it more expansively and poignantly, as a child sees it.

But I must here admit that I have no such confidence in my own readings of these later poems as in those at the beginning of the sequence. It goes without saying that in offering my own summary notions of the import of every one of these pieces I am disregarding a wealth of implication which is precisely what gives the work at its best an easy richness that can be savoured only in properly sympathetic reading. But if in this way I am throughout doing less than justice to the poetry, it seems to me that in another way I am doing more than justice to these last poems, putting the best face on the matter for the poet's sake, in a way that he doesn't altogether deserve. For here I am no longer so sure that the poet is in complete control of his material; the implications that I have to ignore strike me hereabouts as a fuzz of vagueness rather than meaningful ambiguities. My discomfort is justified by such a passage as this:

> We were as Danes in Denmark all day long
> And knew each other well, hale-hearted landsmen,
> For whom the outlandish was another day
>
> Of the week, queerer than Sunday. We thought alike
> And that made brothers of us in a home
> In which we fed on being brothers, fed
>
> And fattened as on a decorous honeycomb.
> The drama that we live – We lay sticky with sleep.
> The sense of the activity of fate –
>
> The rendezvous when she came alone,
> By her coming became a freedom of the two,
> An isolation which only the two could share.

I have fought shy throughout of describing these three-line groups as 'stanzas'. And yet in the first half of the sequence they are genuine stanzas, no less truly so for not being self-contained. The sense is cunningly made to run over from one stanza to another (note how often I have had to start a quotation with the last line of a stanza rather than the first), and this weaving through and over the divisions between stanzas enacts very often just the theme that is being presented, of flux, continual transition, and change. In the passage just quoted, however, the sense is no longer run over but wrenched across the gap between stanzas; and because I can find no significance in the violent effect thus attained, I cannot help thinking that the apparent stanza-form here is no more than a typographical convenience. There is, in the penultimate stanza quoted, what seems like an analogous breakdown in syntax.

The last poem in the sequence stands back and tries to see for what it is, this whole picture of the nature of the world and man's destiny in it. What phrase will cover it? 'An unhappy people in an unhappy world' – no, the case is not so bad as that. 'A happy people in an unhappy world' – no, that means nothing. 'A happy people in a happy world' – that's mere comic opera. Nothing will do to define it but, 'An unhappy people in a happy world'. And the reason for this? The poet decided that man's destiny is as it is because God requires in His Creation, before it can satisfy Him, an element of conflict to be reconciled, and hence a margin of freedom for man that leaves him capable of heroism: 'Like a blaze of summer straw, in winter's nick.' This is the last line of the whole poem, a fine full close in which the heroic affirmative tone is mixed with an acknowledgment of man's smallness, and so is shot through with pathos. This recovery at the end is effected in nearly every one of these poems, but some of them, as we have seen, start very lamely indeed, and this last poem is no exception:

> An unhappy people in a happy world –
> Read, rabbi, the phases of this difference.
> An unhappy people in an unhappy world –
>
> Here are too many mirrors for misery.
> A happy people in an unhappy world –
> It cannot be. There's nothing there to roll
>
> On the expressive tongue, the finding fang.
> A happy people in a happy world –
> Buffo! A ball, an opera, a bar.
>
> Turn back to where we were when we began:
> An unhappy people in a happy world.
> Now, solemnize the secretive syllables.

Is it really presumptuous to think that, in this consideration of possible formulae, the judgements that we made on each in the course of para-phrase are clearer, more succinct than those the poet passes in his verse? 'No, that means nothing', or 'No, this formula is meaningless' – isn't that natural phrasing better, even as poetry, than lame poeticisms such as 'finding fang'? And in the last stanza quoted, with the pointless vulgarity of the alliterative sibilants in the last line, is the poet not telling himself what he ought to do, rather than doing it?

At this point my admittedly summary analysis is complete. I have no wish, nor do I see the need, to draw a moral. That can be safely left to persons more interested in the arguments of poems, or in the personali-ties of their authors, than in the poems themselves. One point only may not be clear. I treat this poem in its two aspects, as communication and as artifact, because it seems to me to deserve such treatment. Most poems, especially poems so ambitious in intention as *The Auroras of Autumn*, deserve nothing better than to be brought in as evidence of a common or characteristic tendency or pattern or dilemma. All the poems of Wallace Stevens deserve the more rigorous scrutiny that we give to poems in and for themselves, not as material for making a case or advancing an argument. They demand this sort of attention by virtue of a power in them which makes itself felt immediately, when we have hardly begun to understand them. If I had to define this power in a word, I should fall back upon one that I have already used more than once, though loosely. It is *splendour*. There is splendour in *The Auroras of Autumn*, and it is that which forces us to get quite clear in our own minds what we understand by these poems, and (quite precisely) what we think of them.

First published in *Perspective* VII (Autumn 1954). Reprinted in *The Achievement of Wallace Stevens*, eds Brown and Haller (Lippincott, 1962).

8 Two Ways Out of Whitman

William Carlos Williams, *Pictures from Brueghel and Other Poems* (MacGibbon & Kee, 1964)
Theodore Roethke, *The Far Field* (Doubleday, 1964)

The case of William Carlos Williams remains the rock on which Anglo-American literary opinion splits. And ready as we may be to cry out on British taste for its confident insularity, I do not find myself sorry or indignant that British readers, by and large, hold on to their misgivings about what Williams's achievement amounts to. This is no more than Williams himself seems to have expected: he was sure that American poetry must break free of British precedents, and applied himself so resolutely to this end, that it is no surprise if the British reader finds himself shut out from Williams's poetry. This makes it sound as if Williams were an old-fashioned cultural nationalist, parochially American all through, and the poorer for it. And for many years, especially when Williams the stay-at-home was set up against Pound the cosmopolitan, it seemed that the case was indeed as simple as that. But no one can think so any longer. Williams was not simple-minded, though it was part of his rhetorical strategy often to seem so; he was an elaborate and sophisticated theorist of poetry, though the affectations of his prose conceal the fact; and in his way he was thoroughly cosmopolitan, though his court of appeal was French rather than British, and French painting more than French poetry. And so younger Americans have been able to make a programme for themselves out of what Williams and Pound have in common. One may agree with the Black Mountain poets that this programme, or something like it, represents indeed 'the tradition' in American poetry of the present (more than, for instance, the currently fashionable poetics of exhibitionism derived from Lowell's *Life Studies*), and yet one may still believe that Williams's achievement is altogether more precarious and perverse than such poets will admit. One may admire Williams's disciples (I think of Edward Dorn and Robert Creeley), more than one admires Williams.

Or rather, more than one admires Williams's poems. For Williams himself was obviously an exceptionally amiable man, upright and unswerving in his vocation. He earned the windfall which undoubtedly came to him (and this is touching) at the very end of his life, in three collections all published when he was over seventy: *The Desert Music and Other Poems* (1954), *Journey to Love* (1955) and *Pictures from Brueghel* (1962). These now appear in London, in a book confusingly entitled after the last of them. They ought to be read in chronological order, which is not how they are printed.

Some of Williams's best pieces are here: in *Desert Music* 'The Descent', 'To Daphne and Virginia' and (less certainly) 'The Host'; in *Journey to Love*, 'The Ivy Crown' and (much less certainly) 'Asphodel, that Greeny Flower', as well as a slighter piece, 'Address'; and in *Pictures from Brueghel*, 'The Polar Bear', 'The Dance', 'The High Bridge above the Tagus River at Toledo', 'An Exercise' and 'The Turtle'.

The poems in *Pictures from Brueghel* are mostly slight, though deft and graceful at their best. Many pages are both self-indulgent and self-regarding, and the pretentiousness of, for instance, 'Some Simple Measures in the American Idiom and the Variable Foot' will raise the blood-pressure of all but the most committed devotees. (I agree with G.S. Fraser that British readers cannot *hear* Williams's rhythms; I often doubt if Americans can hear them either.) In this, his last collection, Williams is much of the time writing as *chef d'école*, there are many 'exercises' or examples of how-to-do-it, and the poems about Brueghel paintings, for instance, talk about 'art', and therefore about themselves, in a way which in any other writer would be stigmatized as the most constrictive sort of aestheticism. On the other hand, there is a new departure here: *Pictures from Brueghel* experiments, as the earlier poems do not, with suppression of punctuation-stops, so as to achieve syntactical ambiguities of great complexity, yet controlled.

Even in the more ambitious and impressive poems from the other collections, Williams spends a lot of time talking about what he is doing even as he does it. For example, in 'Asphodel, that Greeny Flower',

> And so
> > with fear in my heart
> > I drag it out
> and keep on talking
> > for I dare not stop.
> > > Listen while I talk
> against time.

Or, later in the same poem,

> Begin again.
> > It is like Homer's
> > > catalogue of ships:
> it fills up the time.
> > I speak in figures,

> well enough, the dresses
> you wear are figures also,
>   we could not meet
>   otherwise. When I speak
> of flowers
>   it is to recall
>   that at one time
> we were young.

This is a poetics of ad-libbing; the poet starts at a point very far from his subject, and talks his way nervously nearer and nearer to it. Wherever we pick up the poem we find Williams speaking with a blunt and vulnerable directness which is peculiarly his, and very appealing, but because of his doctrine of 'figures', the poem as a whole is not direct at all, but extremely oblique and circuitous in the way it approaches the subject.

Among the 'figures' which Willliams uses most often are flowers. We think of him, on the basis of his earlier anthology-pieces, as remarkable particularly for finding his figures (or his 'images', as we tend more laxly to call them) in unpoetical places – in the waste lot, the rubbish heap, the suburban by-pass; and, sure enough, he seems to admire Brueghel for finding figures that are unpoetical by Italian Renaissance standards. But in these later pieces we are more often disconcerted by figures such as flowers which by our standards are very poetical indeed. Not only asphodel but daisies, mustard-flowers, jonquils and violets, even, and indeed especially, roses – flowers, or rather the names of flowers, are all over the place. The device is at its lamest in 'The Pink Locust':

> The poet himself,
>   what does he think of himself
>   facing his world?
>
> It will not do to say,
>   as he is inclined to say:
>   Not much. The poem
>
> would be in *that* betrayed.
>   He might as well answer –
>   'a rose is a rose
>
> is a rose' and let it go at that.
>   A rose *is a rose*
>   and the poem equals it
>
> if it be well made.

This is something worth saying. But the way of saying it! From whatever standpoint this is surely wretched writing, ad-libbing at its most poverty-stricken. In a slightly better poem, 'Deep Religious Faith', or in one of the positively good ones, 'The Ivy Crown', flowers still have a symbolic significance which is fixed and inert, imported into the poem as a stock response, not created nor re-created in language. (The same is true of the flowers in Olson's *Maximus Poems*.) And not only flowers get this treatment. In 'The Desert Music' the music which is appealed to is as much of an inert talisman, as little created or re-created, as near to the unsupported assertion, as in many of these poems flowers are. And under the influence of this the valuable directness of utterance degenerates into something stolid and glib, as at the end of 'A Negro Woman':

> holding the flowers upright
>   as a torch
>   so early in the morning.

To my ear the same tone sounds at the end of 'The Gift', where none of the stock 'figures' are in play:

> The very devils
>   by their flight give praise.
>   What is death
>   beside this?
>   Nothing. The wise men
>   came with gifts
>   and bowed down
>   to worship
>   this perfection.

One can admire the courage of this directness in confronting a subject so awesome as Christ's Nativity, and it is perhaps our nervousness with the subject which makes us hear as mawkish what in fact is tender. But the flatulence of this ending is another matter. It is, I suspect, the very note of the *faux-naïf*. And I suspect also that no American ear can register this as off-key, simply because so much of American literature from the first has been committed to recovering Adam's innocence, a valuably child-like *naïveté* of perception. If Williams, like other devoted Americans, lapses into the *faux-naïf,* this is the price he cannot help but pay for what he sometimes triumphantly achieves, the tone of the true *naïf* piercing and unforgettable. Almost certainly the British reader values this less than he should; we are nervous at being found so much in the open, unprotected by any armour of wit. And so the poems we shall find it easiest to admire are 'The Descent', where Eliot's 'Burnt Norton' in the background (Williams triumphantly survives the comparison) gives a sort of witty double perspective; and 'To Daphne and Virginia', where the tone becomes momentarily, and untypically, sardonic:

> We are not chicadees
>   on a bare limb
>   with a worm in the mouth.
> The worm is in our brains

In Theodore Roethke's posthumous collection, *The Far Field* , we have only to turn the first page to come upon 'The Rose exceeds, the rose exceeds us all', and we are back in the language of flowers all over again. The last of a sequence of longish poems called 'North American Sequence' is entitled 'The Rose'. It concludes:

> And in this rose, this rose in the sea-wind,
> Rooted in stone, keeping the whole of light,
> Gathering to itself sound and silence –
> Mine and the sea-wind's.

The betraying repetitions – 'this rose, this rose', 'the rose exceeds, the rose exceeds' – point up by contrast Williams's economy and elegance, the clean spareness of his perceptions and procedures. On a later page Roethke exclaims: 'Be with me, Whitman, maker of catalogues'. And except for some lyrics in short-lined stanzas, mostly love poems, where the intrusive voice is Yeats's, Whitman is indeed ubiquitous. In profound ways Williams too is writing in a Whitmanesque tradition, but his Whitman has been made over and made new; the influence is at a level far below similarities of syntax and metre. But in Roethke the allegiance is plain for all to see; syntax and metre are indeed those of the 'maker of catalogues'. And coming to Roethke after Williams, the effect is fatty and wasteful, coarse; the method lends itself to incantation, but its poverty shows up when it can contrive an emphasis only by rhapsodically excited repetition. As for the flowers, Roethke in a memorable early collection, *The Lost Son*, used flowers very strikingly indeed by re-creating the world of hot-houses and unnaturally thriving vegetation in which he grew up as the son of a florist. There are incidental references to this in *The Far Field*, most pleasingly in a poem called 'Otto', but they do not add up to a frame of reference for the whole. Instead, the scene most often referred to is the seashore, presumably near Roethke's last home on an island in Puget Sound, and their state of mind is what used to be called 'the oceanic feeling'. Unhelpful because hackneyed expressions like 'the immensity of nature', or even 'Wordsworthian pantheism', are what come to mind. And one can sympathize with Roethke: these experiences are real enough, and powerful, though both the reality and the power have drained away from the words we use in speaking of them. Roethke's words are not a lot better; and in fact to proceed by excited cumulative catalogue is almost to admit defeat, spattering the target instead of aiming for the bull.

Postscript: This piece has annoyed many of my American friends, for whom Roethke's last poems, and Williams's also, are precious and admirable achievements. They are at liberty to believe that what is manifest here is the inability of a British ear positively to *hear* one distinctively American sort of voice – a deafness not just to its cadences, but also its tone. At the risk of immodesty however I must say that I don't believe that is the case. At least, that isn't the whole story.

The Review 14 (December 1964). Reprinted in *The Poet in The Imaginary Museum*.

9 Coming to Terms with Whitman

A Choice of Whitman's Verse, selected by Donald Hall (London: Faber, 1968)

Donald Hall admits that he spent many years evading Whitman, 'finding innumerable ways to resist him'. This resistance was typical of several generations of American poets, and much of it can be laid at the door of T.S. Eliot, their mentor, who deplored Whitman and what he stood for in American culture. The poem which turned the tide, so many people have thought, was Allen Ginsberg's 'Howl', though what effected Donald Hall's conversion was a less ambitious poem of our time. Louis Simpson's 'Walt Whitman at Bear Mountain'.

With the zeal of the convert Hall is now less than fair to what made him and others resist and remain unpersuaded for so long. It was not just that in form and content alike Whitman offended against propriety and genteel decorum. So long as he is seen as any kind of moralist (and he seemed to pretend to this, as some of his admirers still pretend to it on his behalf), he has to be declared profoundly and dangerously irresponsible; and one might even go along with Yvor Winters when he argued that Hart Crane's suicide was the logically inevitable consequence of the morality which he imbibed through Whitman from Emerson.

We can admire Whitman, or (to speak for myself) one can justify the admiration one feels for him, only by classing him with a kind of confessional poet who claims, and must be allowed the right, to be irresponsible. More and more Americans of recent years have conceded this right to Whitman and to other poets; in Britain inarticulate readers (including some of our younger poets) will make the concession, but most articulate readers don't.

We shall have to learn to do so. For reluctantly and with embarrassment I record for what it is worth my own testimony: reading *Song of Myself* in this selection I found myself reading a great poem, invigorating and liberating. The experience was undeniable and at whatever cost my ideas about poetry and morality will have to be changed to allow for it.

Nothing less is called for if we are to come to terms with what Leslie Fiedler has called 'the poet of the twenty-first century'.

Guardian, 10 May 1968.

10 A Demurral

The Collected Poems of William Carlos Williams, Volume I: 1909-1939. Edited by A.Walton Litz and Christopher MacGowan (New Directions, 1986; Carcanet Press, 1987)

Williams is the most embarrassing poet in the language, surpassing even Whitman. Good for him, it may be thought; he gets under our skin, strikes through our genteel subterfuges. But it isn't so. We are not embarrassed by Williams; we are embarrassed *for* him. He doesn't get under our skin; he makes it crawl. The dust jacket to *Al Que Quiere!* (1917) reads:

> To Whom It May Concern! This book is a collection of poems by William Carlos Williams. You, gentle reader, will probably not like it, because it is brutally powerful and scornfully crude. Fortunately, neither the author nor the publisher care much whether you like it or not. The author has done his work, and if you *do* read the book you will agree that he doesn't give a damn for your opinion ... And we, the publishers, don't much care whether you buy the book or not. It costs a dollar, so that we can't make much profit out of it. But we have the satisfaction of offering that which will outweigh, in spite of its eighty pages, a dozen volumes of pretty lyrics. We have the profound satisfaction of publishing a book in which, we venture to predict, the poets of the future will dig for material as the poets of today dig in Whitman's *Leaves of Grass*.

'Brutally powerful and scornfully crude' may or may not seem apt for 'The elm is scattering / its little loaves / of sweet smells / from a white sky!' or 'Daisies are broken / petals are news of the day'. In any case, where may one find a piece of hype that more embarrassingly shoots over or wide of its mark? Such gaucheness was to be typical of Williams first and last. And the fiction is maintained that these are the words of the publisher, not of the author. But can we believe that the author didn't at least approve them? Certainly such shrill bluster comes from Williams himself throughout his career, culminating in what may be the most embarrassing moment in all his work: 'I am a poet! I am. I am. I / am a poet, I reaffirmed, ashamed.' Ashamed is perhaps what he then was; but if so, unashamed is what he now forces himself to be, like a man who compels himself to strip in public, though he hates it. And for us who are present at the performance, observing it, what could be more uncomfortable? We blush for him; we don't know where to look.

This condition is often described (and applauded) as 'nakedness' – as if there were nothing to put the rest of us out of countenance when, fully clothed ourselves, we meet a man with no clothes on. ('Off, off you lendings' – is that the idea? Clothes are hypocritical?) Since 'naked' obviously means 'disarmed', is it therefore disarming? Williams seems to have thought so, and he traded on the idea constantly in verse and prose alike. As late as 1945 he asked: 'why have I divided my lines as I have?' He answered, in a piece meant for public delivery, 'I don't know.' And sure enough, he never once showed himself aware of the term 'enjambment'.

Is this disarming? Or is it not, rather, shameless; that is to say, impudent? Williams's refinement of the ploy comes clear when we realize that he didn't mean to follow 'I don't know' with 'And I don't care'. Not for him that Whitmanesque insouciance. Williams's audience in 1945 was to understand that his ignorance made him anxious; he really cared, and if he couldn't say why he divided his lines as he did, he would go on trying to find out (though he never succeeded). His impudence thus has a special quality, is screwed up another turn. He would present himself as, though ignorant of enjambment, in intention a *poeta doctus*, a learned craftsman. Hence his insistence on that most hallowed and ancient principle, measure – a term that, as Stephen Cushman has shown in *William Carlos Williams and the Meanings of Measure*, was paraded by Williams constantly, yet never had for him any fixed determinate meaning at all.

Yvor Winters decided that Williams was incapable of consecutive thought. This may be right; certainly there is nothing in Williams's discursive prose that suggests otherwise. But Winters missed the point. Muddleheadedness, whether real or pretended, innate or acquired, was the strongest card in Williams's hand. At the start of his career Ezra Pound amiably told him as much. And although Williams resented Pound's condescension both then and later, he was shrewd enough not to discount Pound's judgement and advice: there was room for a dumb ox in American poetry, and if only Williams was patient and played his cards right, the place was his for the taking.

Like other predictions by Pound, this one was borne out, and for thirty years now Williams has been accorded the adulation and affection that the intelligentsia reserves for its dumb oxen. The dumbness is, and perhaps is meant to be, disarming. Critics at any rate find it lovable. Winters himself, notoriously the hardest of all critics to disarm, did not escape the trap. Though he changed his mind about Williams and grew steadily more grumpy about him as his star rose, Winters, proudly and professedly the scourge of anti-intellectualism, made especially indulgent concessions to

the anti-intellectualism of Williams. (At the end of his life he tried to clear
this up with a sentence that is entertaining, but too clever by half: 'He is
not even an anti-intellectual poet in any intelligible sense of the term, for
he did not know what the intellect is.') Robert Lowell testified that for
his generation it was Winters's praise of Williams that at a crucial time
tipped the balance in Williams's favour.

Williams's best poem, Winters thought, was 'By the road to the contagious hospital'. And if, with A.Walton Litz and Christopher MacGowan,
we leave off reading Williams at mid-career in 1939, this choice seems
reasonable:

> By the road to the contagious hospital
> under the surge of the blue
> mottled clouds driven from the
> northeast – a cold wind. Beyond, the
> waste of broad, muddy fields
> brown with dried weeds, standing and fallen
>
> patches of standing water
> the scattering of tall trees
>
> All along the road the reddish
> purplish, forked, upstanding, twiggy
> stuff of bushes and small trees
> with dead, brown leaves under them
> leafless vines –
>
> Lifeless in appearance, sluggish
> dazed spring approaches –
>
> They enter the new world naked,
> cold, uncertain of all
> save that they enter. All about them
> the cold, familiar wind –
>
> Now the grass, tomorrow
> the stiff curl of wildcarrot leaf
>
> One by one objects are defined –
> It quickens: clarity, outline of leaf
>
> But now the stark dignity of
> entrance – Still, the profound change
> has come upon them: rooted, they
> grip down and begin to awaken

One good reason for preferring this to other Williams poems is that it is
by his standards quite densely punctuated. All the same, the punctuation

is manifestly both sparse and inconsistent – as it has to be if he is to continue to seem, as he must, incapable of consecutive thought. For full and consistent punctuation would testify to an ordering clarity that Williams, as a dumb ox, must seem to be innocent of. The fuzz that indeterminate grammatical relations thus install at the poem's centre is – and how can we be surprised? – thickened by the diction: not 'red' but 'reddish', not 'purple' but 'purplish', not 'twig-like' but 'twiggy'.

To be sure, 'twig-like' is not in the lexicon of that American spoken by Polish mothers that Williams once declared to be his chosen linguistic medium; but then, would Polish mothers personify spring by describing it/her as 'dazed'? It is the observer who is dazed, and so are we if we go along with him, registering only approximate colours, approximate shapes. And rightly so; the time of year that is being registered is a betwixt-and-between season, when the fuzz in our perceptions corresponds to the fuzz that we see, or think we see, on branches about to bud. And so we find a deeper reason for thinking this poem pre-eminent: for once, the chosen subject calls for and responds to, adventitiously perhaps but very happily, the style's characteristic preference for approximation over exactness, daze over definition.

Poets' punctuation is seldom attended to. In Williams's work it is more than usually revealing. For as late as *Sour Grapes* (1921), probably his best collection, Williams had shown himself ready and able to punctuate conventionally and correctly. Moreover, in lovely poems such as 'To Waken an Old Lady' and 'The Widow's Lament in Springtime,' he had expertly and with feeling played off the pauses of punctuation stops against the pauses enforced by line-endings. This is, so some will think, damning evidence that the disorderliness of Williams's mind was not innate but acquired, or at least sedulously cultivated, perhaps in obedience to Pound's rash and in effect cynical advice that disorder, clumsiness with concepts, and slow muddle would be Williams's strong suit.

Two years after *Sour Grapes*, Williams, in the inchoate prose of *Spring and All*, was already declaring himself – with pride? certainly without shame – a muddle-head: 'Being of a slow but accurate understanding, I have not always been able to complete the intellectual steps which would make me firm in the position.' At the same time he begins to grind his teeth at anyone who calls a poem 'lovely'. The loveliness of 'To Waken an Old Lady' is out of keeping with what he invokes without irony as 'the modern trend'; and Williams, still trying to be 'brutally powerful and scornfully crude', dismantles all the resources, among them conventionally correct and sensitive punctuation, that had made 'To Waken an Old Lady' possible. The feelingful and delicate lyricist is possessed of higher ambitions – ambitions that would eventuate in the would-be epic *Paterson*, which the volume before us mercifully exempts us from contemplating. In the process, the poems would cease to be lovely or lovable to just the extent that their author would in the minds of his admirers, become both.

'By the road to the contagious hospital' stands first in the very elaborate though wayward structure that Williams erected in 1923 under the title *Spring and All*. And we have to ask if we take the full force of the poem when we remove it from that context. The question is very difficult, if not impossible, to answer. The reason for this is the peculiar nature of the original *Spring and All*. The folksily expansive or inclusive 'and all' may be thought to give the game away from the start – or, more precisely, to wrap up the game before it has started. For the phrase asserts the author's right to the broad and fuzzy margin of approximations that indeed seems to have enveloped Williams's every enterprise – as it had to, if he was to preserve his invaluable persona of the earnestly wellmeaning muddlehead.

Over the years the muddle became so elaborate that now we can't even say what *Spring and All* is, what it consists of. Mostly we understand by the title a sequence of 27 or 28 poems, every one of which, however, appeared independently as publishing occasions offered, thus suggesting that the *Spring and All* context was no more than a temporary convenience anyhow. Moreover, on its first appearance in 1923 *Spring and All* had the format of many pages of discontinuous, hectic, and obscurely polemical prose, out of which the poems rose at irregular intervals like so many knobby outcrops from a sea of lava.

That lava, cooled into a pumice of barely grammatical prose, protested its volcanic origins by the most sophomoric inventions of the 1920s international avant-garde: 'Chapter XIII' was preceded by 'Chapter 19' and followed by 'Chapter VI', which in turn led to 'Chapter 2' (five sentences). Shock tactics, this used to be called, or *épater le bourgeois*. (In those heady days the bourgeois was supposed still to exist, though in precipitate retreat before, as Williams put it, 'the social energized class – ebullient now in Russia'.) The prose passages of *Spring and All*, now restored by Litz and MacGowan, certainly constitute a period piece, and supply the wan pleasure that period pieces can provide. What they add to 'By the road to the contagious hospital' is the perception (which we might or might not have guessed) that 'spring' in that poem is, though literal, also a metaphor for the historical period in which the author conceived himself to be writing.

Certainly some of the other poems profit from being returned to their original context. One such is 'The Red Wheelbarrow', which by now has surely bored everyone to tears; it is better when returned to the sequence than as the trivial and self-preening squib that, considered in isolation, has received so much grave and reverent attention from so many critics. But the best poems – XVIII, 'The pure products of America / go crazy', and XIX, 'This is the time of year' – soar quite free of *Spring and All*. In gratitude to Litz and MacGowan I must name also XIV, 'Of death / the barber', unnoticed by me in the past, which, if I'm allowed to punctuate it (and who shall stop me?), I can find both witty and tender.

Decorum whispers into one ear, and prudence into the other, that it is high time for a paragraph beginning 'And yet …' If I had a third ear, there would be heard in it the hurt and protesting voices of several friends, including undoubtedly James Laughlin, who as publisher has crowned many years of devoted service to Williams by commissioning this handsome and reasonably priced edition. And yet… 'And yet he is a great poet.' I am quite sure, as Winters was, that Williams is nothing of the kind. Still, having named three or four poems that I am grateful for, I could without much trouble specify a dozen more. That would be graceful. But it would slide away from the troublesome question of how we have come to devalue the notion of greatness in poetry, and perhaps of poetry itself, when the label 'great poet' is affixed to Williams, as it customarily is. Despite the fervent and frequent and of course embarrassing assertions by Williams about poetry's supreme status, his practice and his belated reputation have debased the dignity of the poet's calling.

Very well, talk of ploy and stratagem is spiteful and tendentious. Very well, Williams probably wasn't consciously a con artist. Let's grant for the sake of argument that he was genuinely as simpleminded and as muddleminded as he seemed. The fact remains that the man who resented being patronized by Pound got himself into the situation of being patronized by everyone else. For that is what recognition, when it belatedly came to Williams, amounted to: not respect, not esteem, but alas *love* – the condescending love of powerful minds for a weak one. It hardly required much power of mind to see that 'the variable foot' is a laughable contradiction in terms; or that 'No ideas but in things,' the slogan that Williams was so proud of, represents a consummation devoutly not to be wished, supposing it to be possible (as fortunately it isn't). As Octavio Paz gently recalled, 'His conversation induced you to love him rather than admire him.'

As for Williams's lovableness, consider a piece often recalled with chuckling affection, 'This is Just to Say':

> I have eaten
> the plums
> that were in
> the icebox
>
> and which
> you were probably
> saving
> for breakfast

> Forgive me
> they were delicious
> so sweet
> and so cold.

The word for this, the *only* word for this, is 'cute'. Technically, if we must break a butterfly on a wheel, this little squib is like that other squib 'The Red Wheel-barrow': in each case, the expanses of white page around the printed words enforce (visually, for Williams had a pictorial, not an auditory, sensibility) a hushed portentousness that the words in themselves, whatever the trickiness of spacing and lineation, do nothing to earn. This apparently (and really) trivial item must have significance, else why is the statement of it framed with so much white paper? The manoeuvre is just that simple. And of course significance is claimed not just for the goodness of plums but for the ritual of raiding the icebox, and for the wrist-slapping, smiling low tension between modestly affluent man and wife. No wonder we all feel cosy with it – until we remember that such cosiness is hardly the effect aimed at or attained by poets of the past whom Williams on occasion measured himself against.

Williams, unaware apparently that in such a poem he had underwritten the suburban lifestyle, would in his next collection, *An Early Martyr* (1935) – which includes 'The Yachts' – display a bleeding heart on behalf of the victimized and dispossessed proletariat. His heart was in the right place – on his sleeve; where his head was, it is as usual impossible to say. A poet who was, or pretended to be, mindless – is this the effigy we are to hang our garlands on? If we persist in doing so, the consequences may be far-reaching, and not just for poetry.

New Republic, 20 April 1987.

11 Robert Lowell

Life Studies (Faber and Faber, 1959)

Very little, in Lowell's *Poems 1938–1949*, is of the standard of 'The Quaker Graveyard in Nantucket'. And yet in this and a handful of other poems Lowell's achievement is so central that it earns him the pre-eminence that is generally accorded him in his generation: what is new is not a distinctive tone or outlook, but something impersonal, a new or renewed range of resources in the medium, of opportunities suddenly opened to the tradition. It has the quality of a signal breakthrough for all of us who write. What it amounts to, this first perfected style of Lowell's, is a rediscovery of impetus, of a drive through from the first word of a poem to the last. Into a world of poems that more and more offered themselves under the image of interlocking verbal structures, of internal tensions balanced, locked together or reconciled, came suddenly these poems that were, on the contrary, a sequence of verbal *actions*, poems with a trajectory. Technically speaking, Lowell's innovation was simple and obvious, once he had made it: the impetus which pelted through the poems came from enjambment fiercely wrenched over, very clear and clangorous end-rhyme:

> To Cape Cod
> Guns, cradled on the tide,
> Blast the eelgrass about a waterclock
> Of bilge and back-wash, roil the salt and sand
> Lashing earth's scaffold, rock
> Our warships in the hand
> Of the great God ...

When the verse goes with such a rush as this, the meaning of a word no longer stands around it in a penumbra of overtones. A word may have more than one meaning, but successively not simultaneously: 'rock' for instance is a noun as we come up to it – 'earth's scaffold, rock' – but a verb as we go away from it – 'rock our warships'. The word turns over in the palm of the hand, as a lodged pebble might, or as a sculpted plane turns over and twists inside itself before the eye that imagines touching it. This is possible only because the line ends where it does, and because the syntax

tugs us so peremptorily round that ending. It is the forward tug of grammatical sense from line to line, fighting against the constant backward tug
of would-be conclusive rhyme, which forces us to feel the poetic energy,
driving always forward through the time the poem takes in the reading.
And syntax therefore – a grammar and punctuation correct by the standards of prose – is essential to this poetry, as to any poetry in which
enjambment is significant. Moreover a syntax thus invigorated by over-
coming one rhyme after another, rapid and close, can carry as many
densely concrete images as the poet can cram together. And so Lowell's
achievement is to solve what has been the central technical problem ever
since Pound started the *Cantos* and Eliot wrote *The Waste Land* – how to
combine their rapidity of transition from image to image, their poetic
equivalent for the cinematograph 'cut', with the musical dynamic of
syntax, ordering and unwinding.

Yet this is the style, such a brilliant and necessary invention, which
Lowell in his latest collection has jettisoned altogether. When I first saw
what he was up to, reading some of these later pieces in the *Partisan
Review*, it seemed like a monstrous folly:

> ... Oh my *Petite*,
> clearest of all God's creatures, still all air and nerve:
> you were in your twenties, and I,
> once hand on glass
> and heart in mouth,
> outdrank the Rahvs in the heat
> of Greenwich Village, fainting at your feet –

There is no good to be said for this. Everything is wrong with it, even to
the comical misfortune that the name of the Greenwich Village friends is
straight out of jabberwocky. But then, why should the Rahvs be there at
all? This jauntiness with proper names was a maddening tic that had gone
out, one thought, with early Auden. Now that we have *Life Studies* as a
whole, and find them full throughout of the names of relatives and
personal friends, our first reaction is to see in this, as in early Auden, a
damning confusion in the poet's mind between his public role as poet and
his private life, a spurious vitality injected into the first from a coy exhibitionism about the second. We may even reflect that this is a confusion
which a Lowell might easily fall into in the USA just as a Sitwell may (and
of course does) in England. In fact, however, in Lowell's strangely
touching, jagged and painful poems about his parents and grandparents
and uncles, it is precisely their being Lowells or Starks or Winslows which
saves them and makes them public documents. For it seems true that to
be born into one of these Boston mandarin families is to find one's self
with a public role willy-nilly, from birth. 'The Rahvs', however, remain
as much of an embarrassment as ever; and mostly, when the poet treats of

intimate affairs like his marriage, his child or children, and his spells of mental illness, I am not so sure as I should like to be that I'm not peeping through keyholes. It's only fair to say (and in fact a great deal could be said about it) that even here the tone is astonishingly often under control; still it's a precarious success at best.

What is certain is that this new departure of Lowell's, so far as it's successful, has nothing to do with any other poet. This later style represents no break-through for the rest of us, and in fact it's hard to see how it can serve even Lowell himself any further. Nevertheless the one or two poems in the earlier manner which appear in this volume show how necessary it was for Lowell to make the change. For the earlier style to work, every poem had to go at a fast and furious pace from first to last; and this inability to maintain the impetus at a slower rate of striking drastically limited the range of possible tones of voice, hence of possible attitudes and ultimately of possible subjects. In these circumstances to abandon a rhetoric so brilliant and powerful represents a sacrifice not much short of heroic, a splendidly courageous starting out afresh. And when all reservations are made, the risk is justified here, by the results.

For the Union Dead (Farrar, Straus, 1964)

> Work-table, litter, books, and standing lamp,
> plain things, my stalled equipment, the old broom –

This opening to a poem is in a familiar idiom for the British reader. Lowell is known to admire Philip Larkin. And Larkin or even Kingsley Amis might start a poem:

> Homecoming to the sheltered little resort,
> where the members of my gang
> are bald-headed, in business...

Of course, even when he starts in this British throw-away style, Lowell is soon trusting his tropes and images further, and driving them harder, than his British contemporaries have the nerve to do. He's got a nerve, this poet has – nerve in the sense of courage (courage to seem, and sometimes to be, ridiculous), and nerve in the sense of impudence, as when he shamelessly draws on his private dilemmas for poetic means and ends.

Even so, what a British ear picks up as familiar is something new for Lowell, and neither illusory nor incidental. Being anxiously lazy, being short-sighted, suffering from eye-strain, returning to a boyhood home, looking back on early years in wedlock – these are the themes of a Larkin or an Amis, the stock-in-trade of middle-aged domesticity which has, more or less wryly, settled for half a loaf better than no bread; and they are now the themes of this poet who in the past has dealt rather with eschatological dramas of salvation or damnation, with shocking disclosures of conflict and strain in intimate relations, and with hectically-coloured treatments (often monologues) of characters from history.

These earlier Lowells have not vanished without trace. Quite apart from the flawed but fine title-poem, there are poems for instance on Caligula and Ralegh and Jonathan Edwards – all to my ear strident, or else arbitrary at crucial places; the same goes for a poem on Florence and one on a rail journey from Rome to Paris. More strikingly, God and Grace and Free-will are named in a delicate poem, 'The Flaw', which to my mind surpasses any of the melodramas on these themes, which Lowell wrote when, as he dryly says, he wanted his fling

> with those French girls, Mediterranean
> luminaries, Mary, Myrtho, Isis –
> as far out as the sphinx!

Such dryness implies no narrowing of range; for the lines come from a poem which begins and ends in anguish. The difference is that the anguish is no longer played for all it is worth. So with the metaphysical hunger in 'The Flaw'; it is as keen as ever, but Hardyesque and subdued, no longer vaunted.

It takes courage, when your readers expect fireworks, to write poems in so low a key as 'The Old Flame' (no irony in the title, or hardly any), 'Going to and fro', 'Returning', 'The Drinker,' 'Soft Wood', 'The Flaw'. This is an uneven collection, as all Lowell's are, because he is always on the move. He has shown before, with *Life Studies*, the courage to disappoint his readers' expectations; and in this collection he disappoints those readers who expect him to be at least always sensational. To more deserving readers, who are a little behind the times, these poems will indeed appear sensational, in their methods and strategies; readers ought to be patient at least with the poems named, so as to see below the harsh and sometimes glittering surface into the honesty and sobriety of the substance.

Manuscript, dated October 1959; *Guardian*, 26 February 1965.

12 The Lowell Verse-Machine

History (Farrar, Straus & Giroux, 1973)
The Dolphin (Farrar, Straus & Giroux, 1973)
For Lizzie and Harriet (Farrar, Straus & Giroux, 1973)

Elizabeth Bishop was quoted triumphantly on the dust jacket of the 1969 *Notebook*: 'Somehow or other, by fair means or foul, and in the middle of our worst century so far, we have produced a magnificent poet.' I feel no need to demur, though strictly I've no right to an opinion, being British and so no part of that 'we', that 'our'. Plenty of people must have felt, though, as the original *Notebook* of May 1969 was already changed in July of that year and radically changed as well as expanded for the London edition of 1970, that the Lowell verse-machine was not just overheating but also throwing up ever more sludge and waste. In a poem at the end of one of his new books, *History*, Lowell quotes somebody, perhaps himself, on his own career:

> surviving to dissipate *Lord Weary's Castle*
> and nine subsequent useful poems
> in the seedy grandiloquence of *Notebook*.

But the fact that the poet has anticipated an objection shouldn't stop us from raising it, if we think it just. And in fact something of the kind is unavoidable once we realize that of the three new books, two once again announce themselves as quarried out of *Notebook*. What sort of game is this poet playing with his public – apart, of course, from making money out of us? How resist the suspicion that *Notebook*, at least in its first version, if not indeed in its second and third, was just an unconsidered emptying out on to the page of every scribble and doodle that Lowell had perpetrated over several years? Of *History* Lowell says: 'About 80 of the poems … are new, the rest are taken from my last published poem, *Notebook* … All the poems have been changed, some heavily. I have plotted. My old title, *Notebook*, was more accurate than I wished; i.e., my composition was jumbled. I hope this jumble or jungle is cleared – that I have cut the waste marble from the figure.' Fair enough. But 'plot' was already being claimed for *Notebook* in its first version: 'My plot rolls with the seasons,' he said then. And when we discover that the 370 poems of *History* are mostly

arranged in the simple chronological order of the dates at which their
overt subjects (Alexander, Caligula, Mary Stuart, Lincoln, etc.) appeared
on the stage of history, we cannot but think that the Michelangelesque
metaphor about the waste marble being cut away from the figure is indeed
grandiloquent, and that it promises a lot more than is performed. Can we
call it plotting, let alone 'sculpture', when all the poet has done is sort his
poems into loose categories merely by subject matter?

However, this is unfair. There is indeed sculpturesque energy of a very
imperious and exciting sort when we find three sonnets (out of four) in
Notebook under the heading 'Searchings', compressed into one called
'Statue of Liberty':

> I like you like trees ... you make me lift my eyes –
> the treasonable bulge behind your iron toga,
> the thrilling, chilling silver of your laugh,
> the hysterical digging of your accursed spur,
> Amazon, gazing on me, pop-eyed, cool,
> ageless, not holding back your war-hoop – no chicken
> still game for swimming bare-ass with the boys.
> You catch the frenetic spotlight we sling about
> your lighthouse promontory, flights an inch
> from combustion and the drab of ash ...
> While youth lasts your flesh is never fallen –
> high above our perishable flesh,
> the icy foam rubber waterfall stands firm
> metal pear-pointing to eternity.

The first line is from one sonnet, lines 3 to 7 are from another, lines 8 and
9 and also lines 10 to 14, (adapted), from yet another. Moreover, the original poems all belonged to private life, whereas the new poem is public
(though with valuable private resonances – the statue is American woman-
hood as well as Liberty). Also, we pick up a thread of plot, since 'Statue
of Liberty' follows a sonnet, much revised from a quite different place in
Notebook, about walking in pinching shoes in Buenos Aires:

> the Republican martyrs lie in Roman temples;
> marble goddesses calm each Liberal hero
> still pale from the great kiss of Liberty ...
> All night till my shoes were bloody – I found rest
> cupping my soft palm to her stone breast.

Though the strain of the adaptation shows through, for instance in the
musical shapelessness of line 6, still this is an impressive example of the
merely anecdotal purged and lifted to a new power. The anecdotal should
not have been published in the first place; but let that pass. (What
happened, by the way, to the practice of indexing books of poems alpha-

betically by titles and first lines? Neither Faber nor Farrar, Straus do us this courtesy, though these books cry out for it urgently.)

In any case, each edition of *Notebook* carried a clear warning that in Lowell's usage, 'plot', was an unusually capacious notion: 'Single poems and sections are opportunist and inspired by impulse. Accident threw up subjects, and the plot swallowed them − famished for human chances.' And a sonnet for Berryman that survives through both *Notebooks* into *History* makes the same point:

> John, we used the language as if we made it.
> Luck threw up the coin, and the plot swallowed,
> monster yawning for its mess of pottage.

Which enables us, leaving all sorts of questions unanswered, at least to begin answering one question we've posed already: what sort of game Lowell is playing with us. We can begin by saying that it's an exceptionally *intimate* game: we are to be with him, we *have* to be with him, as he runs a distracted hand through his hair, leafing through his old files and trying to see what his recent writing amounts to; where and how, if at all, it 'adds up'. As much with *History* as with any of the *Notebooks* we are really left to do the adding up for ourselves − *if we can,* the poet himself having virtually admitted that for his part he can't. And so, for 'intimate' in this sense we might as well read 'democratic'. From that demotic idiom which has become, since Williams, ever more *de rigueur* for American poets, Lowell is excluded because of his early schooling in the drumming decasyllable, 'the mighty line'; his coquettish habits of publishing are his way of achieving by other means a sort of unbuttoned welcome of the reader in the workshop, something that other American poets have achieved through a low-key idiom that he's debarred from.

All the same, 'coquettish' is an abusive word, and it has to be. For as readers we just don't know where we are, or what is expected of us. For instance, if from one point of view these procedures are democratic, in another light they are just the opposite, for the poems seem to come to us under the lordly rubric, 'Never apologize, never explain'. The whole collection *For Lizzie and Harriet* appears to assume that we know about Lowell's marital arrangements and how they've changed lately. If we don't know about this, we don't know where to go for information; and we feel like people absentmindedly invited to a party where everyone else is in the know and knows everyone else. The least we might expect is to be introduced to at least one other person in the room; and in his 'Afterthought' to the 1970 London *Notebook*, Lowell did that much, explaining the poem that stood first in *Notebook* and that now stands first in *For Lizzie and Harriet*:

> Half a year, then a year and a half, then

> ten and a half – the pathos of a child's fractions, turn-
> ing up each summer. God a seaslug. God a queen
> with forty servants, God ... she gave up – things whirl
> in the chainsaw bite of whatever squares
> the universe by name and number. For
> the hundredth time, I slice through fog, and round
> the village with my headlights on the ground,
> as if I were the first pilosopher,
> as if I were trying to pick up a car
> key ... It can't be here, and so it must be there
> behind the next crook in the road or growth
> of fog – there blinded by our feeble beams,
> of face, clock-white, still friendly to the earth.

Of these lines, which he said were 'as hermetic as any in the book', Lowell wrote in 1970: 'The "fractions" mean that my daughter, born in January, is each July, a precision important to a child, something and a half years old. The "Seaslug etc." are her declining conceptions of God.' With this note to help, we can admire the order of ideas and images through the poem, in particular the propriety by which the moon, measure of time, in the end escapes 'name and number' by being pointed to only in a riddling circumlocution. But in *For Lizzie and Harriet*, there is no note and all we are given instead is the child's birthdate: 'January 4, 1957'. Moreover the new version gives, for lines 9–11,

> Like the first philosopher Thales who thought all things water,
> and fell in a well ... trying to find a car
> key ... It can't be here, and so it must be there

– which switches the whole thing on to a track of frigidly playful pedantry.

What I've been saying smacks fustily of those rightly suspect argu-
ments, once so common in America and still to be heard in England, which begin: 'The reader has his rights also ...'. The trouble with this is that it presupposes certain assumptions, shared by the poet and his public, about what poetry is or what it does. And the truth is, on the contrary, that even less than his readers is the poet nowadays (a poet such as Lowell) clear about what he is doing, and why. In those circumstances, it might be said, the only honest thing for him to do is to let it come, let it tumble out, pell-mell – in hopes that someone, somewhere, will discern the design and the purpose that escape him. If he still talks incongruously about cutting away the waste marble, we need only suppose that he's less good at writing blurbs than at writing poems. However, this doesn't explain how he can still revise. For if he doesn't know what he is doing, or why, how can he decide that one set of words suits his purpose better than another? And in any case, such decisions crop up at every moment

in composition as in revision: the puerile enjambment, 'turn/ing' – why did Lowell perpetrate it in the first place, and then adhere to it when he came to revise? He must have had *some* reason; can we believe it was the sort of thing that dazzles the freshman writing seminar, a disposition of line-endings so as to (get it?) *enact* the turning that it talks about? Such odds and ends of reach-me-down 'technique' are quite worthless in the absence of any conviction about the point of the poetic enterprise as a whole. One takes the point easily enough that he's sick of the well-made poem, the expensive art object, as an end in itself; but if that is thrown out the door, along with it have to go related fantasies about 'enactment'. And no amount of coquettish publishing can mask, or make up for, directionless composing.

However, for the poet who has lost direction (or deliberately abjured it, as Lowell for honourable reasons seems to have abjured the prophetic and denunciatory direction of *Near the Ocean*, for instance), another option is open: he can bring it about that the life he lives brings him into situations at once extreme and typical in such a way that poems skimmed off that life, though they have in themselves no more direction than entries in a journal, feed upon and take over the direction that the life has. And this seems to be the case with *The Dolphin,* much the best of these three collections and the one that owes next to nothing to *Notebook*. One extreme and typical situation here is that of exile, the self-sought exile of Lowell in England which naturally and inevitably becomes for him the paradigm of exile in general:

> Is it honorable for a Jew to die as a Jew?
> Even the German officials encouraged Freud
> to go to Paris where at least he was known;
> but what does it matter to have a following,
> if no one, not even the concierge, says *good day*?
> He took a house in London's amused humdrum
> to prove that Moses must have been Egyptian –
> 'What is more monstrous than outliving your body?'
> What do we care for the great man of culture –
> Freud's relations were liquidated at Belsen,
> Moses Cohn who had nothing to offer culture
> was liquidated at Belsen. Must we die,
> living in places we have learned to live in,
> completing the only work we're trained to do?

'London's amused humdrum' is brilliantly just and caustic, to characterize the peculiarly English brand of philistinism; and it may serve, as well as any of dozens of equally quotable throw-aways, to show how the marmoreal conclusiveness of the mighty line survives into Lowell's most recent writing, even now when pentameter and sonnet alike are consis-

tently violated and, as it were, disembowelled. In fact, part of the superi-
ority of *The Dolphin* to *For Lizzie and Harriet* can be seen in the readiness
of the later poem to stay with the iambic pentameter quite comfortably
for several lines at a time; the compulsion to disrupt it, at whatever cost
in arbitrary ugliness, seems to be something that Lowell has for the
moment worked out of his system.

All the same, *The Dolphin* stays within the framework of *Notebook* and
the poems that came out of *Notebook,* to the extent that 'Lizzie' and
'Caroline' and 'Harriet' are characters in a drama we're supposed to know
about. And in fact *The Dolphin* pushes intimacy to a new extreme; of
poems like 'In the Mail' or 'Exorcism' or 'Foxfur' the first thing to say is
that they are acutely embarrassing. Or so any one will feel who remembers, perhaps wistfully, the proprieties that went without saying up to
twenty years ago. It was Lowell's own *Life Studies* that put an end to such
automatic reticences; and the course which he then adopted, of making
public what had been thought to be inviolably private, is the course that
he sails on still. The privacies which he betrays are for the most part not
those of the bedroom, but of the living-room, the telephone booth, the
mailbox. To my mind this makes them no less shocking, for I agree with
George Steiner that fornication and buggery on stage and screen are
alarming not because they expose sexuality, but because they expose
privacy. The right to privacy for one's self, and the right not to look when
the privacies of others are exposed, are rights that are now derided, if not
yet explicitly denied. And for this surely baleful development, Lowell has
to take some of the blame.

And yet there's no reason to think him a compulsive exhibitionist. He
could have come to this practice by a line of argument which does him
credit. For indeed everything I've noticed so far – Lowell's ways of
publishing no less than his ways of writing (style as well as subject) – make
sense only if we see them as one more desperate phase in the struggle,
waged ever since the Romantics, to cut poetry clear of rhetoric.
According to the Romantics' logic, as soon as the poet looks outside the
circle of his intimates, and thinks of his public (of an anonymous third
party – to be interested and intrigued, in short, to be *persuaded*), he is operating no longer as poet but as rhetorician. And Lowell, because he has
been famous for so long, has to go to desperate lengths so as not to write
with his avidly interested public in mind. He can do this (so I guess) only
by writing much and writing fast – by, as it were, jumping himself into
each poem; also by cramming into the poem things that will be meaningful only to his intimates; also by refusing to distinguish between the
private and the public. It is a real bind for him; and his struggles in it, from
Notebook onward, are heroic. But of course the facts of his situation, if he
can suppress them from his mind as he writes, catch up with him unavoidably when he publishes. At that point it becomes impossible to pretend

any longer that the faceless public doesn't exist. Writing poems may or may not be a rhetorical operation (I believe it is, in part, and has to be), but certainly publishing them is. And so as Lowell continues to publish, his struggles not to be a rhetorician, though they may be heroic, are certainly in the last analysis fatuous.

Fortunately, by the time he finished *The Dolphin* – perhaps before he started it, certainly by the time he passed it for publication – Lowell had reached these conclusions for himself. He has had the grace to allow that the poems which present themselves as literal transcripts of letters and phone calls may be nothing of the kind (I am devoutly glad to hear it, and over-ready to believe him); he has by implication taken the side of the arch-rhetorician Yeats: and he has 'plotted' the book in an acceptable public sense, by way of a cluster of dominant images signalized by the title – images of fishnets, stirred mud, eels, salmon-trout. When he says,

> After fifty so much joy has come.
> I hardly want to hide my nakedness –
> the shine and stiffness of a new suit, a feeling,
> not wholly happy, of being reborn,

he seems to be referring in the first place to his new marriage and his new child; but his public, which is interested in *public* meanings, comes across enough evidence that the new life is a new life of his art also, a shucking off at last of the self-contradictions that snarled him in *Notebook* and the collections that came out of *Notebook*. In this new dispensation, if it's still true that 'Everything is real until it's published' – why, that's just the name of the game, the shadow of the rhetorician's dishonesty that necessarily falls on all of us who 'go on typing to go on living'.

Parnassus II: 1 (Fall–Winter 1973). Reprinted in *The Poet in The Imaginary Museum*.

13 *Robert Lowell's* Collected Prose

This may be Lowell's most winning book. But it should not be read straight through, nor taken in big gulps. Robert Giroux, faced with more than forty pieces, nearly all short and scrappy, some incomplete, has sorted them into three sections plus an appendix. This arrangement is reasonable, and on balance probably the best possible. But it has certain disadvantages. If we want to know what Lowell thought of William Carlos Williams, we find him taking three bites at the cherry – 1947, 1948, 1962; and whereas this is enlightening about how he changed his mind (the two bites at John Berryman, eight years apart, are very illuminating in this way), on the other hand we are confused about how far his second thoughts cancelled out his first. At any rate, it's only by sorting out the chronology that we can construct a narrative of Lowell's life in and out of, but mostly in, literature.

A narrative thus reconstructed, we can read out of it several plots. I write from Tennessee; and that must be allowed for when I draw out one plot that might be called 'the Defection from the South'. The outline is well known: Lowell wasn't secretive about it, and here it's documented in the famous 'Visiting the Tates', in a two-part tribute to John Crowe Ransom (the two bites at this cherry twenty-six years apart), and in a piece on Ford Madox Ford, that unwieldy British survivor from the heroic age of Modernism whose largely adventitious connections with the Old Confederacy drew the young Lowell southwards in the first place. Without in the least minimizing the solidity of Lowell's educational grounding in New England (we have here an astonishingly precocious essay on *The Iliad* by the eighteen-year-old Lowell at St Mark's School), still he himself insisted that it was from Southerners, from Allen Tate in the first place, then from Ransom after he had moved north to Ohio, that Lowell imbibed the notion of the poetic calling as a strenuous, dedicated and above all erudite discipline. This was something he never reneged from, but he did repudiate the particular sorts of erudition and discipline that his Southern mentors first instilled in him. Here the plot thickens, and turns painful; for whereas Tate, a master who never lost touch with his protégé, seems never to have complained of being betrayed, yet he might well have done so. For the drastic turn-around in taste that Lowell and Randall Jarrell (the latter himself a Southerner) effected in the 1950s left

Tate for his last twenty-five years a poet bombinating into a void. Between his poetry and the poetry of William Carlos Williams there was no common ground, and no accommodation was possible. Did Lowell feel guilt at this betrayal, this defection? Between the lines there is some evidence that he did. But he didn't dwell on it; and why should he? Jarrell and he were right: however rigorously correct in the abstract Tate's and Ransom's poetics may have been, neither of them fathered a single poet writing to any purpose in their chosen and mastered styles. (For that matter, as Lowell shows himself shrewdly aware, Ransom it was who *mastered* his style, not the more ambitious poet Tate.) The revealing document is Lowell's 1953 essay on Robert Penn Warren's *Brother to Dragons*, wherein the author of *The Mills of the Kavanaughs*, adept of New England gingerbread Gothic, sees into and through Warren's Southern Gothic – all under the suave surface of respect and admiration. It is not just that Lowell and Jarrell read the signs of the times; they detected an obfuscating dishonesty in what was accepted as the appropriate rhetoric for poetry, particularly in the South. What was historically unprecedented was that the South, in the persons of the Fugitives and the New Critics (often the same persons) had buttressed and vindicated its rhetoric by a poetic theory so sophisticated that Lowell and Jarrell, indoctrinated in it, could never thereafter disprove it or disown it. Unable to disprove it, unwilling to disown it, they went by rule of thumb, that is to say by *practice* and ignored or flouted the principles that all the same they could not deny.

Probably the strangest piece here, now published for the first time, is called 'Art and Evil'. It was put together from a manuscript supplied by Elizabeth Hardwick, with a continuation that turned up at Harvard. It is unfinished, though the last extant paragraph begins 'Finally': and so Giroux suggests that only a couple of concluding sentences are missing. However that may be, he must have felt when he noted 'The manuscript breaks off at this point', that it could hardly have done anything else. For the discourse had become so wayward and rambling that any sort of drawing together was impossible; the piece could only have broken off as it does, it could not have reached an end. Some of it seems to date from the 1950s, other parts from as much as twenty years later; but much of it surely was composed during the onset of one or other of Lowell's manic phases. Certainly it gets more excited and unnaturally confident as it goes on. And yet it has more than clinical interest. For the relation between Lowell's art and his apprehension of evil is for us the most vexing question about him, as it was (and he shows himself aware of this) for us and others in his lifetime. And this may have been his most strenuous attempt to explain himself to himself on this matter.

He begins with a brilliant and rapid survey of how the writers of his generation had changed in their apprehension of evil from where they started, with the posturing diabolism of the French and English Nineties, and of Jacobean playwrights seen through Nineties spectacles, into perceiving the black and sinister undersides of supposedly robust and 'wholesome' writers like Shakespeare, Tennyson and Dickens. Then Lowell turns to T.S. Eliot's *After Strange Gods* of 1933, with its contempt – the easy and eager contempt of the lately converted – for all those to whom 'the doctrine of Original Sin is not a very real and tremendous thing'. Lowell thinks that Eliot's 'tremendous' gives the Devil too much dignity, or at least that it registers in the Devil's presence a *frisson* such as by 1956 (Lowell's date) no one could feel any longer; after Buchenwald and Vorkuta and Hiroshima, Lowell suggests, we know the Devil as a familiar, an old acquaintance in whose company we are more at home than with his heavenly Antagonist. There is some re-writing of history here; for in poems of strained religiosity like 'Colloquy at Black Rock', written after Buchenwald, Lowell himself had made much play with 'tremendousness'. After an airy excursus into theology and Christian apologetics, which assures us that Cain and Lucifer and Christ are alternative names for a figure called 'the criminal', Lowell announces that the rest of his paper will be concerned with eight figures, catalogued two by two: Rimbaud and Milton's Satan; George Eliot's Grandcourt from *Daniel Deronda* and Virgil's Aeneas; Dickens's Sarah Gamp and Faulkner's Popeye; Goethe's Mephistopheles and Shakespeare's Iago. And so it proves: one by one, these eight are taken up. The passionately criminal Rimbaud (or Satan) is judged to be less evil than the cold man Grandcourt – a view not unfamiliar and not unappealing, which can however exonerate much that looks like wickedness, including the heartless sort called frivolity. There is such intellectual frivolity (Lowell calls it 'recklessness') in the way he flouts the principles that the New Critics had impressed on him. He had surely read in his youth L.C. Knights's *How Many Children Had Lady Macbeth?* with its demonstration of the ruinous muddle we get into when we mistake a fiction inside a fiction, Lady Macbeth or Iago, with people we have met or might meet in the street or in a drawing-room. Yet here, quite as if he were Knights's whipping-boy, A.C. Bradley, Lowell considers on a par the historical person Arthur Rimbaud and Satan, that fiction inside the fiction called *Paradise Lost;* and Aeneas and Dido in the Fourth Book of *The Aeneid* are envisaged and discussed quite as if we had access to them otherwise than through the sensibility of Virgil. This is one more instance of 'the defection from the South': Lowell blithely or flippantly reinstates one of the worst habits of the belle-lettrist criticism from which Knights and Ransom, Brooks and Warren and others, had for a time weaned him along with the rest of of us. Did he know what he was doing? I judge that he did, and didn't care. Give him credit, he never published this piece. But he was familiar with evil, no doubt of it.

Of course the old belle-lettrists, practising their impressionist criticism, had their own ways of succeeding and delighting. A.C. Bradley himself, author of *Shakespearean Tragedy*, is not a wholly discredited figure, nor should he be. It is natural and proper that, as New Criticism was succeeded by other schools ever more grimly and glumly professional, we should sigh for the verve and speed that characterized *belles lettres* at its best; and should have applauded when Randall Jarrell in particular reinstated the old ways of proceeding. There is a sparkling performance here, on Ovid's *Metamorphoses*, where Lowell I think surpasses Jarrell at his best: an astonishing nine pages of lightly carried learning. Lowell professed not to take himself seriously as a critic; but here he must be taken very seriously indeed. When he wrote criticism, he wrote it as *belles lettres*. In this and in other ways the post-modernism that he and Jarrell with others inaugurated was really a harking back, thoroughly reactionary.

He was wonderfully well read, in many languages. There is no poet now writing in English, so well-educated; and this makes Lowell seem, so soon after his death, a figure from a lost age, the last of his kind. Often he alludes to other writers so as to say obliquely something about himself and his work that he would not say directly. A striking instance is an encomium of some late poems by Heine, interjected suddenly and fiercely into a conversation with Ian Hamilton, one of two interviews here reprinted; this throws aslant a clear and self-justifying beam of light on Lowell's last four collections. Back then in 1971 Hamilton conscientiously needled Lowell about newly fashionable manifestations he was thought to have sponsored: confessional poetry, extremism, political mass violence, a welcome to popular song and verse. Lowell responded civilly and sourly; his fame, which he knows about, is for him a burden. We believe him, and think it does him credit.

And yet there were striking *lacunae* in Lowell's knowledge. Challenged as to living British poets, he remembers neither Basil Bunting nor Thom Gunn; challenged as to Americans, he has nothing to say of Charles Reznikoff or Carl Rakosi, George Oppen or Louis Zukofsky. The plot-line called 'defection from the South' twists in upon itself; the deafness of the New Critics to poets like those named, American and British, is one coarse plank in the Southern rhetoricians' platform that Lowell unfortunately did *not* defect from.

He names me in talking to Hamilton, remarking on my escape to America almost simultaneous with his to England. 'Davie and I', he says, 'are taking vacations from our Furies.' I have always felt honoured that he thought me, at least in some respects, his peer.

Typescript, signed but not dated (the *Collected Prose* was published in 1987).

14 Two Poets

'I used to lie with an ear to the line'
      – Seamus Heaney

You said it, and you had in mind
  The railway line. Or did you? There's
That other line to be listened to, maybe lied with:
'Each verse returning like the plough turned round.'

  Too much Lowell in your latest.
  All of us suffered that contagion
While he lived. But much that is beyond him,
And beyond me, is your 'Glanmore Sonnets'.

  The line that you lied with an ear to was
  His, at times. But while you ploughed
Dogger and Dread, your field, the narrow seas,
His metalled velocity glittered 'Near the Ocean'.

  Your Irish English, though it croons
  Too soon you think, is yours; unlike
My British English, dry and tetchy; his,
Drinking America like 'iron vodka'.

  For yes, you said that: oceanic
  Swell it has, yes his proud verse
Was never under sail, but locomotive;
His keel ran ironclad on railway tracks.

  In his idiom the pun on 'line'
  Wouldn't arise. All said and done,
It is a wretched quibble after all:
His pistons jabbered, but they never lied.

Agenda 18 (Autumn 1980).

15 John Berryman's
Freedom of the Poet

In J.D. O'Hara's picture book, *A History of Poetry* (1975), there appears a familiar photograph of the aging John Berryman, with gurulike beard, flowing, grizzled, unkempt. On the same page are pictures of Robert Lowell, Sylvia Plath and Anne Sexton; and to all of these the caption reads: 'Lowell … was the first American poet to write in the intimate, intro- spective verse style that has since been dubbed "confessional" poetry. This new approach to poetry was to prove the undoing of at least one of Lowell's contemporaries and two of his disciples.' And in case we have any doubt who the contemporary is, and who the disciples, the caption makes it plain: 'John Berryman … along with Sylvia Plath … and Anne Sexton …, all harbouring unresolved personal torments, wrote poems filled with angst and death wishes that were ultimately fulfilled by suicide.' Perhaps unintentionally, this conveys the clear impression that Berryman was a confused character who lost his head – as did, more excusably, a couple of much younger poets – because of the example of a stronger poet, Lowell, and the critical brouhaha that Lowell's developing career provoked. It should be said at once that this pitiably veering weathercock is not at all the figure that emerges from the volume of Berryman's erst- while uncollected essays and reviews and stories.

For the moment we need take up the matter of Berryman's suicide only so far as to confess ourselves baffled by it – as does Berryman's friend and publisher Robert Giroux, who reveals that a bare seven months before he jumped to his death not only was Berryman assembling this book and getting a new child christened, but he was planning a half-dozen further books to be written through the 1970s. Whatever the reasons for Berryman's suicide, such evidence as we have certainly doesn't *prove* that it was what his writing career was pointing him towards, the only way out that his own poems left open before him. And in fact we look in vain, in Berryman's criticism, for the postures and the arguments or pseudo- arguments that are the stock-in-trade of the apologists for a 'confessional' or an 'extremist' poetry. From 1936, the date of the earliest piece here, through to 1967, the date of the latest, Berryman is thoroughly and unashamedly an *academic* critic and reviewer, though in a way that doesn't preclude his being also a lively and readable journalist. As much could be said of Randall Jarrell, one of Berryman's and Lowell's contemporaries who predeceased them, as did Delmore Schwartz. This was Berryman's generation, and these were his peers – as it seems he was happy to acknowledge.

And after all, to call him 'academic' isn't quite good enough. Particularly when he writes of Jewish authors (Anne Frank, Isaac Babel), but in fact throughout, early and late, Berryman is in love with erudition – ultimately with wisdom, but he takes it for granted that the way to wisdom is through erudition; and that erudition is arrived at and transmitted in contexts that are *authoritarian* and *institutional*. Berryman makes this point, as it may be defiantly, by printing in the forefront of this collection and occupying its first eighty pages, the most scholarly articles of all – on Shakespeare and some of his contemporaries; and I think this is a pity. However that may be, Berryman comes through as every inch a university man; there is nothing of the Bohemian about him – it comes naturally to him, writing to a friend in the last year of his life, to give the syllabus of the seminar he is conducting. And it's no surprise to find that a story of his, discovered in his papers, concerns a professor in his classroom teaching Milton's 'Lycidas'. It's very important, I think, to recognize that none of this testifies to any timidity on Berryman's part, still less to his having in any sense divided aims. For him the vocations of poet and scholar fit together perfectly; and he's in no danger of thinking that the experience he gets from books is less authentic than what he gets from bed or bar-room.

On the contrary, a subsidiary but very notable value that this book has, as in effect a chronicle of American literary opinion, is that it should renew our respect for a chapter of American cultural history that at present tends to get condemned as 'the New Criticism', if not as 'ivory-tower academicism'. I have in mind, particularly in essays on Henry James and Theodore Dreiser, Berryman's sharp but respectful dealings with that distinguished suicide of an earlier generation, F.O. Matthiessen. And more important than that, because even more honourable to Berryman, is an exacting implication to that very word *chronicle,* an implication that has everything to do with Berryman's scholarly conscience, his erudition: people have said or done things, books or stories or poems have been written, which deserve to be remembered though they're in danger of being forgotten – and the chronicler recognizes and acts upon the obligation to save them from oblivion. In all of this Berryman's idea of the life devoted to art and to erudition is uncompromisingly austere and strenuous. As he wrote of Ring Lardner in 1956: 'All the artists who have ever survived were intellectuals – sometimes intellectuals *also*, but intellectuals. The popular boys cannot understand this. When Shakespeare mocked

Chapman and Ralegh and their school of intellectual art, he did it with a higher brow than theirs. Hemingway studied Turgenev and everyone else he thought useful. Lardner never studied anybody.' And that is, for Berryman, a death sentence on Lardner.

It's against this severe and inflexible background that we have to make sense of the very fierce and shocking and disconcerting poet that Berryman ultimately became. It cannot be denied that at some point in mid-career Berryman momentously shifted his stance towards his art and the experience that his art fed upon, just as Lowell did with his *Life Studies* (1959). And the shift seems to have to do, not surprisingly, with that inescapable figure in every American poet's heritage, Walt Whitman. Berryman's 1957 essay on Whitman, here printed for the first time and deliberately placed by him so as to introduce all his pieces on modern poetry, is thus a document of capital importance. On the other hand, if Berryman thus belatedly weds himself to the Whitmanesque strain in the American tradition, this doesn't in the least mean – as it too frequently does in what passes for informed discussion on these matters – a rejection of the European, or of 'formalism'. Berryman remained a poet to whom it came naturally, as late as 1965, to talk of 'problems of decorum', and as late as 1968 to go for a title – *His Toy, His Dream, His Rest* – to Giles Farnaby in the sixteenth-century *Fitzwilliam Virginal Book*.

The view of poetry that Berryman reads out of Whitman's *Song of Myself* is what plenty of others have found there: 'The poet ... fills with experience, a valve opens; he speaks them.' To the layman this may seem banal, self-evident, and innocuous; it is none of these things, least of all the last – as Berryman undoubtedly recognized when he said, 'I am obliged to remark that I prefer this theory of poetry to those that have ruled the critical quarterlies since I was an undergraduate twenty-five years ago.' How questionable the Whitman theory is appears when Berryman remarks of it, 'It is as humble as, and identical with, Keats's view of the poet as having no existence, but being "forever in, for, and filling" other things.' For only eight years before, in a very perceptive essay on Pound that deserves to be a landmark but isn't, Berryman had cited the same tag from Keats's letters, and had declared austerely: 'For poetry of a certain mode (the dramatic), this is a piercing notion; for most other poetry, including Pound's, it is somewhat paradoxical, and may disfigure more than it enlightens.' Properly to explain the shift in Berryman between the Pound essay (1949) and the Whitman essay (1957) would go far beyond what can be expected of a reviewer. Let it suffice to say that Berryman isn't muddled, but he's certainly using 'dramatic' in a very special sense, since Pound, the creator of 'personae', can be seen, and has been, as very much a 'dramatic' poet. And in Berryman, the author of *Homage to Mistress Bradstreet* (1956) – which is very clearly in one obvious sense a dramatic, not to say histrionic, performance (and one that as late as 1965 he was deservedly proud of) – the term 'dramatic' is obviously a very tricky one. My own guess is that the significance of *Song of Myself* for the later Berryman isn't to be charted in terms of poetic theory, however generously interpreted, but has to do with two aspects of the Whitmanesque poet that have often been remarked on – first, his egalitarianism (his 'democracy'), and second, his shamelessness. In that case, the pathos and the distinction of Berryman's career reside first in his having a haughtiness which Whitmanesque democracy was permitted to chastise (in 1947, in Cambridge, England, the lordly urbanity of Berryman of Clare Hall was vividly remembered); and second, in his having a natural shamefastness which Whitmanesque openness was permitted, with the help of alcohol, to outrage.

As a young American in England, nearly forty years ago, Berryman appears to have hopped aboard the Dylan Thomas bandwagon, then vociferously rolling. And it is tempting to date from that experience, not from the encounter with Whitman fifteen years later, Berryman's conversion to some vulgarly debased notion of the poet as society's sacrificial scapegoat. Biographical documentation, yet to come, may establish that indeed the Dylanesque life-style did have its attractions for Berryman. But in the present state of our knowledge it is prudent, as well as charitable, to suppose that the young American – knowledgeable though he undoubtedly was – was bamboozled by the cherished and sedulously promoted fictions of a foreign culture into thinking, for instance, that Dylan represented a Celtic, an indigenously Welsh, imaginative tradition challenging the received and authenticated English establishment. Berryman's 1940 puff of Thomas gives us no evidence one way or the other; it is strangely statistical – 'Colours are frequent, especially green, which occurs twenty-eight times and connotes origin, innocence....' The chief interest of this as of some other pieces of the 1940s is to transport those of us who are old enough to remember back to a world in which Lowell's *Lord Weary's Castle* was contemporaneous with *The Selected Writings of Dylan Thomas* (preface by John L. Sweeney, 1947). And indeed:

> Gospel me to the Garden, let me come
> Where Mary twists the warlock with her flowers...

This is early Lowell; but might it not be Thomas?

Another piece now printed for the first time, dating from about 1960, is an essay on *Don Quixote*, which I suspect is even more important than the Whitman essay for getting our bearings on the late Berryman. It is extremely scholarly; the learning, though it is worn lightly and deployed only to be serviceable, is very impressive. It is also a profoundly Christian piece of writing, which insists, if I read it right (for it's written with admirable clarity, yet needs to be much pondered), that Cervantes's comic masterpiece comes into focus only if we read it as a work of fervent though disenchanted piety. This is important, because the notion is abroad that Berryman in his last two collections wobbled or wavered into an unconsidered sort of Christian salvationism. On the contrary, his Christian allegiance dates from much farther back in his life. And remembering how the astonishingly sustained six-line stanzas of *The Dream Songs* (1969) make up a minstrel-show colloquy between 'Henry' and 'Mr Bones', how can we fail to make the connection with Quixote and his interlocutor Sancho Panza? Berryman's suicide was 'quixotic'; just so – and we owe it to him to learn what he thought the quixotic figure signified. (One thing it signified was 'humility', as one thing the Whitmanesque figure signified was 'humiliation'; and one way to regard all Berryman's poems of the 1960s is as one long penitential exercise in self-humiliation.)

As for death wishes – yes, they do crop up, quite insistently; notably in 'Thursday Out', which is presented as a story but seems to be rather a section of travelogue, a highly wrought meditation on that grandest of mausoleums, the Taj Mahal; and in 'Shakespeare's Last Word', here printed for the first time, an essay on *The Tempest*. But death wish sounds too glib, too clinically dismissive. If that is anywhere near the right diagnosis of Berryman's trouble, we can be sure he arrived at it himself long before we did. In any case the possibility doesn't in the least qualify my sense that the man behind this book was not only one of the most gifted and intelligent Americans of his time, but also one of the most honourable and responsible. I take no satisfaction in saying this. The time to say it to him was when he was alive. And now it's too late.

This article first appeared in the *New York Times Book Review* 25 April 1976. © 1975/76 by The New York Times Company. Reprinted by permission in *Trying to Explain*.

16 A Bee in His Sonnet

John Berryman, *Collected Poems 1937–1971*, edited and introduced by Charles Thornbury (Farrar, Straus & Giroux, 1989)

It would be nice, and just about possible, to write about John Berryman without mentioning Robert Lowell. Lowell's shadow fell heavily on Berryman while they were both alive, though there's reason to think this was more of a problem for Berryman's readers than for Berryman himself. But now they are both dead and thereby 'historical', driving a wedge between them would serve little purpose. They were the two male voices (their female peers are another matter) of the American *imperium*. Lowell at a certain stage of his career discerned, or thought he discerned, that such an *imperium*, an American Empire, had come into being; and thereafter he wrote poems leaning on the assumption that there was a 'rhyme in history' between the Roman Empire, that held together for centuries, and an American Empire that held together for perhaps only thirty years. This was a myth; not in the sense that it was a transparent fiction (for it wasn't), but in being enforced by a compelling rhetoric – Lowell's pre-eminently, but also President Kennedy's, President Johnson's. Berryman, who didn't naturally think along these lines, was by this mythological but not false logic cast, he too, as a laureate of North American imperialism. He didn't mean to be, and yet he was, a poet of Empire.

In 1966, author of *Homage to Mistress Bradstreet* published ten years before, recipient of awards from The National Institute of Arts and Letters, of the Pulitzer Prize (for *77 Dream Songs*, 1965), and of a Guggenheim fellowship, Berryman departed with his third wife and his daughter for nine months in Europe, initially and most permanently in Ireland. And it was from Dublin that he sent to his publisher his 110 'Sonnets to Chris' which, supplemented by seven new sonnets and a prefatory poem in the 'Dream Songs' stanza, would come to be known as *Berryman's Sonnets*.

He needed money, or he thought he did. And his drinking habit, which the Irish domicile did nothing to allay, no doubt weighed heavy on the domestic budget. Still, Berryman at his most drunken was a poet in earnest, not a cynical sponger; and so the question inescapably arises – what did he think he was doing, dredging up from twenty years before poems that, for all their audacity and inventiveness, were irretrievably compromised by being in thrall to a rhyming and metrical strait-jacket long discredited? Berryman was no fool, no *naïf*. He was knowledgeable in particular about those Shakespearean decades that saw the sonnet-sequence acclimatized in England. Can he then have thought, as 'a Renaissance specialist', that what worked in sixteenth-century England must work in twentieth-century North America? Plainly not, not quite; for his diction and syntax incorporated, quite radically, nineteenth-century usages, notably those of Gerard Manley Hopkins. And yet his implicit claim is quite clearly that, given a few Hopkinsian adjustments, the Petrarchan sonnet could accommodate twentieth-century American actuality as certainly as fifteenth-century Italian or sixteenth-century English.

Plainly, it isn't so. The social and particularly the amorous conventions that frame Petrarch's addresses to Laura are to this day largely baffling to Old World scholars, Italian or English or whatever. And yet thrice-married Berryman could, he seems to have thought, strike through their hesitations. Splendid of course for a poet thus to bypass scholarly equivocations. One has seen it happen, and applauded. But Berryman's appropriation of Petrarch is hardly a case in point. For what we seem faced with is Berryman's determination – supposedly in 1947, more certainly on publication twenty years later – that Petrarch's sonnets should (*must*) be made to fit an adulterous (doubly adulterous, it appears) liaison in the United States of the 1940s. The 'fit' is just not there. And Berryman's *willing* the fit reveals him as not what the overt record suggests, a New World poet exceptionally aware and respectful of Old World precedents; but on the contrary a thorough-going New World imperialist, determined that no Old World precedent – not even one so outlandish as the Petrarchan – should resist being assimilated into the social and amorous situations of twentieth-century North America.

This is harsh, however. And the *Sonnets*, both the writing of them and their belated publication, can and should be seen more indulgently. Charles Thornbury makes the right suggestion: it was in and by the *Sonnets* that Berryman broke free of the 'period style', Audenesque and Yeatsian, that he had mastered for his first collection, and fashioned instead the style that became distinctively his. Thornbury's word for this mature Berryman style is agreeably capacious; he calls it 'nervous'. Another name for it might be 'deliberately indecorous'. And one sees easily enough how the labour at the Petrarchan rhyme-scheme could have effected this: the rhyme-words are so much harder to come by in English than in Italian, that to get them at all the writer must be ready to swoop and veer from one register of English to another. The decorum that would prescribe a consistent level of diction has to be flouted repeatedly, continuously. Berryman's distinctive style, the style of *Dream Songs* (excluded from this volume), brilliantly makes a virtue of this necessity, vertiginously swooping and swerving from high to low, from pedantic to racy to raucously comical, in a way we came to recognize as peculiarly his, and peculiarly poignant as well as entertaining. If Berryman recognized that the labour on the *Sonnets* in 1947 brought him this breakthrough, then it is beside the point that they are, one by one and as a whole, 'failures'. They had served their purpose for him, technically; and publishing them in 1966 was not an aberration nor a miscalculation, but a justifiably proud setting of the record straight. Their overt subject is of no account; they represent a sustained and risky stylistic experiment, one that bore fruit.

We need to recognize just what stage Berryman was at. In 1966 he was 52, and had reached what Lowell called the terrible moment when a poet becomes too large for critics to challenge and criticize. (That moment comes earlier in American than in European careers.) Michael Schmidt in his *Reading Modern Poetry,* pondering what Lowell meant by this judgement, elaborates usefully: 'At that point his poet friends have embarked upon their different journeys, too, and are either jealous and competitive, or have no time to take him to task for his mistakes, excesses, aberrations. He is met with adulation or hostility: "The odds is gone". For Lowell, this was the point at which the poet becomes most vulnerable. He must fall back upon himself, and he is even more alone and exposed than he was when he set out. He must weigh his own work, and nothing is more difficult ...' Weighing his own work was what Berryman was about when he published his *Sonnets*.

It is from this perception of the threat that adulation poses to the poet (especially to a poet like Berryman who always anxiously solicited the advice of his peers), that we can get into perspective *Love & Fame* (1971). Never mind the love; so long as Berryman knows what he is doing, it is the fame that worries him:

> My tough Songs well in Tokyo & Paris
> fall under scrutiny. My publishers
> very friendly in New York & London
> forward me elephant cheques.

The sprained word-order of these sentences is another of the indecorums that he had learned to tolerate in the *Sonnets* and to exploit in the *Dream Songs*. But of course the larger indecorum is in the choice of subject. A not very prissy reader could well be shocked by the explicitness of some of Berryman's treatments of 'love'; but he violated a more jealously guarded taboo when he undertook to puzzle over what it was like for him to be famous. 'Fame is the spur', thought the Renaissance; Berryman, weeping all the way to the bank (he knows he cuts a comic figure), cannot persuade himself that fame in that glorious sense is the same as the celebrity he has, with fat royalties, and *carte blanche* to make amorous conquests.

I recall with some discomfort that when *Love & Fame* first appeared, I like others thought it self-indulgent. We had been bamboozled not by Lowell himself but by some of his admirers who had, on the basis of his *Life Studies*, proclaimed the emergence of a new kind of modern poetry called 'confessional'. Confessional was what *Love & Fame* seemed to be; and I confess that even today I am disconcerted by not seeing where the distance is, between the alcoholic drying out in a mental ward and the man who writes poems about it. Berryman tells us:

> Amplitude, – voltage, – the one friend calls for the one,
> the other for the other, in my work;
> in verse and prose. Well, hell.
> I am not writing an autobiography-in-verse, my friends.

To this day I have sympathy for the reader who should respond, raucously, 'You could have fooled me!'

There was still to come *Delusions etc. of John Berryman* (1972), which the author did not live to see through the press. I'm not aware that any one has annotated this, so as to make any of us confident about it. (Charles Thornbury's annotations are austerely textual.) A lot of it – though it is wonderfully various – is more dependent on Gerard Manley Hopkins than anything since *Sonnets*. Its first section – 'Opus Dei', an exercise on the offices for the day (Matins, Nones, and so on) – rather plainly takes off from what was in the end the last section (Part Four) of *Love & Fame*, subtitled 'Eleven Addresses to the Lord'. Whereas there has been no lack of voices deploring these late poems as a belated lurch into religiosity, there is in fact much evidence from earlier in Berryman's career that even at his most bawdy and arrogant he was always, and consciously, a son of the Church. Accordingly the poems of *Delusions etc.* deserve much more respectful and instructed attention than they have yet received. To my ear they come off the page with a rhythmical authority that commands such attention. Cheating a little, I quote from this last collection (since we began with Berryman the American imperialist) his 'Lines to Mr Frost':

> Felled in my tracks by your tremendous horse
> slain in its tracks by the angel of good God,
> I wonder toward your marvellous tall art
> warning away maybe in that same morning
>
> you squandered afternoon of your great age
> on my good gravid wife & me, with tales
> gay of your cunning & colossal fame
> & awful character, and – Christ – I see
>
> I know & can do nothing, and don't mind –
> you're talking about American power and how

somehow we've got to be got to give it up –
so help me, in my poverty-stricken way

I said the same goddamn thing yesterday
to my thirty kids, so I was almost ready
to hear you from the grave with these passionate grave
last words, and frankly Sir you fill me with joy.

There speaks a poet who recognizes civic responsibilities; not, as too many commentators would persuade us, a man entranced by his own image in the mirror.

17 Berryman

(i)

New surprises? No. No new surprises:
The course my life takes has begun to bore
Me, as to interest others. Berryman's
Cross-talk, however, now he is safely dead ...?
Ah but forget it! Palpitations and
Palpations of the ego ... My good friend
Amboise survives its builder, Shakespeare's sonnets
Silly Will Shakespeare. (Emendation: 'sully'?
By no means.) Count them: halfway into nine,
or ten now, lines of verse. This looks like being
A sonnet, then. Trust me, trust Robert Lowell:
That's how the thing resolves itself, the problem
Of form? There is no problem. There's the problem
Of how to write down anything at all.

(ii)

Not that we lack for certainties. Of those
We've had enough since time began, and more
(As muddled, wretched Berryman recognized)
Since Calvary. No, no, we have enough
Of things worth saying; but it's how to say them ...
How, with such bite, such necessarily vulgar
Acridity as may etch them on to such
Pliant plates we hardly can call them 'minds',
Flit as they do, as they are meant to do ...
Well, here's a stab at it: in Harvey Road,
In Cambridge, England, some one recalling then
And there the remembered, imperturbably armoured
Berryman of Clare.
                        His polished, empty
Poems of those years I carried off under my arm.

18 Randall Jarrell

Kipling, Auden & Co. (Farrar, Straus & Giroux, 1980; Carcanet New Press, 1981)

This volume of *Essays & Reviews 1935–1964* is the fourth and final collection of Jarrell's uncollected pieces, following *Poetry and the Age* (1953), *A Sad Heart at the Supermarket* (1962) and *The Third Book of Criticism* (1969). Noting that five pieces from one of these previous collections, and one from one of the others, are here reprinted, and noticing too the after all quite perfunctory title given to this book, we would be less than human if we did not suspect: 'scraping the barrel'. And our suspicion is at least partly confirmed: the second half of the book, which is arranged chronologically, does indeed seem wearisomely eclectic, with the galvanic and ultimately monotonous liveliness of lively journalism when its performances are pulled out of their periodical contexts and offered as turns in a non-stop vaudeville of knowledgeable smartness. However, the *young* Jarrell is on this showing that same brave and perceptive, trenchant and cleansing critic whom we remember from other books. And indeed the sympathetic reader can hardly avoid formulating a necessarily sad hypothesis, called 'what went wrong?' about how the young Jarrell, unmistakable and irreplaceable, turned into the older Jarrell who had only a little better taste and only a little more energy than a dozen critics and reviewers among our contemporaries.

The story as I read it tells of a poet and critic who never had, nor did he need, a theory either of poetry or criticism; but had until 1945 or so what served him better – a firm view, partial indeed but sensible and independent, of the literary and cultural history which had led up to, and still conditioned, the world in which he was trying to write poems. That world was dominated by something that he called 'modernism', and what concerned him most was to decide how that was related to something in the recent past called 'romanticism'. The perception he came to, which he hammered away at through the first decade of his career, was that the writers who thought themselves 'modernists', though they mostly supposed they were anti-romantic and often wrote remarkably searching criticism which tilted against romanticism, themselves in their own imaginative writing used thoroughly romantic procedures. This case is by no means so novel and challenging as it was when Jarrell first formulated it – which is to say that in large part we have come round to seeing that he was right. Himself, he was neither in favour of romanticism nor in principle opposed to it; but he argued, surely rightly, that the romantic procedures taken over by the modernists, (not American nor yet British procedures, but for the most part French) had been pushed to a point where there was no further way forward along that path. And accordingly he saw it as necessary for himself and his contemporaries to strike out on a new track, one that he was too shrewd to map in advance.

Quite suddenly, at the end of the Second World War, all of this disappears from Jarrell's criticism, and thereafter he was to manage without any effective historical perspective at all. The reasons for this change of front are not hard to find, and they do Jarrell credit: having experienced modern warfare at first hand and through first-hand witnesses (like the famous reporter Ernie Pyle, to whom he pays tribute), Jarrell perceived how for accredited modernists like E.E. Cummings and Marianne Moore war is something that happens to other people, and happens in ways that the serving soldier would not recognize. If one had to find a turning-point in this volume, it would be the page of *Partisan Review* in 1945 in which he castigated Marianne Moore's 'In Distrust of Merits' – a wonderfully well-managed piece of criticism, unsparing and indignant, and yet informed throughout with respect and regret. The same charge, of being inexcusably 'literary' about warfare, is laid at the door of Allen Tate, when Jarrell in 1945, welcoming *Land of Unlikeness* by his friend Robert Lowell, none the less says of Lowell: 'airplanes he treats as Tate does, only more so – he gives the impression of having encountered them in Mother Shipton.' This is particularly significant, because up to 1945 Tate was at the centre of Jarrell's admirations, to such an extent that even when Tate isn't named but only 'the modernist', that modernist seems unmistakably cast in Tate's image.

Jarrell, author of 'The Death of the Ball Turret Gunner', undoubtedly had the right to be furious with 'In Distrust of Merits', or with Tate's 'Seasons of the Soul', or with Cummings's 'plato told'. But what follows, for us? What are we to think of that Modernism which, at the hands of these distinguished practitioners proved so incapable of responding with common humanity to the atrociously common predicament of modern warfare? Must we settle for humanitarianism, as Jarrell seemed to do sometimes in his late enthusiasm for W.C. Williams? Must we agree with Wilfred Owen (whom Jarrell extolled) that 'the poetry is in the pity'? Hardly. For there is a component of Anglo-American modernism which, because it never meant much to Tate, Jarrell too was deaf to: the strain that at various times has been called 'imagism', 'objectivism', even 'projectivism'.

H.D. is the one representative of this kind of writing whom Jarrell took note of; and his confident superciliousness towards her is painful. For H.D., and the imagists and objectivists generally, wrote in a style inoculated against the sort of grandiloquence that can convert bomber aircraft into something out of Mother Shipton. For lack of contact with this style, or of appreciation of it (even though he approximated it himself in 'The Death of the Ball Turret Gunner'), Jarrell became the sort of critic who, when historical perspective is called for, prefers to quote an apophthegm of Goethe – just like that Matthew Arnold whom in his ardent youth, when still influenced by Allen Tate, Jarrell had been ready to deride for thinking Dryden and Pope classics of our prose, not of our poetry.

19 Theme and Action

Of Allen Tate's poem 'The Buried Lake' (1953), it has been rightly said that it 'appeared just as a new poetry began to rise in America':

> This new poetry's obsessions with oratory, romantic gesture, and exhibitionism have ... altered the way poetry works in the modern world. Even some of Tate's friends shifted eventually toward the new mode, among them Robert Penn Warren, Robert Lowell, and John Berryman.

This 'new mode' is as firmly established still as it was when Radcliffe Squires wrote of it thus in 1971. There are no signs that it has run its course, or is likely to do so at all soon. And accordingly public taste is no better prepared for Tate's *Collected Poems 1919–1976* than it was for his *Poems* (1960). Not many poets in any time have had to survive for so many years a change in taste (or in fashion) which so comprehensively brought into disrepute all, or nearly all, that the poet in question had set most store by in his art. It is an unenviable fate; and Allen Tate deserves our sympathy. I shall argue that he deserves a great deal more than that; but sympathy at least is what none of us should deny him.

As for the drastic change in expectations which put Tate in mid-career out of key with his age and his public, the most telling sign of it, to my mind, is that in all the four hundred pages of Tate's forty-five-year-long literary correspondence with Donald Davidson the name of William Carlos Williams rates not a single entry, whereas belated admiration for Williams's performance in poetry has been perhaps the defining characteristic of the years from 1953 to the present day – a development inaugurated if by any one person then by Randall Jarrell, a Vanderbilt man like Tate, and at one time quite close to him. By contrast, among Tate's contemporaries and associates through earlier decades, only Yvor Winters I think made any claims for Williams's poetry, and those claims were much more severely qualified than what it has become usual to claim for him through the last quarter-century. This sudden but sustained veneration for the author of *Paterson* could not help but damage Tate's relations with his readers. For Williams struggled – in the end very successfully – to present American readers with an either/or choice between his sort of poetry and T. S. Eliot's; whereas by 1953 Tate had for many years conspicuously aligned himself with Eliot – with Eliot's world view, however, more than with Eliot's verse style.

If it be objected that Radcliffe Squires's formulations – 'oratory, romantic gesture, and exhibitionism' – point somewhere away from Williams, I would for my part contend rather vigorously that Williams's performance answers to all these prescriptions: it is oratorical, it *does* make romantic gestures, and it *is* exhibitionist. I could even be quite bitter about it. For I can still recapture the sense of inexcusable affront that I had twenty-five years ago in England when, having learned to esteem American poetry in the work of Tate and John Crowe Ransom, and having worked out from that bridgehead to make more or less rewarding contact with Hart Crane, with Winters, and the early Penn Warren, I found myself made a monkey of, asked to esteem what seemed by contrast the unlicked and *faux-naïf* writing of Williams's *Collected Earlier Poems*. I remain convinced today that a sort of sentimental populism in Williams himself, in an influential admirer like Jarrell, and among American readers generally, overrates Williams's sort of poetry, and is grievously unfair to the incompatible sort of poetry that Allen Tate has written.

I cannot help being personal. For like any other literary man of my generation in the English-speaking world I find myself, as I turn the pages of Tate's *Collected Poems*, repeatedly brought up short by poems and parts of poems that recall my past to me – so constantly, though by no means always consciously, has Tate been a presence in my thinking from the time when I first began considering what serious writing might be. That presence was always minatory and challenging, never reassuring. The demands which it made of writing and of writers (also of readers) were always far too exacting for comfort. As early as 1929 the author of *Mr Pope and Other Poems*, published the previous year, wrote to Donald Davidson from Paris:

> Tradition is the intensest expression, or communication, the past has reached. This is always difficult. What most people mean by tradition is the debased and diluted version of the great masters which the second rate poets have passed on. Like Tennyson. It is worthy of remark that the only Victorian poet who is in the great tradition (Arnold) is put aside for Browning and Tennyson. These latter give the reader all the illusion of reading poetry, without forcing him to extend himself to the great effort of reading poetry itself. It is almost as difficult to read poetry as it is to write it. I find it so, and so should the reader, I believe.

In 1929 there was perhaps some excuse for this. And in fact there is an account of an older Tate teaching 'Tears, Idle Tears' in Minnesota, which suggests that he was not always so disrespectful to Tennyson. But it was surely wrong in 1929, as it was less excusably wrong in 1940 when I heard something similar from my teachers in England, and as it is quite inexcusably wrong in 1978, to relegate Tennyson to the second rate and elevate Arnold above him. In short, the Whitmanesque strain in American poetry was not the only legacy from the past which Tate exhorted us to disown, and sometimes when we of my generation bowed to his authority we cheated ourselves out of certain bequests that we have only lately and at some cost recovered for ourselves. And so the powerful presence that speaks to us from these poems was not always in the past beneficent. The 'tradition' that Tate proudly claimed to prolong and to speak for was less capacious than it should have been.

It was the same when one turned from Tate's criticism to his poems. Those too one regarded with respect and even awe, but hardly with love. Particularly if one read them, as I did, along with Ransom's, one could not fail to remark in them the lack of that seductive suavity which won us over to Ransom. The 'great effort' required of us as readers was apparent; what was not clear was the payoff, quite simply the pleasure, that our efforts were supposed to earn. Ransom, Hart Crane, even in his austere way Winters, were *winning* writers in a way that Tate has seldom deigned to be. That winningness which these others had, which he disdained, might take the form of haunting and plangent cadence; but equally it could be no more than the explicit making of common cause with his readers, by alerting them to a topic or an occasion which they could share with him, either actually or in imagination. Thus, when a poem called 'Picnic at Cassis' was dauntingly retitled 'The Mediterranean', the reader was denied the chance of making common cause with the poet in the familiar occasion signified by 'picnic'; and he was left to work out for himself that something as familiar as a picnic was being talked of – no easy matter, after a cunningly adapted epigraph from Virgil, and in view of the grand sonority of the diction:

> Let us lie down once more by the breathing side
> Of Ocean, where our live forefathers sleep
> As if the Known Sea still were a month wide –
> Atlantis howls but is no longer steep!
>
> What country shall we conquer, what fair land
> Unman our conquest and locate our blood?
> We've cracked the hemispheres with careless hand!
> Now, from the Gates of Hercules we flood
>
> Westward, westward till the barbarous brine
> Whelms us to the tired land where tasseling corn,
> Fat beans, grapes sweeter than muscadine
> Rot on the vine: in that land were we born.

The point is not in the least that this grand diction is excessive for recounting a boating picnic by expatriate Americans in the south of France; on the contrary, the truly imaginative act was precisely in moving from an occasion so trivial to a peroration so grand and yet so well earned, and the winningness of that progression, that 'rise', was forfeited as soon as the intrinsically trivial occasion was suppressed, or buried so deep that we have to delve to find it. This is a great pity. For these verses are very moving, and incidentally exemplify – consider the inventive vigour inside the pentameter – how Tate could adopt the world view of the American Virgilian expatriate Eliot, while being not in the least indebted to Eliot in movement through the verse line, or from verse to verse. Great and memorable as it is, this poem of 1933 still suffers from having (perversely as it must seem) curtailed the imaginative movement from the particular to the general, by ill-advised second thoughts concealing the particularity of the occasion it started from.

An even more striking and regrettable instance of this perversity is the ambitious poem in four parts, 'Seasons of the Soul' (1944). The four parts, headed 'Summer', 'Autumn', 'Winter', 'Spring', can be, and have been, glossed in other terms: for instance, 'Air', 'Earth', 'Water', and 'Fire'; also the soul of man (1) as political figure, (2) as abandoned sufferer, (3) as sexual being, (4) as desperately appealing before death for spiritual insight. But what is there in the poem, as immediately experienced by the reader, which could tempt him to consult the erudite commentaries – by Vivienne Koch, for instance, and Katherine Garrison Chapin – which tease out these further 'levels'? (And what a whiff of the recent past, by the way, comes up from that very word, 'levels'!) Well, there is this, as early as the third stanza:

> It was a gentle sun
> When, at the June solstice
> Green France was overrun
> With caterpillar feet.
> No head knows where its rest is
> Or may lie down with reason
> When war's usurping claws
> Shall take the heart escheat –
> Green field in burning season
> To stain the weevil's jaws.

But that vivid evocation of the 1940 blitzkrieg on France is the only concession that Tate makes to his reader, to advise him that the immediate occasion of the poem is one that he shares with the poet – the experience of World War II. And without Donald Davidson's privileged insight ('the four parts. ... as reflecting *throughout* the disastrous implications of World War II'), how would any of us identify – among the distracting echoes of Virgil and Dante, Wyatt and Lucretius and Traherne – *submarines* as the subject of the second stanza of 'Winter':

> A shark swift as your dove
> Shall pace our company
> All night to nudge and tear
> The livid wound of love?

Once again, as in 'The Mediterranean', the particular occasion of the poem, instead of being made to release symbolic or emblematic resonances, is suppressed *in favour of* those resonances – with the result that every reader, except the most attentive and instructed, will hear those resonances bombinating in a void. As with 'The Mediterranean', so here with 'Seasons of the Soul' we have a poem of very great accomplishment (the siren song here is Yeats, the Yeats of 'The Tower', as there it was Eliot) erecting quite gratuitous and perverse obstructions between itself and the well-disposed reader.

With this endemic fault (for so I take it) there goes another, which is graver since it concerns not the poet's relation with his reader but his relation with his language. Cleanth Brooks detected it many years ago, though without reprobation. 'Almost every adjective in his poetry,' said Brooks, 'challenges the reader's imagination to follow it off at a tangent.' Typical instances in 'The Mediterranean' are 'a gull white-winged along the *feckless* wave', and 'When lust of power undid its *stuffless* rage' (NED knows no such word as 'stuffless'); from 'Seasons of the Soul', 'time's *engaging* jaws', and (an ill-judged acquisition from Thomas Wyatt)

> I saw my downcast mother
> Clad in her street-clothes,
> Her blue eyes *long* and *small*....

And then there are the three terza rima poems of the 1950s (three parts of a projected autobiographical poem, planned first to have nine parts, later six). Here we find, in the first of them, 'The Maimed Man':

> ... By eye I mean the busy, *lurked*, discrete
> Mandible world sharp as a broken tooth.)

> And then rose in the man a small half-hell
> Where love disordered, shade of *pompous* youth,
> Clutched shades forbearing in a family well; ...

where the dictionary gives no warrant for 'lurk' as a transitive verb, and where 'pompous' is there for a pun with the Greek *'pompos* as applied to Hermes. And the second poem, 'The Swimmers', begins:

> Kentucky water, clear springs: a boy fleeing
> To water under the dry Kentucky sun,
> His four little friends in tandem with him, seeing

> Long shadows of grapevine wriggle and run

>   Over the green swirl; mullein under the ear
>   Soft as Nausicaa's palm; *sullen* fun
>
>   *Savage* as childhood's *thin harmonious* tear: ...

– where every one of the last four adjectives seems indeed, in Brooks's
sense, 'tangential', and thereby as far as possible from what Pound
applauded in Johnson's 'Vanity of Human Wishes': 'the lexicographer's
weighing of the epithet'. In fact, this persistent mannerism in Tate's verse
ought to give pause not only to those who too readily describe it as 'classical', but also to those who describe it as 'modern' – insofar as 'the
modern' in Anglo-American verse may be thought to derive as much
from Pound's precedent as from Eliot's.

What I am suggesting is that the besetting fault of Tate's writing, early
and late, has been an impatient neglect of the literal meaning of his poems
in favour of their symbolical or (his own word) *anagogical* meanings. To
give just one more instance, in the very beautiful 'Shadow and Shade' of
1933 – a poem admired by Winters though by few others, and another
that stands at least as far from Eliot as from Williams – the only flaw,
though a serious one, is the impossibility of knowing where the two actors
in the poem are standing (indoors, that is, or out-of-doors).

And I believe this may be the point to engage with Tate's identity as a
Southerner – though a captious and restive one. For it seems to be characteristic of the literature of the Southern Renascence – of that literature,
and of the criticism which attended and explained it up to Walter
Sullivan's remarkable *Death by Melancholy* (1972) – that it insists on
'theme', as distinct or distinguishable from 'action'. This distinction, it has
been pointed out, has no justification in any Aristotelean scheme, though
other components of that scheme (for instance 'plot' and 'character') are
taken over by Southern critics. But in any case the distinction offends
against common sense. For all the critical commentaries agree that the
stories and poems of the Southern Renascence have one theme, and one
only: the myth – by which one does not mean the fiction, still less the illu-
sion – of an antebellum Southern civilization destroyed by the Civil War,
or by that war's aftermath. To be sure, there were distinct shadings in the
different retellings of the myth: differences, for instance, about how far the
seeds of its destruction were in the antebellum South from the first; or
again, more urgently, differences about what should be the attitude and
the aspirations of the self-conscious Southerner in the here and now of the
1930s and 1940s. But these were only shadings; the myth was massively
one and the same, so we were told, in Andrew Lytle's *The Long Night* and
in Tate's 'Aeneas at Washington'. But if that were so, and if the theme
were what one read for, why bother reading Mr Lytle's novel when one
had read Mr Tate's poem, or vice versa? Since it's a fact of experience that
a reading of the one work doesn't spoil one for the other, it follows that

what one reads for and responds to isn't in the first place the theme, but on the contrary, in Aristotle's sense, the *action*.

It is obviously easier to detect the action in a narrative or a drama than in a poem like 'Aeneas at Washington' which is not in any usual sense either narrative or dramatic. Yet every poem of any sort *has* an action – an action consisting of the sequence of its words and images exploding on the reader's consciousness, now fast, now slow, now pushing forward, now circling back. The action, of course, need not be continuous, but will develop through stages, incorporating a jump or break from one stage to the next. In a scrupulous poet like Tate, we may expect to find such 'jumps' indicated by typography. So it is in 'Aeneas at Washington' where, after the first sixteen lines of magnificent (and yes, winning) translation and adaptation from the *Aeneid*, there is a break signalled by a space and the beginning of a parenthesis:

> (To the reduction of uncitied littorals
> We brought chiefly the vigor of prophecy,
> Our hunger breeding calculation
> And fixed triumphs.)

For Lillian Feder these four lines are 'a brilliant transition'; but she can think so because she is reading the poem for its theme, and thus can gloss it from Tate's essays. But if it should be read, like any other poem, for its *action,* does not the abrupt desertion of the pentameter in the first and third of these lines make one hear in the diction the Eliot of 'Gerontion'? And in that case, does this not strike us as a parenthesis in a damaging sense, not a resumption or a switching of the action, but a standing aside from it, not a break in the action but a damaging breach of it, a wandering of attention, both ours and the poet's?

The action then resumes, magnificently. The destroyed South is named in 'Blue Grass', rammed hard against 'Troy' in controlled synaesthesia bringing conflagration and fruition together. The action now is indeed 'explosive' and rapid:

> I saw the thirsty dove
> In the glowing fields of Troy, hemp ripening
> And tawny corn, the thickening Blue Grass
> All lying rich forever in the green sun.

There is to my ear a lapse three lines later into telltale sub-Eliotic diction signalled by the mannered epithet, 'singular':

> The singular passion
> Abides its object and consumes desire
> In the circling shadow of its appetite ...

– lines which Cleanth Brooks, reading for 'theme' as Lillian Feder did with the parenthesis, can seem to vindicate by a gloss from Tate's essay, 'Religion and the Old South'. But after that the action proceeds with authority and magnificence to its tragic conclusion when the speaker on the banks of the Potomac asserts bleakly:

> Struck in the wet mire
> Four thousand leagues from the ninth buried city
> I thought of Troy, what we had built her for.

('Struck', I'm afraid, is a misprint for 'stuck'.)

Thus, even in this, which I take to be one of the great poems of our time and one of the greatest American poems of all time, there are flaws more or less damaging. And this seems to be the rule: if I were asked to name any one poem by Mr Tate that is flawlessly consummated, I doubt if I could find one. But what follows from that? Only that in the act of composition he is mastered by forces which he can only with difficulty, and not consistently, master. It is a sort of definition of what an older criticism would recognize as a poet of genius, rather than talent. Tate as critic and pedagogue has had a noble contempt for the too easy understanding of the artist as one who knows not what it is he does; yet his own work shows that he too, despite his analytic intelligence and his principled civic responsibility, was, when he wrote his greatest poems, carried out of himself, overmastered. Properly to take leave of him, we need not prose but verse. Conceivably, thus:

> Rue for remembrance: not
> A tribute he would slight.
> And yet of us he asks
> That what we say be right.
>
> The Man of Letters as
> Hero was not the mark
> He aimed at, but it was
> The chaplet of Petrarch.
>
> Praise then no scrupulous voice
> That chose, and chose right. Those
> The Muse takes have no choice;
> He was of those she chose.

This essay first appeared in *Parnassus* 6, no. 2 (1978). Reprinted in *Trying to Explain*.

20 A Tribute to Allen Tate

[...] Several times in the months since I came to Tennessee I have found myself saying that I first became aware of Allen Tate's poetry when I went up as a freshman to Cambridge in 1940. However, now that I have really applied myself to think back, it seems to me that I have been making myself out to be more precocious than I really was; and that the time which I remember, when Allen Tate was on the lips of my contemporaries and myself, must have been 1947 or 1948, when I returned to Cambridge after the Second World War. That is borne out by the dates in my copies of the Selected Poems of Allen Tate, John Crowe Ransom, and Robert Penn Warren. All are dated 1947 or 1948, London publications, and one of them (Warren's) from a London publisher so fugitive and little reputable that I suspect the edition was pirated, and the author received no royalties for it. Of course these American poets had been known in England before that, but they had not been widely known, nor were their writings widely available. At any rate, to me and my contemporaries in the late 1940s they came as a revelation of what American poetry had come to be in the twentieth century. You must understand that for us foreigners that was how they figured – as Americans, not Southerners. In due course, indeed, it came to seem that all these American poems we were admiring had been written on one or other of two campuses – Vanderbilt and the University of the South. Where these favoured haunts of the muses were located on a map of the United States was not at all clear to us; and indeed I am not at all sure that we realized how they were two distinct places, and not one nest of singing birds under alternative names. Similarly, though we knew in a vague way about the War between the States, I am sorry to confess that we found it difficult to remember which side called itself 'Confederate', and which, 'Unionist'. There is no doubt of course that in our ignorance of, or at best very hazy information about, such matters, we missed a great deal of the resonance and poignancy of these poems that we admired. On the other hand it does seem worth emphasizing that the poems could and did surmount these gulfs and barriers of incomprehension; we admired them for their assurance and audacity, as works which uncompromisingly profited from the innovations of T.S. Eliot and W.B. Yeats, and particularly from the precedent of the seventeenth-century poets whom Yeats and Eliot had taught us all to admire with a new fervour. From Tate's and Ransom's poems, and increasingly from their criticism, we moved out – my friends and I in England – to make the acquaintance of other American poets; of Wallace Stevens and Hart Crane, even of a poet so far in the past as Emily Dickinson.

I am speaking of a climate of opinion about poetry which disappeared long ago. Radcliffe Squires, the most learned and scrupulous student of Tate's poetry, points out that already, a quarter century ago, there was emerging a new poetry which denied many of the principles on which Allen Tate had proceeded. As Mr Squires says, 'This new poetry's obsession with oratory, romantic gesture, and exhibitionism have ... altered the way poetry works in the modern world. Even some of Tate's friends shifted eventually toward the new mode, among them Robert Penn Warren ...' Not only did Allen Tate live his last twenty-five years in the knowledge that fashion had decisively and indeed aggressively moved away from the sort of poetry which he advocated and practised, but those of us throughout the English-speaking world who had taken more or less notice of his practice and his precepts have also found ourselves, to a lesser degree, left aside by the preference for more oratorical and exhibitionist behaviour among poets. Those preferences are still prevalent and dominant in the circles where poetic reputations are made, whether in London or New York or wherever else, and there are no signs that they are running out of steam.

At any rate, you will see that I am moved to claim some part in Allen Tate for non-American poets like myself. And I will go so far as to say that there are certain of Tate's poems which may, without excessive falsification, be read in a British or an Australian – at any rate a non-American – accent. One such poem I venture to think is 'Aeneas at Washington'. The Aeneas who speaks this tragic poem is undoubtedly, I suppose, a survivor from the ruined Troy of the old Confederacy, moving and brooding in the capital of the victorious Unionist Greeks. More certainly, he is one of those Englishmen (Scotsmen, Irishmen, Welshmen) who in history's yesterday crossed the Atlantic to found a new nation cleansed of the errors and evils of the Europe they came from. But I remember that through many centuries in the Middle Ages Englishmen too regarded the City of London as 'Troynovant', New Troy, substantiating with a bizarre and half-believed mythology the idea that as the ruined Prince of Troy, carrying on his back his aged father and his crucial household gods, sailed the seas to found a new Troy in Rome, so at some later date another hero transferred the destiny of Rome to England. Thus I can, and I do read this great poem as having to do with the situation of any man or woman who has devoted any considerable part of his energies to re-establishing on a new base the life not of himself and his immediate kin, but of his tribe, his

nation, his people. In other words, the Aeneas who speaks this poem and
figures in it seems to be indeed the character that appears in Homer's *Iliad*
and Virgil's *Aeneid*, as well as later versions of that same heroic prototype
of our own day, speaking varieties of English as once he spoke Latin, and
before that Greek.

> I myself saw furious with blood
> Neoptolemus, at his side the black Atridae,
> Hecuba and the hundred daughters, Priam
> Cut down, his filth drenching the holy fires.
> In that extremity I bore me well,
> A true gentleman, valorous in arms,
> Disinterested and honourable. Then fled:
> That was a time when civilization
> Run by the few fell to the many, and
> Crashed to the shout of men, the clang of arms:
> Cold victualing I seized, I hoisted up
> The old man my father upon my back,
> In the smoke made by sea for a new world
> Saving little – a mind imperishable
> If time is, a love of past things tenuous
> As the hesitation of receding love.
>
> (To the reduction of uncitied littorals
> We brought chiefly the vigor of prophecy,
> Our hunger breeding calculation
> And fixed triumphs.)
>
>   I saw the thirsty dove
> In the glowing fields of Troy, hemp ripening
> And tawny corn, the thickening Blue Grass
> All lying rich forever in the green sun.
> I see all things apart, the towers that men
> Contrive I too contrived long, long ago.
> Now I demand little. The singular passion
> Abides its object and consumes desire
> In the circling shadow of its appetite.
> There was a time when the young eyes were slow,
> Their flame steady beyond the firstling fire,
> I stood in the rain, far from home at nightfall
> By the Potomac, the great Dome lit the water,
> The city my blood had built I knew no more
> While the screech-owl whistled his new delight
> Consecutively dark.

> Stuck in the wet mire
> Four thousand leagues from the ninth buried city
> I thought of Troy, what we had built her for.

On the only occasion when I spent any time with Allen Tate (about two years back) he greeted me by saying, 'Arthur Winters died ten years ago.' This was, I suppose, characteristically direct; but also delicately tactful. It showed that he was aware how I had been rather closely associated with Arthur Yvor Winters in past years, and how I had in *some* respects carried on in Stanford the work that Yvor Winters had begun there. Winters, when he was alive, had talked to me of Tate. Back in the late 1920s, when Allen Tate's centres of operation had been New York and Paris, and Winters's had been New Mexico and California, they had corresponded actively, if not furiously. In particular, Professor Thomas Parkinson of Berkeley, in a recent book centred upon the letters which Hart Crane wrote to Winters, has shown in a most moving way how Tate on the one side and Winters on the other were co-operating (though quarrelsomely sometimes) to save from his own self-destructive drives the doomed genius of Hart Crane. Tate wrote the crucial introduction to the first collection of Crane's poems, and Winters manoeuvred so as to write the crucial applauding review of that book. Of course, Winters and Tate failed; Hart Crane duly destroyed himself in 1932 – but not before he had left a score of brilliant and astonishing poems which are permanent acquisitions to the canon of American poetry, and indeed of poetry in the English language. I wanted particularly to draw attention to this episode because both Tate and Winters were fiercely uncompromising and severe in everything that concerned the difficult art to which they had devoted themselves; and so both of them made enemies, around each of them cluster anecdotes which show them merciless in condemnation of inferior workmanship and self-deceiving workmen. It seems the more necessary to remember that in both cases the severity was linked to, and was in the service of, an unsparing generosity towards 'the real thing' when they were sure that they had found it. Their services to Hart Crane, surely in human terms one of the people it was most difficult to help, show this clearly.

It's not only in this connection that I find myself thinking of Allen Tate and Yvor Winters together. Sharply as they sometimes disagreed, and differently as Tate's poems and Winters's poems come at us from the page, they shared a conviction that American culture must derive from and must repeatedly be refreshed by, that cultural cradle of the Mediterranean whose records are available to us in Greek and Latin and Hebrew. Moreover, Tate and Winters stand together in my mind as representing an astringent and sophisticated temper in American poetry which is very rare indeed in American writing of the last twenty-five years. That more recent poetry has on the whole navigated by sea-marks quite different from those which Tate and Winters instituted for their students and apprentices to sail by, in the treacherous shoals of modernity and fashion.

Address delivered at Vanderbilt University, 1981.

16 Zion

Mired in it! Stuck in the various
rust-coloured, dove-coloured, yellowish
or speckled muds of history, you mistook
clarity, the dayspring from on high,
for a satisfaction of art, or the condition
of addressing the untutored.
                                    (As you never
did, they were otherwise tutored.)

Once, stuck in the mud by the Capitol,
you thought of the ninth buried city,
Richmond, Montgomery, what you had built them for,

of Troy, and of Rome, of Richmond, of Rome, not Zion;

of Troy, of Troynovant, of London,
the West Country, sometimes Geneva,
never of Zion;

of New Caledonia, New
Amsterdam, New Zealand,
Rome (Georgia), other Romes
and Athenses of the North,

New Delhi, Athens, Syracuse, not Zion.

Tutored in computer-processing,
still they may learn of Zion.

Trained in marketing techniques they
may discern in that murk the clarity
of a city not built on seven hills,

not guarding a river-crossing
nor plugging a gap in the mountains.

Unskilled in Islamic culture, they
may still make a Mecca of Zion.

Having heard or not heard of Lindisfarne, Iona,
are not the lot of us pilgrims?

The variegation of muds,
the iridescences,
constitute for some
in youth a passion,
in age a distraction from boredom

which, if designedly aimless
for long enough, merits the name of
Zion or some say Eden.

This poem is included here, as a postscript to the foregoing essay.

22 The Persistent Alternative: Cassity, Pinsky, Others

When I called this paper, 'The Persistent Alternative', I must admit I had an overweening and perhaps paranoid suspicion that I should be inviting admiration for a sort of American verse-writing that would go unnoticed or else under-esteemed by the other contributors to this symposium. But in this I was wrong. Harold Bloom has applauded one of my poets, Robert Pinsky, and another, Turner Cassity, has been generously appreciated by Richard Howard. The five sparkling pages with which Mr Howard introduces Cassity's latest collection, *Yellow for Peril, Black for Beautiful* (George Braziller, 1975), have I find sharpened invaluably my sense of this strange and strangely isolated poet. So I'm grateful; and if in due course I shall begin to wonder if Richard Howard doesn't esteem rather different aspects and parts of Cassity's achievement from those that most compel my admiration, or if, even when we concur in admiring the same writings, Mr Howard and I seem to admire for rather different reasons, that doesn't remove my sense of obligation. Such civil disagreements among the six of us are, I take it, just what this symposium is meant to provide for.

At any rate, if I'm to justify my promise to provide an *alternative*, I must start by posing that alternative in a very modest way. And I can do so by remarking that Turner Cassity is very markedly and self-consciously a writer of *verse*, in the sense that central to his awareness of what he is doing is the integrity of the verse-line, and particularly the value of the *turn* from one line into the next. This is not quite the same as saying, what is none the less true, that Cassity writes in metre – an alternative that, in the case of younger generations of American poets, is I think rather seldom considered. It's in a poem from his second collection *Steeplejacks in Babel* (Godine, 1973), that Cassity announces most defiantly his espousal of this alternative. But open defiance is not at all his way; and his act of defiance is conveyed, with characteristic obliquity, in a poem which overtly isn't about writing at all but about the harbour of Sydney, Australia:

> Cruise ships are, for the young, all that which varies.
> The aged disembark with dysenteries.
> Always, it is middle age that sees the ferries.

They hold no promise. Forward or reverse
Impels them only to where what occurs,
Occurs. Such is, at least, the chance of being terse,

And is their grace. The lengthy liners, fraught
Sublimely, shrill for tugs. If they're distraught,
That is because the thoughts of youth are long, long thoughts –

Save those of gratitude. The slow, massed force
That frees them they will cast off in due course,
To learn, or not to learn, the ferries' sole resource:

How, in the crowding narrows, when the current
Runs in opposition and the torrent
Claws the wheel, to locate in routine, abhorrent

For the storm, the shore that makes it specious;
Where one calls the vicious, curtly, vicious,
And the scheduled ferry, not the cruise ship, precious.

Richard Howard says very handsomely and justly, of this poem, that we
see in it 'that old ceremonial of keeping, of returns and recuperations
which we call verse, meaning thereby something that keeps turning'. And
indeed the turn round a line-ending was surely never managed more
suavely than in 'where what occurs,/ Occurs ...' All the same, suavity isn't
what this poet is chiefly concerned with, but on the contrary what the
continually turning verse is after is, he says explicitly, 'terseness', 'curtness'
– a quality or an effect for which he readily foregoes the sublime and the
distraught, all those feelings that might be called 'oceanic', of which therefore the appropriate emblem is the wandering cruise-liner, not the
cramped and dependable to-and-fro of the ferry-boat. It's not often that
'the chance of being terse' is valued so highly; and it's particularly unlikely
that we should find this alternative opted for by a writer whose home-
ground is the same as William Faulkner's. But of course we may well think
he came by this preference not in Jackson, Mississippi, but in Stanford,
California, where in his youth he heard an older poet declare:

Passion is hard of speech,
Wisdom exact of reach;
Poets have studied verse;
And wit is terse.

Richard Howard entertainingly recognizes this early conditioning of
Cassity when he speaks of him as 'crisp from his encounters with the Yvor
Winters memorial frigidarium'. And it is doubtless because I've spent time
by Winters's side or in his shadow (though never quite at his feet), that
my awareness of this early allegiance of Cassity's bulks rather large in my

sense of him. It is, so far as I know, an allegiance that Cassity has never disowned. Nor should we expect that he would – after all, the harshest thing that he has to say about his young 'cruise-liner' poets is that they lack *gratitude*. It's true that the tone of Cassity's voice is at nearly every point very far from the tone of Winters. But perhaps that's the best reason for insisting on the connection between them; it may show, what is customarily denied, that the principles of the Wintersian alternative in American poetry can carry over and be profitable in the service of a quite different emotional temperament from Winters's own. That temperament – Winters's – was one that trapped him into seeming, and perhaps being, at times overweening, at other times paranoid; and when he promoted what he certainly saw as an alternative to the main drift of American verse in his lifetime, the overweening set many teeth on edge, and offends still. Which is a great pity. For, when disentangled from the particular emotional and tonal peculiarities that Winters's temperament gave to it, the alternative that he promoted seems to me as viable, and as little regarded, now as in his lifetime. One feature of that alternative has so far emerged – to poets of this persuasion (and I am glad to subscribe myself among them) the rhyme of 'verse' with 'terse' is, if fortuitous, the happiest and most meaningful sort of fortuity.

Cassity's 'In Sydney by the Bridge', though invaluable as a sort of programmatic poem (by a poet to whom the programmatic comes hard and seldom), represents him, just because it is programmatic, at less than his best. I'd define what is deficient about it by remarking that it could have been written by a poet who had never actually *been* in Sydney, New South Wales; or else (the same point the other way round) that we as readers have really no more sense of the scene of Sydney Harbour when we finish the poem than before we began reading it. Much better, to my mind, is a poem about Amsterdam which really *is* about that Dutch city – a city which, as it happens, I have never visited:

> Neutral and dull, the bricks that serve as shores
> Enforce their color on the channeled water;
> And if a distant movement, as of oars,
> Has made that mirrored brick, its mortar scatter,
> Now, as the soon abated force goes slack,
> A leveling inertia lays them back.
>
> Surface on surface to a depth of peace –
> How little stirred to be so far from stagnant!
> As if reflection and its slow release,
> Its visions idly on that water regnant,
> Themselves were substance and renewal; beat
> Or silence; action, and the act complete.

As if our shadows, lengthening below,
Received us bodily to calm, to vision,
Always to rock with lifted oars; where, low
Beside the mirror, sense and its precision
Give to the arching sky, the dormered town,
A motion one brick up and one brick down.

A lovely poem, surely, which I unaffectedly envy him! And if I say that I read it as a true and vivid report on one specified place on the globe's surface, I don't mean to class it with those rhymed picture-postcards from foreign parts with which our poets, on their Guggenheim years in Europe, regale the folks back home. It is of course a *paysage interieur* as much as it is a *paysage* locatable on the map, and a season of the soul as much as it is a tourist season, or part of one. The double-meanings of 'reflection' and 'vision', to go no further, give to the reader so inclined sufficient provocation for allegorizing. But we should beware, I think, of allegorizing too promptly and too eagerly: Cassity is very much a world-wandering poet, a globe-trotter, and although the places that he responds to have something in common (mostly, for instance, they are post-colonial places), still the sheer irreducible variety of visitable places and climates is something brought powerfully home to us as we read Cassity; and to some unPlatonic minds, the compelling assurance of that available diversity is in itself a pleasure and a comfort.

There could hardly be a starker contrast to Winters who, vividly though he responded to places and climates, never left the United States, and through much of his life could only with difficulty be lured more than a hundred miles from San Francisco. In this indeed – his refusal to travel, whether in fact or imagination, beyond the parameters of North American experience – Winters lamentably presented *no* alternative to the prevailing temper of American letters in his time, a temper even more marked and constricting in the years since he died, for which the only precise name is, I'm afraid, *cultural chauvinism*. Winters to be sure never pretended, as many have pretended since, that for the just assessment of American poetry one needs no other language than English; his study of some French poets was assiduous, and is amply documented. But it was part of his exaggerated esteem for literature that he should suppose assiduous reading of Rimbaud and Valéry had given him a comprehensive acquaintance with the French mind and sensibility such as could only be distracted, in no way enhanced, by first-hand acquaintance with the sights and sounds and smells of Paris or Charleville. In the same way I remember how baffled I was, thirty years ago, when I was first in correspondence with Winters, by his objurgations against a Romanticism which seemed not to be the Romanticism that I knew from my own British tradition; as of course it was not – it was the specifically American Romanticism of Ralph Waldo Emerson, from which Winters regarded the romanticisms of Blake and Coleridge and Wordsworth as marginal and not very noteworthy variations. That the British societies which nurtured these British poets were geographically, ethnographically, demographically very different from the American society that nurtured Emerson – this he presumably knew, but shrugged impatiently aside. Such considerations bulked large only in sorts of history which he had by that time agreed with himself to consider as trivial, compared with the two sorts of history that absorbed him – that is to say, the history of literary forms, and the history of ideas. It seems to me a characteristic defect of American criticism today, that it still takes account of these two sorts of history to the virtual exclusion of other sorts – of social and economic and political history. At any rate how unlikely, and how impossible to account for in Winters's scheme of things, that one of the poets he schooled should by choice or chance spend many years in the Union of South Africa, and should give a more nuanced and affecting image of life in that strange society than has been given, to the best of my knowledge, by any English-speaking South African, whether black or white or yellow or brown! If that is Turner Cassity's achievement, or one of his achievements, it is hard to see how any of the currently influential American schools of criticism is able to come to terms with it, or to value it, any better than Wintersian criticism does. For a criticism which, whatever other disputes may divide it, still agrees to take as the central task of American poetry the defining of *American* identity, there is no way to account for an American poet whose most noble and moving verses are imagined as spoken by the ghost of President Paul Kruger hovering over his own effigy in Pretoria:

> Too literal to wonder what myth is,
> I have become one. Servants, misfits, you
> Who serve your princes, I was raised a shepherd.
> Now, an idol like a cast-iron stove,
> I rule my city. Birds, I am informed,
> Nest in my top hat. They are *regte boere;*
> Let them. Lime or homage, what the harm?
> Safe in the fold the undone flock, and mine
> The golden fatherland, the strapping sons.

(Let restive liberals, prompt with right-minded indignation at the society that Paul Kruger brought into being, rest assured: there are other Cassity poems about South Africa which take account of their indignation, though here he chooses not to.) Confronted with this phenomenon, we either damn with faint praise ('Cassity is a limited poet, but ... performs candidly within his range'), or else, more disastrously, we decide that he can't be serious. Of this second way of turning the force of Cassity's challenge to our preconceptions Richard Howard has remarked, with fine distaste:

Architecture, as Walt Whitman once observed, is what you do to a building when you look at it, and our transactions with this poet's oeuvre suggest that we turn a building into a 'folly' when we don't look at it enough. It is our neglect which is playing the fool here, not Cassity's capacity, not Cassity's veracity, not Cassity's sagacity.

And yet even Mr Howard sees an element of 'the folly' in the extraordinary edifice that Cassity erected in 1970 on the pages of *Poetry* magazine, a narrative poem in twelve sections about a 1917 German airship expedition to South West Africa, story-line and dramatis personae both and all entirely solid and clear; or again, in the verse-play, *Men of the Great Man*, set around the death-bed of Cecil Rhodes. This last Mr Howard describes as 'a Lament for the Dead Hero which is this poet's own snarling version of the collapse of the Knights of the Grail – a kind of *Boys Own Parsifal*, wherein the Fellowship dissolves into ...Rhodes scholarships!' This is certainly an accurate as well as admirably compact description of this play. And undoubtedly the decline of imperial grandeur to Rhodes scholarships calls for some sort of astonished exclamation mark. It would be a pity, though, if Mr Howard's exclamation-mark carried too much the implication of 'What an amusing thing to have thought of writing about!'

Cassity himself, unfortunately, invites that sort of snickering reading. Too often his titles are arch and cute. The poem about Amsterdam, for instance, has the dandified title, 'A Somewhat Static Barcarolle'. It is a mannerism that we have been resigned to ever since Wallace Stevens, and I've never seen a convincing explanation of what purpose Stevens meant his dandified titles to serve. In Cassity's case very often they seem to signal only a nervous giggle. A more grievous case is his entitling his poem about the German dirigible, 'The Airship Boys in Africa' – which certainly seems to imply that if we take the poem seriously (as for my part I certainly do – it is too well written for me to take it otherwise), we are making fools of ourselves.

And Cassity's giggle sounds elsewhere than in his titles. On his way to 'The Airship Boys in Africa', he had written for instance a poem in his first book, 'The Afterlives of Count Zeppelin'. (Somewhere behind them both, I would guess, is Winters's solemn and impressive 'Elegy. For the U.S.N. Dirigible, Macon'.) The Count Zeppelin poem begins with a good joke, then deteriorates rapidly:

> Inflated, yet elliptical, of epic size,
> What great Teutonic riddle hangs there in the skies?
> It is the *Graf von Himmel*, bearing far from Jews
> And postwar debt true Germans on eternal cruise:
> Teachers of counterpoint, and, wives in braided locks,
> Cherubic manufacturers of cuckoo clocks;
> Ex-Kaiserin, Big Bertha, other Krupps, and – *echt* –

> A mid-air cellar tanker planes refill with *Sekt*.
> For cabin class, a *Turnverein,* a skating rink,
> And fourteen cabin boys, to hum them Humperdinck.
> Moreover, in the steering gondola, her odd,
> Stiff navigator may, conceivably, be God.

I haven't the heart to go on to the second strophe. It should be clear that the self-conscious 'wicked' outrageousness of the rhymes has taken hold of the poem and wrenched it out of any possibility of shapeliness; it is as if the Sydney Harbour ferry crashed full tilt into the pier on every second traverse – this verse never turns, it shudders to a stop, then painfully starts again. 'Dandified' is hardly the word for this effect; yet the motive behind it seems the same – the compulsion to always astonish, outsmart, upstage any conceivable reader. And for this we now, thanks to Susan Sontag, have a better word than 'dandified'; it is 'camp' – not just an effect, but the sensibility which seeks out such effects and revels in them, a sensibility which since 1964, when Ms Sontag published her momentous 'Notes on "Camp"', we have no excuse for not defining quite precisely, and recognizing as a powerful strain in American poetry of our time. 'Camp', I would say, is Turner Cassity's besetting temptation, and one he has succumbed to lamentably often.

Fifteen years ago Susan Sontag confessed to feeling very ambivalent about 'camp'. She said for instance in her essay 'On Style':

> No doubt, in a culture pledged to the utility (particularly the moral utility) of art, burdened with a useless need to fence off solemn art from arts which provide amusement, the eccentricities of stylized art supply a valid and valuable satisfaction. I have described these satisfactions in another essay, under the name of 'camp' taste. Yet, it is evident that stylized art, palpably an art of excess, lacking harmoniousness, can never be of the greatest kind.

Yet on the whole, despite misgivings, she welcomed 'camp' as an ally in her polemic 'Against Interpretation'. In this I think she was mistaken. None of us who are involved in institutions of allegedly higher learning can think that 'interpretation' as she defined it is any less of a menace now than it was fifteen years ago; the *interpreters*, bearing in upon the content of texts, operate in every classroom up and down the land, breeding there more of their own kind – that is to say, people who under pretence of serving art in fact emasculate it, and *tame* it. But what stops these colleagues of ours in their tracks are not the 'camp' texts which brazenly are more concerned with form than with content, but on the contrary texts which leave the interpreter with nothing to do precisely because their content is unchallengeably obvious, texts which in the most obvious way mean implacably just what they say. Ms Sontag, wistfully yearning for just such an overt and undeviating art, found it only in the cinema; but if she had looked a little further, she would have found it in our poetry also – though in a sort of poetry which goes largely unregarded because it does not suit the vested interests of the institutionalized 'interpreters'; and also (it must be said) because our students are so obtuse about the resources of their native language that no content, however overt, is overt enough for them not to miss it or get it wrong. Turner Cassity has written such admirably overt poems, though rather often he obscures the fact by giving them foppish titles; but he has also written 'camp' poems, in which the overt subject is scanted in favour of the supposedly 'delicious' sensibility that plays upon it and around it.

Such a poem is 'The Return of Ming the Merciless', part of what Mr Howard calls 'the luminous fabric Cassity has woven out of Movieland cobwebs'. It's just here that I find my taste diverging from Richard Howard's, and so in all fairness I must let him explain himself. He says:

> It is a reclaiming, a civilizing process, this career of Cassity's as I trace it, in which 'anecdote falls heir to all', and 'style gives back a time but takes its terrors.' *Where id was, there shall ego be* is the swamp-draining motto of our modern Faust, which Cassity recasts: where *kitsch* was, there shall culture feed. The energies of a bitter wit, a *turner*, indeed, of the most intricate contours upon the lathe of prosody, are bent or at least curved to transform what had been merely waste – public consumption, rated G – into particular delights, the significance speech has when it is no longer public but personal, obsessively individual, idiopathic, its own man: rated X.

The difference between us will be obvious: my argument requires me to attach a minus-sign to those attributes – 'personal', 'obsessively individual', 'idiopathic' – to which Richard Howard assigns a plus.

I think it's rather important to get this right. Certainly the point is not that old movies, and our memories of them, are insufficiently dignified subjects for poetry to deal with. On the contrary, consider only the opening lines of Mr Hollander's 'Movie-Going':

> Drive-ins are out, to start with. One must always be
> Able to see the over-painted Moorish ceiling
> Whose pinchbeck jazz gleams even in the darkness, calling
> The straying eye to feast on it, then fall
> Back to the sterling screen again. One needs to feel
> That the two empty, huddled, dark stage-boxes keep
> Empty for kings. And having frequently to cope
> With the abominable goodies, overflow
> Bulk and (finally) exploring hands of flushed
> Close neighbors gazing beadily out across glum

> Distances is, after all, to keep the gleam
> Alive of something rather serious, to keep
> Faith, perhaps, with the City.

This speech may be 'personal', but not in any way that stops it from being *public*; it is not 'obsessively individual' but *communal*; it is not 'idiopathic' but *social* or *sociable*. If we had any doubts of this, we lose them at the point where I broke off reading, where 'the City' announces the presence of the late W.H. Auden, that most public of poets, who is never far absent thereafter from the rest of the poem. And one consequence of the Audenesque presence is that John Hollander's poem can be argued with, where Cassity's 'Return of Ming the Merciless' cannot be. It is possible to ask, after reading Hollander's poem: 'Is he right about the significance of the movies, or is he wrong?' And that, from my point of view, is abundantly to his credit. He made the point himself in another movie-going poem, 'To the Lady Portrayed by Margaret Dumont': 'The camp was to make sex grotesque, but when / Was anything more grave?' Just so: the matters raised by the Marx Brothers movies are quite *grave* matters, they deal with 'something rather serious' – which doesn't in the least mean that we need find them anything but hilarious, nor need we feel ashamed of the rapt affection with which we remember our younger selves first revelling in them. The movies are however, or they were, a social, a public phenomenon; and they accordingly deserve to be taken as seriously as John Hollander takes them. Auden bequeathed us one idiom in which such seriousness was possible; thirty or more years ago Winters had perfected another. Each idiom has its dangers; the Audenesque tends to be garrulous, as the Wintersian tends to be glum and portentous. All the same, I think the current scene would be a more heartening spectacle if one or other or both of these idioms were more practised, more in evidence.

Instead what we have is a great deal of 'camp'. There is a certain awkwardness about using this term because, as Susan Sontag noted, 'camp' in a narrow sense has been taken over as a sort of badge by the homosexual community; and so, if we demur at it, we may think we must go in fear of the vigilantes of the Gay Liberation Front. But fortunately the fit between 'camp' and homosexuality is far from perfect: many heterosexuals practise 'camp', and some avowedly homosexual writers won't touch it. (Consider, in the second category, my admirable compatriot Thom Gunn.) In any case, we need to use the term in a broad sense, to embrace for instance all those mannerisms and rhetorical postures that Robert Pinsky in *The Situation of Poetry* called 'daffy' or 'dopey' – engagingly unpretentious words, to which however I find that I can't attach any certain meaning. Elsewhere in his remarkable book Pinsky points to the same quality when he speaks of 'the playful, or jackanapes strain' so prominent in contemporary verse, distinguishing it (because of its 'cool') from the 'surrealist' strain with which we have too long, too laxly, confounded it. Pinsky's example is a 'poem about hurling 78-rpm records at Holstein cows'; and no one who has attended even a little to current verse-magazines and anthologies can fail to recognize the variously arch or cute writing that he has in mind. It is writing in which the overt subject, if there is one (and often there isn't), is only the pretext for the display of what it is hoped will seem an intriguing or amusing sensibility, the poet's. This I take to be at the opposite pole from Cassity's poems about South Africa; poems about which, taken together, one might argue whether they present a plausible or implausible account of that very special society.

Pinsky stands in much the same relation to Winters as Cassity does, though he sat in Winters's classroom twelve years or more after Cassity had sat there. His emblematic and artistically compacted account of what Winters said in that classroom is in a section of his 'Essay on Psychiatrists', from his first collection, *Sadness and Happiness* (1975):

> ... But it is all bosh, the false
> Link between genius and sickness,
>
> Except perhaps as they were linked
> By the Old Man, addressing his class
> On the first day: 'I *know why you are here*.
>
> *You are here to laugh. You have heard of a crazy*
> *Old man who believes that Robert Bridges*
> *Was a good poet; who believes that Fulke*
>
> *Greville was a great poet, greater than Philip*
> *Sidney; who believes that Shakespeare's Sonnets*
> *Are not all that they are cracked up to be ... Well,*
>
> *I will tell you something: I will tell you*
> *What this course is about. Sometime in the middle*
> *Of the Eighteenth Century, along with the rise*
>
> *Of capitalism and scientific method, the logical*
> *Foundations of Western thought decayed and fell apart.*
> *When they fell apart, poets were left*
>
> *With emotions and experiences, and with no way*
> *To examine them. At this time, poets and men*
> *Of genius began to go mad. Gray went mad, Collins*
>
> *Went mad. Kit Smart was mad, William Blake surely*
> *Was a madman, Coleridge was a drug addict, with severe*
> *Depression, My friend Hart Crane died mad. My friend*

> *Ezra Pound is mad. But you will not go mad; you will grow up*
> *To become happy, sentimental old college professors.*
> *Because they were men of genius, and you*
>
> *Are not; and the ideas which were vital*
> *To them are mere amusement to you. I will not*
> *Go mad, because I have understood those ideas …'*

Elsewhere in 'Essay on Psychiatrists' we have a long quotation from the
Imaginary Conversation between Philip Sidney and Fulke Greville, as
imagined and composed by Walter Savage Landor, that figure secure in
Winters's constricted pantheon until ejected in the last desperate years
which produced *Forms of Discovery* and the posthumous anthology (with
Kenneth Fields), *Quest for Reality*: Landor, who was the admired subject
of Pinsky's first and little noticed book, *Landor's Poetry* (1968). It is necessary to insist on this, because otherwise Pinsky's derivation from Winters,
and his continuing allegiance to him, will go unnoticed. *The Situation of
Poetry* is, for instance, as thoroughly a work of Wintersian criticism as is
the earlier and more vulnerable *Landor's Poetry*, though in the later book
the Wintersian allegiance is for thoroughly honourable reasons professed
only obliquely, and in his pages on Wordsworth and Keats Pinsky is at
pains tacitly to distance himself from the aberrant judgements of Winters
in his last tormented years. But the distinction between those to whom
ideas are 'vital' and those to whom they are 'mere amusement' is no more
lost sight of in *The Situation of Poetry*, despite its suavely accommodating
tone, than it was in *Landor's Poetry*. Those to whom ideas are 'mere amusement' are those who practise 'camp', in whom Pinsky detects, from a
seemingly urbane and impartial stance, 'the playful or jackanapes strain'.

It is the same with Pinsky's verse. For those who care to take the
trouble, there are in the magazines of the late 1960s or early 1970s poems
by Pinsky which bear the Winters stamp as indelibly as poems by Edgar
Bowers or Scott Momaday. But through those years Pinsky, like some of
his contemporaries (James McMichael for one), was concerned to ingest
the Wintersian principles at a level where what ultimately emerged would
have none of the readily recognizable Wintersian mannerisms. The poems
that in the event emerged – in *Sadness and Happiness,* and more lately in
An Explanation of America (1979) – are particularly hard to associate with
the Wintersian bequest because, apparently in defiance of that crucial
rhyme of 'verse' with 'terse', they make great play with the illusion of
garrulity, very much as Wordsworth did in some of *Lyrical Ballads.* The
garrulity is an illusion; as (of all unlikely people, and how very much to
his credit!) Hugh Kenner perceived when *Sadness and Happiness* came out.
What we may be forgiven for registering at first as garrulity is in fact (to
invoke a term that Pinsky has been at some pains to re-instate respectably)
discursiveness. Discourse (*dis-currere*) ; a running over – not the running

over of moods available to a refined sensibility, but a running over of topics naturally and rationally suggested by a subject that is a *true* subject; for instance, in *An Explanation of America*, America. The poem can be argued with. For instance, is America, whether as land-mass, as historical entity, or as an aggregate of individuals calling themselves 'Americans', quite so *frightening* as Pinsky clearly perceives it to be, when he conceives of explaining it (the doggedness of 'explaining' and 'explanation' is at the heart of his enterprise) to his young daughter? The question is a real question, and should be debated. The poem truly is what it declares itself to be: an explanation. And of an explanation one may and should ask that it explains all that is to be explained. If it seems to fail, then it is open to objections on those grounds; but those objections will not be raised so long as this poem is taken to be (like all poems, so our sophisticates tell us) not an explanation of the historical and physical entity, America, but only of the sensibility of its author.

The same goes for John Ashbery's 'Pyrography' in his collection, *Houseboat Days*. This is (so James A. Powell persuades me) 'a traditional Independence Day oration – commissioned, no less' (by the Department of the Interior). Ashbery's poem, which in its movement uncannily resembles those passages which I most admire of Pinsky's *Explanation of America*, most feelingfully commits itself to certain propositions about Americans' sense of history or lack of that sense, about Americans' responsibility or irresponsibility towards their recorded past. Those propositions could be, and ought to be, argued with; they are true or they are false, partisan or else comprehensive – and unless they are questioned in those terms, poetry is being taken less than seriously, as a merely optional and tolerated murmuration in the margin of our corporate life. But of course, for those readers who read 'Pyrography' as on the contrary 'a journey poem in the tradition of Rimbaud's "Bateau Ivre"', there is abundant excuse; for all the poems that John Ashbery had published earlier had been poems that could *not* be argued with, explorations not of a subject but of a sensibility – in short, an exquisitely refined and inventive species of 'camp'. 'Pyrography' is for the moment in Ashbery's *oeuvre* the exception that proves the rule; it is permissible to hope that it is only the first of other poems he will write, that will have, as 'Pyrography' has, a subject distinct from its author and describable in terms of social and cultural history. If it helps him to be given commissions by Government Agencies, may such commissions come upon him thick and fast!

Lecture, Folger Shakespeare Library, Washington (November 1979).

23 Louis Zukofsky

All. The Collected Shorter Poems, 1923–1958 (New York: Norton, 1965)

For those who need to know that Picasso could draw a likeness if he chose, Exhibit A is Zukofsky after Sir Charles Sedley:

> Not, Celia, that I look for rest
>   In what I do or am;
> In its own time this song addressed
>   To you is not for them:
>
> The hurrying world, our hastes have
>   No part in you like me;
> Faces stop showing what they crave
>   In my attempt to see.
>
> 'All that in woman is adored'
>   Grows my phrase, and your mind
> Sings some hundreds of years to afford
>   My cadence in kind.
>
> And if your ears hear me I store
>   It in our book *Anew*
> Where we last who make Sedley – more
>   Than he was perhaps – true.

Would he had writ thus always? Hardly. The high gloss on this elegant pastiche obscures rather than clarifies – certainly on a first reading, and even on a second: the suavity of the phrasing conceals its compactness, although it is the compactness that makes the poem both difficult and rewarding. 'Like me', for instance, means both 'such as I have' and 'such as they (our hastes) have in me'. Again, the colon after the first quatrain explains 'them' as being 'this hurrying world' and 'our hastes'; and yet when it turns out that these are the joint subject of another sentence, we make a rapid retrospective adjustment, and read 'them' as the speaker's doings and beings ('what I do or am'). And this is not to mention the allusive sense of the faces that stop showing what they crave. This is a language to which the norms of prose syntax are esssential (hence the very sedulous punctuation), though it breaks the norms even as it respects them.

Zukofsky respects and uses grammar because many of his poems, early and late, are tight argumentative affairs. And this means that, although he belongs in the Poundian tradition with which he aligns himself, he is quite often within hailing distance of a quite distinct tradition which for a long time was more influential among us – the wit writing of Allen Tate, say, or William Empson. As Empson writes about cleaning his teeth into a lake while camping out, so Zukofsky addresses his wash-stand and, through elliptical allusions to designs half-glimpsed in accidental scratchings on its marble tiles, he comes to the noble humaneness of Empson at his best:

> so my wash-stand
> in one particular breaking of the
>   tile at which I have
> looked and looked
>
>   has opposed to my head
> the inscription of a head
>   whose coinage is the
> coinage of the poor
>
>   observant in waiting
> in their getting up mornings
>   and in their waiting
> going to bed
>
>   carefully attentive
> to what they have
>   and to what they do not
>   have.

The Empsonian or 'new' criticism ought to have appreciated the many poems by Zukofsky which are dense with compressed conceits in the seventeenth-century manner, or (as with a piece about barberries in snow) in the ultimately different manner of Hopkins. But in fact that criticism ignored Zukofsky and among his peers it was Pound and Williams who appreciated and helped.

The ties which bind him to Pound are thus in the first place personal and grateful. But he is indebted to Pound also for concepts and preoccupations, as appears from the notes which in one or two cases he appends to poems. And not only concepts but perceptions also come to him sometimes from the same source, as in a poem about a privet leaf in winter, which ends:

> it happens wind colors like glass shelter,
>   as the light's air from a vault
>   which has a knob of sun.

Surely the most Poundian lines not written by Pound!

But above all what aligns Zukofsky with Pound and Williams, what removes him from the world of wit-writing, is his concern first and last with the musical measure of verse. The poem about the wash-stand is in places obscure. But it is less obscure than the poem after Sedley which at first seems so straightforward. And it is less obscure because, being so much further from counting off syllables to the verse-line, it can use line-endings, as apparent on the printed page and to the listening ear, to compel meaningful inflections:

> carefully attentive
> To what they have
> and to what they do not
> have ...

This is rudimentary. Zukofsky's more elaborated music offers itself most frankly in the opulent orchestration of a poem to Tibor Serly midway in a first section headed '55 poems 1923-35'. (This poem is still full of witty conceits, and excellent ones.) It is at its most elusive in the section 'Anew 1935-44,' where it most often eludes me – and for reasons which are made clear:

> The lines of this new song are nothing
> But a tune making the nothing full
> Stonelike becomes more hard than silent
> The tune's image holding the line.

In the longest poem in the collection, '4 Other Countries' from 'Barely and widely 1956-58', the music, in its double aspect of submerged half-rhyme and of spaced intervals at the ends of short lines, makes for astonishingly compact expression, and this vindicates more than one would have thought possible that inherently unsatisfactory form, the poem as travelogue.

The Nation, November 1965. Reprinted in *The Poet in the Imaginary Museum*.

24 Lapidary Lucidity

Collected Poems of Carl Rakosi (National Poetry Foundation, 1987)

On a tape I have listened to from the Naropa Institute, Carl Rakosi reading a couple of years ago sounds like George Burns – as imperturbable, with the same insolent knack of timing. It is an extraordinarily assured performance. And on the page as well as in the auditorium, Rakosi, last survivor of the Objectivists, will strike many people as the most engaging of them.

No one can be a purist about Objectivism. Louis Zukofsky dreamed up the label in 1931 when, thanks to Pound, he was given a free hand for a special issue of *Poetry*. When this was followed by *An Objectivists' Anthology* (1932), Rakosi appeared again, along with Charles Reznikoff, George Oppen, Zukofsky himself, but also Pound, Eliot, Rexroth, Williams, Bunting, and McAlmon. However, since 1969 when L.S. Dembo devoted a special issue of *Contemporary Literature* to 'the objectivists', the name has customarily been attached only to Zukofsky, Oppen, Reznikoff and Rakosi. And this is a pity, in several ways. Zukofsky always maintained that for him Objectivism was merely a pragmatic expedient, and this is borne out not only by the woolliness of what he threw together as the group's manifesto, but by his own writing practices both earlier and later; in his later years he conspicuously distanced himself from the rest, and alienated several of them. On the other hand the Englishman Bunting, so Oppen thought no less than Rakosi, was truly of their company; and if so, this is important because it shows that Objectivism was not an exclusively American phenomenon. W.C. Williams, launched on a publishing career before the rest, in the long run and in the public eye pre-empted and somewhat travestied their procedures, so as to monopolize the fame that others like Rakosi should have had a share of. Some would say there was a second generation of objectivists; Lorine Niedecker, a pupil of Zukofsky and Bunting, seems to achieve her deserved stature only in that perspective.

'Objectivist' had nothing to do with 'being objective about' whatever the poetry dealt with. That was a notion too philosophically and psychologically naïve to satisfy men of strenuous intelligence and rather wide learning. On the contrary, it declared an intention, in Rakosi's words, 'to make of each poem an object, meaning by this the opposite of vagueness, loose bowels and streaming, sometimes screaming, consciousness'. This, it may be thought, was always implicit in Imagism before Amy Lowell took it over. But for the Objectivists the implication was not enough; Imagism had stopped halfway towards the more austere and fastidious poetry it had envisaged, which they thereafter aimed at. The best Chinese poetry, for instance, was of a purity beyond even Pound's *Cathay*.

> Of all the old times
>   I'll take Chinese poetry.
> A man could loll under a hemlock tree then
>   and muse
> and nature be
>   as wood to carpenters ...
> a grouse ambling by,
>   a sparrow hopping,
> nothing was of greater consequence ...
>   such sweetness flowing
> as through a membrane through his limbs
>   the universe turned
> into a poet's enclave
>   the great society
> where simplicity is character
>   and character
> the common tongue, the representative
>   of man.
> In those corrupt, bitter times
>   the most obscure clerk
> could attain clarity
>   from these poems
> and his nature
>   and change into
> a superior man
>   of exquisite modesty
> by simply looking
>   at a heron crossing a stream.

Here, in Rakosi's 'The China Policy', 'superior' and 'exquisite' come out of, and take meaning from, 'where simplicity is character' – an austerely moral or moralistic understanding of poetry, such as is only implicit in *Cathay* (though, to be sure, Pound would make it explicit later, in some Confucian Cantos).

It is the same with the occidental tradition of verse-epigram, as Pound had tried to resuscitate it in *Lustra*. Here is Rakosi's version.

Descended
                    from a rumor
of classical
                    irony
filtered
          through Pound
which sits
          so high above wisdom
it appears
          literary
and invulnerable,
                    engraved there
by the style
          and reduces all
to an adversary
                    and runs a spit
through human
                    being
before it can cry
                    'Ouch!'
without revealing
                    who
the ironist
          himself is
or what he feels
                    and in the end
becomes
          its own captive.

(Rakosi's versification is unambitious, in this very unlike Zukofsy's or Bunting's; each verse-line is broken in two merely to retard the reader's apprehension of a sentence that in prose would be congestedly rapid.) This protest at Pound is more sharply focused than any of Williams's protests, chiefly because Rakosi is himself naturally an ironist and epigrammatist, as we can see from his aphoristic prose as well as many poems. It is something in himself that he is quarreling with – 'my gargoyle', he will exclaim before his poem is through.

What Rakosi recognizes and responds to in verse-epigrams is the lapidary, the stony or as-if-stony. Thus, 'How To Be With A Rock':

The explicit ends here.
                    Outer is inner.
It is all manifest.
                    Its character is durity.
There lies its charisma.

By nature it is Pangaea.
                              It has its own face
and its own tomb,
                    the way it stands,
unmoved by destiny,
                      a model for the mind.
We can only be spectators.
                         All is day within.
'Go to the village,'
                  I tell my wife,
'and bring back a chicken,
                          an onion, a goose
and an apple
            and we'll lie here
and repopulate this Siberia.'

It is in Genesis.
A strange god,
             all torso
and without invention or audacity.

It can be accused of both plutonism
and the obvious.
              The closest human thing to it
is the novocained tooth,
                        its Medusa hair now fossilized.

It can be bequeathed to one's heirs
with the assurance that it will not depreciate
or be found irrelevant.

What is winning here is how the very lines that describe the rock as 'without invention or audacity' are themselves both inventive and audacious, wittily declaring it 'A strange god,/all torso'. And this is what one means by calling Rakosi 'engaging'; where in Oppen the moralism comes through as forbidding and exigent, in Rakosi it imposes itself on a temperament that is naturally exuberant and sportive.

Moreover, the temperament has put up a spirited resistance: the poet who began in the 1920s as an *aficionado* of the Wallace Stevens of *Harmonium,* master of Bizarrerie and verbal gymnastics, will late in life still declare, and occasionally prove in boisterous performance, that 'all matter is composed of three elements/and the fourth is comedy'. For comedy with an edge to it, consider 'A Reminder of William Carlos Williams':

How quickly the dandelions
come up

> after the rain.
>
> I picked
>
>   them all
>
> only yesterday.

And for comedy that is many-edged (one of its edges, sadness) see '1924', about Ernest Hemingway:

> They learned first how to handle a rifle
> and went into the woods
> for squirrel and pheasant
> and hooked bait
> with the care of a paleontologist.
>
> At night they sat with whisky
> and said to a companion,
>   'Let's get drunk,'
> And the answer came back,
>   'All right.'
>
> When they went to war and were afraid
> and got shot up
> and found a girl and had a family
>
> or shot lion and climbed Kilimanjaro
> and pursued the dark Iberian
>   gored
> who sighted with his sword
> the place of death
>   behind the bull's neck
> and went in over the horns,
> holding back nothing,
> all they had to say was,
>   'It's good
> when the fall rains come,'
> and the answer was,
>   'Swell.'
>
> Will there be no more larks
>   or Cezanne apples?
> Adieu then.

This is from the sequence 'Americana'; hence, in part, the sadness. But only in part, for who is being mocked in the deliberately stilted 'dark Iberian' and 'Adieu then'? This comedy is discomfiting.

All the same, the steady endeavour seems to have been to purge the writing of this comedy, or to admit it only on rather stringent terms. It is hard to be sure of this, for Rakosi explicitly warns that the collection isn't presented in chronological order of composition or publication, and it's only on a hunch backed by a little evidence that I guess the order is largely back to front, the later poems coming first. (It will all be cleared up, no doubt, when Michael Heller brings out from the National Poetry Foundation his *Carl Rakosi: Man and Poet*.) At any rate, the poems that meet us first are those in which the comic and epigrammatic notes seem to be most subdued, in favour of a greater vulnerability on the part of the speaking voice. Rakosi calls these late poems 'Meditations'. And readers who take their bearings from, say, Coleridge or Keats may take heart from that: these poems indeed confront their big subjects directly, with fewer obliquities than in Rakosi's work generally. However, diction and versification alike still obstruct the crescent fluidity from line to line that we associate with the Romantic lyrical meditation. And when Rakosi alludes to English writing, it is still to pre-Romantic figures like Izaak Walton and Christopher Smart and the authors of the Border Ballads.

With Rakosi no more than with Walter Savage Landor does the reaching after the lapidary preclude the immediately personal. And a section of twenty-seven poems called 'L'Chayim,' all about his relations with his near kin, will be found appealing to those for whom playful wit is not specially pleasant:

> In the biblical vapors
> kindness, sweetest
> of the small notes
>
> in the world's ache,
> most modest and gentle
> of the elements,
>
> entered man before history
> and became his daily
> connection, let no man
>
> tell you otherwise ...

Very reassuring. But these lines are from 'The Old Poet's Tale' which, in five longish sections plus a coda, narrates the protracted death of George Oppen from Alzheimer's disease. This scrupulously dry and factual account of mortal dissolution, from the imagined standpoint of the person who suffers it, is to be recommended only to those with strong nerves and those with a persistent love for the late George Oppen. It is remorseless and pitiful; it is hard to think of another poem like it. If we look in our poets above all for humane feeling, this is the harrowing experience we are likely to be left with.

There is of course wastage, detritus: some dandified pirouettes *à la*

Stevens, some inconsequential anecdotes *à la* Williams. And Rakosi's limitations should be clear – above all, his light-heartedness about versification. Anglo-American syllables can dispose themselves rhythmically in more compacted and demanding and insistent patterns than Rakosi seems to have recognized. But his range and humanity persuade all over again that we can't much longer talk of a 'Pound–Williams tradition' as a sort of accredited counter-culture in this century's American poetry. European though he is by origin and in his sympathies, Rakosi belongs not in the margin but near the centre of what should be seen internationally as distinctively and invaluably American in twentieth-century culture.

25 Braveries Eschewed

George Oppen, *Seascape: Needle's Eye* (Sumac Press, 1972)

For us to come to terms with Oppen, the time has long gone by – if it ever existed – when it was useful to start plotting his place in a scheme of alternative or successive poetic 'schools' or 'traditions'. Imagism, objectivism, objectism, constructivism: if there was ever any point in shoving these counters about, that time is long gone by. In his background and his past there is a good deal of Marxism, and so his attempts to understand the moment in which he writes are a historian's attempts, not, as with most American poets, psychological and/or mythopoeic. It is ironical therefore that when Charles Olson responded to Oppen's review of him he should have protested, 'I wanted to open Mr Oppen to history'; being open to history is one thing, being open to the recorded and unrecorded past is something else. And one may stay closed to that past not out of ignorance or limited imagination but as an act of willed choice. This is an act that Oppen seems to make in a recent poem, called 'The Taste':

> Old ships are preserved
> For their queer silence of obedient seas
> Their cutwaters floating in the still water
> With their cozy black iron work
> And Swedish seamen dead   the cabins
> Hold the spaces of their deaths
> And the hammered nails of necessity
> Carried thru the oceans
> Where the moon rises grandly
> In the grandeur of cause
> We have a taste for bedrock
> Beneath this spectacle
> To gawk at
> Something is wrong with the antiques, a black fluid
> Has covered them, a black splintering
> Under the eyes of young wives
> People talk wildly, we are beginning to talk wildly, the wind
> At every summit

Our overcoats trip us
Running for the bus
Our arms stretched out
In a wind from what were sand dunes

Those who know San Francisco know the ships that Oppen means, and
will share his sense that in the Californian scene such attempts at historical *pietas* have an air of irrelevant conoisseurship. In fact the poem comes
in a sequence of ten with the deceptively modest title 'Some San Francisco
Poems'. But then Oppen is a San Franciscan, once again by will and
choice. He moves about that city and its hinterland seeing it through eyes
that have been conditioned elsewhere. It is an Atlantic eye that looks over
the edge of this continent at the Pacific. The beautiful and precarious shal-
lowness of coastal California, treacherously gummed on to the continent
across the San Andreas fault, is caught by him as by no native or thoroughly assimilated Californian. He is as much a foreigner there as we
might be, and therefore as incredulous, as dubious, above all as apprehen-
sive. It is possible to think that poetry should be responsible for giving to
Californian youth that ballast which we may feel that it so perilously lacks
– 'You were *not* born yesterday!' That was the response of a thoroughly
assimilated Californian, Yvor Winters, in poems like 'California Oaks'.
Oppen does not agree. For him on the contrary sanity is in holding fast to

> 'the picturesque
>   common lot'   the unwarranted light
>
>   Where everyone has been
>   ('Anniversary Poem')

And so 'the courageous and precarious children' (as he calls them) are to
be, have to be, *trusted*, with whatever misgivings. The past will not help
them; and perhaps we only thought that it helped us.

That goes also for the past of Art, including the art of poetry:

> O withering seas
> Of the doorstep and local winds unveil
>
> The face of art
>
> *Carpenter, plunge and drip in the sea*   Art's face
> We know that face
>
> More blinding than the sea   a haunted house   a limited
>
> Consensus unwinding
>
> Its powers
> Toward the thread's end

In the record of great blows   shocks
Ravishment   devastation   the wood splintered

The keyboard gone in the rank grass swept her hand
Over the strings and the thing rang out

Over the rocks and the ocean
Not my poem   Mr Steinway's

Poem   Not mine   A 'marvelous' object
Is not the marvel of things

         twisting the new
Mouth   forcing the new
Tongue   But it rang

We have heard something like this before, from William Carlos Williams. The resemblance is real, and Oppen no doubt would acknowledge it. But the differences are striking too. Williams after all was a mythopoeic poet (*Paterson*) and a historian only so far as he could turn history into myth. He was even a systematizer, and in his last years a master or a prophet looking for (and thinking he found) disciples. Oppen has no such hopes or intentions; his tone is ruminative, intimate, domestic. There is no writer to whom a tag like 'American expansiveness' is more inappropriate. And indeed this goes beyond 'tone'; in a very unAmerican way he seems to offer us, as Hardy did, only 'disconnected observations'. The claims that he makes on us, for himself and his art, are disarmingly modest.

All the same, and in fact even less avoidably than with Williams, the challenge is thrown down to us: the past is irrelevant, a dangerous distraction. Well, is it? For instance, the past of our art ... Much as we may agree that 'a "marvelous" object / Is not the marvel of things', and that the commonplace is fruitfully mysterious in ways that only this sort of poetry can make us see, still, are we Marxist enough, historically determinist enough, to agree that the time is past for so many of the traditional splendours and clarities as this poetry wants us to dispense with? Outside of the San Francisco sequence there is a poem called (and the title is important) 'West':

Elephant, say, scraping its dry sides
In a narrow place as he passes says yes

This is true

So one knows?   and the ferns unfurling   leaves

In the wind

... sea   from which ...

'We address the future?'

Unsure of the times
Unsure I can answer
To myself   We have been ignited
Blazing

In wrath we await

In rare poetic
Of veracity that huge art whose geometric
Light seems not its own in that most dense world West
          and East
Have denied have hated have wandered in   *precariousness*

(I break off at mid-point.) 'Splendours' – is that the word for what an old-fashioned reader would feel the lack of in these verses? Hardly; that elephant, so abruptly huge and patient before us, is himself a splendour. 'Clarities', then? Well, yes; the suppression of so much punctuation certainly makes for obscurity (though the most obscure poem is one called 'The Occurrences', which has no punctuation-stops at all). But the right word, to point for instance to the melodiousness which it seems plain we must not look for in this writing, is surely still to seek. I suggest: '*braveries*'. This writing denies itself certain traditional braveries (rhyme, assonance, determinable auditory rhythm) precisely because they would testify in the poet to a bravery (in the other sense) about his vocation and the art that he practises, a bravery that we cannot afford once we have acknowledged that our condition, though obscured from us by Western and Eastern cultures alike, is above all 'precarious'.

Can we agree? I suggest we cannot. For what we are faced with is a sort of illusionism after all. The poem *has* its own splendour, its own clarities, certainly its own audacities. (Consider only the imperious rapidity of the transitions that it manages.) It has all the braveries; even the melody that it seems to lack may have been lost only in the passage from a Jewish-American mouth to my British ear. The object, willy-nilly, *is* 'marvelous'. It has to be; since it is an articulation in and of the marvel that is human language. That lack-lustre phrase is certainly a shabby rabbit out of any conjuror's hat. But the shabbiness is appropriate as a response to a shabby argument. If we truly want or need to cut loose from our inherited past then we should discard not just poetic figurations of language but any figurations whatever, including those which make it possible to communicate at all except by grunts and yelps. Rhetoric is inseparable from language, even language at its most demotically 'spoken'. And thus, let language be never so fractured and disjointed in order that the saving commonplaceness of common things shine through it, all that is happening is that a new rhetoric is being preferred before an old one. To put it another way, no

Mr Steinway manufactured the instrument, language, on which Oppen performs. And, like it or not, a performance is what each of his poems is – as certainly as a sonnet by Philip Sidney.

This is not in the first place an argument with Oppen or with Oppen's poems. It is a quarrel with those of his admirers – I have met some among 'the courageous and precarious children' – who would explain their admiration by appeal to the untenable positions that Williams's obtuseness trapped him into (from which he later tried to extricate himself by such manifest absurdities as his 'variable foot'). Granted that Oppen does not discard rhetoric for non-rhetoric (which last is an impossibility), but rejects an old rhetoric for a newer one, we have to admire what the new rhetoric permits him to do. In the first place it opens up for him, as it sometimes did for Williams, an extraordinary directness and gentleness in intimacy, as at the end of 'Anniversary Poem':

> To find now depth, not time, since we cannot, but depth
>
> To come out safe,   to end well
>
> We have begun to say good bye
> To each other
> And cannot say it.

Indeed, in the world that Oppen charts about him as he thinks of approaching his end, so hedged about as it is with apprehension and misgivings, this particular tone embodies so much of what he can still feel grateful for and sanguine about, that the newer rhetoric justifies itself on this count alone. And it is quite true that the older more traditional rhetoric cannot encompass this tone of voice. It speaks again on the last page of this little but weighty collection, in a poem called 'Exodus':

> Miracle of the children   the brilliant
> Children   the word
> Liquid as woodlands   Children?
>
> When she was a child I read Exodus
> To my daughter   'The children of Israel ...'
>
> Pillar of fire
> Pillar of cloud
>
> We stared at the end
> Into each other's eyes   Where
> She said hushed
>
> Were the adults   We dreamed to each other
> Miracle of the children
> The brilliant children   Miracle

Of their brilliance   Miracle
of

I would call that (though the word may give offence) elegant as well as touching. And I would say indeed that the elegance and the touchingness depend upon each other.

Shenandoah XXIV: 3 (Spring 1973). Reprinted in *The Poet in the Imaginary Museum*.

26 Lyric Minimum and Epic Scope: Lorine Niedecker

Lorine Niedecker's 'Lake Superior', as it appeared in her sumptuously printed *North Central* (Fulcrum Press, 1968), consists of twelve short or very short passages of verse. Accordingly it can be quoted in full:

> In every part of every living thing
> is stuff that once was rock
>
> In blood the minerals
> of the rock
> ★ ★ ★

> Iron the common element of earth
> in rocks and freighters
>
> Sault Sainte Marie – big boats
> coal-black and iron-ore-red
> topped with what white castlework
>
> The waters working together
>   internationally
> Gulls playing both sides
> ★ ★ ★

> Radisson:
> 'a laborinth of pleasure'
> this world of the Lake
>
> Long hair, long gun
>
> Fingernails pulled out
> by Mohawks
> ★ ★ ★

(The long canoes)

'Birch Bark
and white Seder
for the ribs'
★ ★ ★

Through all this granite land
the sign of the cross
★ ★ ★

Beauty: impurities in the rock
And at the blue ice superior spot
priest-robed Marquette grazed
azoic rock, hornblende granite
basalt the common dark
in all the Earth

And his bones of such is coral
raised up out of his grave
were sunned and birch bark-floated
to the straits
★ ★ ★

                              Joliet
Entered the Mississippi
Found there the paddlebill catfish
come down from The Age of Fishes

At Hudson Bay he conversed in latin
with an Englishman

To Labrador and back to vanish
His funeral gratis – he's played
Quebec's Cathedral organ
so many winters
★ ★ ★

Ruby of corundum
lapis lazuli
from changing limestone
glow-apricot red-brown
carnelian sard

Greek named
Exodus-antique
kicked up in America's
North west
you have been in my mind
between my toes
agate
★ ★ ★

Wild Pigeon

Did not man
   maimed by no
      stone-fall

mash the cobalt
   and carnelian
      of that bird
★ ★ ★

Schoolcraft left the Soo – canoes
US pennants, masts, sails
chanting canoemen, barge
soldiers – for Minnesota

Their South Shore journey
         as if Life's –
The Chocolate River
          The Laughing Fish
and The River of the Dead

Passed peaks of volcanic thrust
Hornblende in massed granite
Wave-cut Cambrian rock
painted by soluble mineral oxides
wave-washed and the rains
did their work and a green
running as from copper

Sea-roaring caverns –
Chippewas threw deermeat
to the savage maws
'voyageurs crossed themselves
tossed a twist of tobacco in'

Inland then
beside the great granite
gneiss and the schists

to the redolent pondy lakes'
lilies, flag and Indian reed
'through which we successfully
passed'
★ ★ ★

The smooth black stone
I picked up in true source park
the leaf beside it
once was stone

Why should we hurry
home
★ ★ ★

I'm sorry to have missed
Sand Lake
My dear one tells me
we did not
We watched a gopher there
★ ★ ★

Faced with such daunting or taunting brevities, our first impulse is to
annotate. Sometimes the impulse should be resisted, and certainly it
shouldn't be indulged at length. But in this case some annotation cannot
be avoided. And so we may start with Sault Sainte Marie, named in the
second section, of which we may learn from Funk and Wagnalls'
Encyclopaedia that it is

county seat and port of Chippewa County, Mich., on the St Mary's
River, opposite the Canadian town of the same name, with which it
is connected by a railroad bridge 1–1/2m. long.
The Chippewa Indians had their favourite fishing grounds at this site
and the first settlement of Michigan was made here. Following visits by
several French explorers, Father Marquette established a mission
(1668). At a great council of Indians held here in 1671, the governor
general of New France claimed for France all country south to the Gulf
of Mexico and west to the Pacific. The British held the area,
1762–1820, when it came into the possession of the United States.
Incorporated as a city in 1887.

What must first strike us is how impassively or indifferently Niedecker passes over those dimensions of her subject that to a writer of another temper might have seemed most 'poetic' – the chequered history through three centuries, the poignant or bizarre juxtaposition, around those dates of 1668 and 1671, between the Versailles of Louis XIV and the wilderness outpost in the middle of untracked North America. Nor is it only the remote past of the Sault (or 'Soo') that is resonant: for the Encyclopaedia entry goes on to record the prodigious feats of engineering which, in the nineteenth century, lifted ships from the eastern Great Lakes up to the level of Lake Superior through two ship canals and five massive locks. As it happens we have evidence of what a poet's imagination of a different temper could make of this material, in Janet Lewis's shamefully neglected masterpiece, *The Invasion. A Narrative of Events Concerning the Johnston Family of St Mary's* (originally University of Denver Press, 1932). An extraordinary intent paragraph on pages 343–4 of Janet Lewis's book, about a ship's passage through the Weitzel lock (completed 1881, 515 feet long), makes a very striking and instructive contrast to Niedecker's blank, almost perfunctory 'big boats/coal-black and iron-ore-red/topped with what white castlework'.

A more famous masterpiece of American historiography, Francis Parkman's multi-volume *France and England in North America*, identifies Pierre Esprit Radisson from St Malo, who in *La Salle and the Discovery of the Great West* (1869) is credited with having discovered, as early as 1658-9, the confluence of the Mississippi and the Missouri. In *The Old Regime in Canada* (1893), Parkman tells how Radisson later, 'having passed into the service of England … wrote in a language which, for want of a fitter name, may be called English'. Hence, we may suppose, 'a laborinth of pleasure' – which is hauntingly unEnglish in more than the mispelling. Radisson's *Second Voyage made in the Upper Country of the Iroquois* was published by the Prince Society in 1885; along with other narratives by Radisson it appears, modernized by Loren Kallsen, in *The Explorations of Pierre Esprit Radisson* (Minneapolis, 1961). He was mutilated by the Mohawks on his first expedition (1652–3); the Lake Superior expedition was his fourth, nowadays dated 1662-3. Thus in Radisson we have a subject that seems to cry out for heroic treatment; and when we look at Niedecker's verses, we have to note how she has either missed the possibility or else firmly set her face against it.

The case is even clearer in the sixth section, with Jacques Marquette (1637–75), French missionary explorer ('Through all this granite land / the sign of the cross'), whose name is commemorated in a Michigan county and port on the south shore of Lake Superior, and also in place names much farther south, near Niedecker's life-long home at Fort Atkinson on Lake Koshkonong in south-east Wisconsin. Marquette's heroic status is as it were official; a marble effigy of him, a gift of the people of Wisconsin, stands in the rotunda of the Capitol in Washington. But as with Radisson so more conspicuously with Marquette, Lorine Niedecker shows no interest in heroic exploits; Marquette in her verses is subdued to, and identified with, what he saw or what he moved among. For the last four lines we can turn to Parkman, in *La Salle and the Discovery of the Great West*:

> In the winter of 1676, a party of Kiskakon Ottawas were hunting on Lake Michigan: and when, in the following spring, they prepared to return home, they bethought them, in accordance with an Indian custom, of taking with them the bones of Marquette, who had been their instructor at the mission of Saint Esprit. They repaired to the spot, found the grave, opened it, washed and dried the bones and placed them carefully in a box of birch-bark. Then, in a procession of thirty canoes, they bore it, singing their funeral songs, to St Ignace of Michilimackinac. As they approached, priests, Indians, and traders all thronged to the shore. The relics of Marquette were received with solemn ceremony, and buried beneath the floor of the little chapel of the mission ...

And in 1877, on the supposed site of the Jesuit chapel at Point St Ignace, there were in fact found buried some human bones with fragments of birch-bark. Thus a beam of pathos is allowed to play on Marquette, as it did on mutilated Radisson. But Niedecker is not centrally interested in the pathetic any more than the heroic; the *sunning* of Marquette's bones, and their being levelled with birch-bark, comes at us as an appropriate consummation of a life – Marquette in death is levelled with those natural presences (horn-blende and basalt as well as birch-trees) which loomed so indifferently above and around him in life. For a word like 'sunned' to bear such a weight of implication, Niedecker's language in this section has to rise above the blank and blunt quality of the earlier passages. And so it does: 'superior' and 'grazed' are both near-puns, lifting the language so as to accommodate the Shakespearean allusion of line 7: 'Of his bones are coral made'. If up to this point Niedecker's words have been, as Hugh Kenner said searchingly of the words of William Carlos Williams, '*stunned*', at this point they come to ramifying life; and of course their live-liness comes with the greater impact because of the stunned drabness that has preceded them. Niedecker, we realize, has *paced* her sequence very carefully.

The drab language now returns, with Québeçois Louis Joliet or Jolliet (1645–1700) who, though his exploits were extraordinary and he accord-ingly gives his name to a town in Illinois, seemed to Parkman – that connoisseur of the heroic, withal so aware of heroism's shadowed and sinister side – conspicuously not epic material:

In what we know of Joliet, there is nothing that reveals any salient or distinctive trait of character, any especial breadth of view or boldness of design. He seems to have been simply a merchant, intelligent, well educated, courageous, hardy, and enterprising.

All the details of Niedecker's section 7 – the paddlebill catfish, the Latin-speaking Hudson's Bay Englishman, the playing of the cathedral organ, and the 'funeral gratis' – are to be found in *Louis Jolliet, Explorer of Rivers*, by Virginia S. Eifert (New York, 1962).

It comes as all the more of a shock that in the next two sections the disconcerting potencies simply of language are suddenly released. For it would be quite wrong to suppose that we can make nothing of this abrupt blaze of: 'Ruby … corundum … carnelian sard' unless we have or can acquire a mineralogist's knowledge about adamantine spar and granular emery. Poetry is not made out of such things, but out of the names that such things bear. The sixth line gives the clue – 'Greek names'; perhaps we have already spent too much time with the encyclopaedia, at this point if not before we must exchange it for the dictionary. It is OED that identifies the Greek word as '*agate*': '1570, a. Fr. *agathe*, ad. It. *agata*, f. L. *achates*, a. Gr. *agates*.' How does it help, after thus tracking the word through its dazzling etymology, to proceed to the definition: 'one of the semi-pellucid variegated chalcedonies'? It does not help at all unless we are mineralogists, and perhaps it does not help even then. Better to stay in excited bemusement with etymologies, which will reveal for instance that 'corundum' comes from the Tamil for 'ruby'. It is the *words* that flash, that turn their hard edges towards us and towards each other. We need not know, and Niedecker need not have known (though I dare say she did), which of the glinting grains that she kicked up between her toes could properly be identified as agate. It is enough that it be *in her mind*, that she be mindful of how there lies on the shores of Lake Koshkonong or Lake Superior a mineral that lay around also (the etymology proves it) in ancient Greece. *That* is the history she is concerned with, and lays claim to. And the record of it is in the dictionary, nowhere else. So it is from the dictionary, if we do not know it from our own usage, that we discover how the names of minerals – 'cobalt', 'carnelian' ('a flesh-coloured deep red, or reddish-white variety of chalcedony') – are also the names of colours, such colours as once glowed on the passenger pigeons whose random extermination by the white man's gun has symbolized, ever since Fenimore Cooper, the heedless exploitation by man of North America's bounties. Williams's 'No idea but in things' is shown up for the sloppy and shallow slogan that it always was. No ideas but in things *as named*, in the *names* of things; that is to say, in words. And what rapidity, what succinctness the words afford us, if only we will trust them! No bleeding hearts need be worn on sleeves, no breasts need be beaten – the point is made simply by moving one word, 'carnelian' from one snatch of verse to the next snatch, taking it away from rocks and putting it with birds.

And the point thus made, that once, does not have to be laboured. For it is not the point of Niedecker's poem, not what she is mainly driving at. It *is*, pretty well, the point of *The Invasion*, though there is no breast-beating by Janet Lewis either – through her 350 pages the indictment gathers and emerges gradually from the historical record recounted seemingly at leisure and with seeming impassiveness. The difference between the two writers appears most clearly in how they deal with Henry Rowe Schoolcraft (1793-1864), explorer and ethnologist, author of *A View of the Lead Mines of the Missouri, Travels in the Central Portion of the Mississippi Valley,* and other books culminating in his monumental *Historical and Statistical Information Respecting the History, Condition, and Prospects of the Indian Tribes of the United States* (6 volumes published by Congress, 1851–7). 'Schoolcraft left the Soo', writes Lorine Niedecker; and does not think to inform us that the departure was from Sault Sainte Marie in 1826, its purpose the signing of the treaty of Fond du Lac, by which (*The Invasion*, p. 239) 'the Ojibways of Lake Superior and the upper reaches of the Mississippi River ceded to the United States, as a token of their good-will, all mineral rights to the great lake basin.' In Janet Lewis's account Schoolcraft is the well-meaning but still inexcusable embodiment of most of what was wrong with the white Americans' treatment of the red man – from his role in engineering treaty after treaty depriving the Indians of their land and rights, through to his supplying Longfellow with the materials for the falsifications of *Song of Hiawatha* (on which, see her biting pages 323–51). If in Lorine Niedecker's treatment of Schoolcraft there is any hint at all of the rationalistic prissiness of which Janet Lewis convicts him, it is at most only a hovering and ambiguous implication. It could hardly be more, since (as we may now notice with something approaching consternation) the Indians, the indigenous and original inhabitants of the Lake Superior region, figure in Niedecker's poem nowhere at all, except as the savages who tore out poor Radisson's finger-nails. What a field-day a perfervidly anti-colonialist critic might make of that! And yet, as we have seen, Niedecker gave us due notice: the only time-spans that interest her are those of geological time, or else those (much shorter, but still to our sense vast), of etymology – the etymology that links classical Greek with current American. No wonder therefore if she asks, in her penultimate section, 'Why should we hurry/home?' And how can it matter, in the last lines, whether she did or did not visit Sand Lake? Why indeed should she hurry, and how indeed could it matter? In terms of what we usually understand as history, Niedecker's treatment, though it adverts to and uses historical documents like Joliet's, Marquette's, Radisson's, Schoolcraft's, is profoundly *un*historical – certainly as compared with Janet Lewis's. Indeed we are forced to go further and say that, since the minerals of the

Lake Superior region are in a real sense the only true 'heroes' of the poem first and last, that poem seems to imply that the mineral riches had to be excavated and thus *known* – a process impossible until the indigenous inhabitants had been expropriated in the ways that Janet Lewis indignantly chronicles.

Philip Sidney said that poetry is essentially superior to history. A European reader of Lorine Niedecker may reflect spitefully, and yet to some purpose, that for a poet of Fort Atkinson, Wisconsin, Sidney's dictum would be readily palatable since there is in Wisconsin so little history for poetry to be superior to. There is *some* history, however; rather more, and more signifcant, than we had thought – as Janet Lewis's book makes us realize. And for a poetry that does *not* rise superior to history we may recall certain long narratives, mostly by Canadian poets, in which Father Marquette and his martyred fellows, being celebrated straightforwardly as heroes of human history, are reduced to figures in a fancy-dress pageant. For that matter, Lorine Niedecker was not the first North American poet to suppose that in an epic of her country the heroes might be rocks and minerals, rather than men. Robinson Jeffers, the rhapsode of Point Sur, declared as much; but while Jeffers declared, it was Lorine Niedecker, in her astonishing isolation, who simply *did* it. What she did, for instance in 'Lake Superior', cannot help but seem to us of the Old World, and to some of the New World like Janet Lewis, forbidding and even repellent in the consistency with which it proceeds from that initial premise. But the consistency is there, impressively; and it ought to be, with whatever private qualms, saluted.

PN Review 25 (Winter 1981); *Sagetried* 1: 2 (Fall 1982).

27 Postmodernism and
Lorine Niedecker

Ten years ago, when considerations of Niedecker's poetry were few and far between, I published in *PN Review* a brief appreciation of her 'Lake Superior' under the title, 'Lyric Minimum & Epic Scope'. Quite by accident and much to my astonishment I discover that this modest piece has been made a *casus belli* between me and Joseph M. Conte, in the latter's *Unending Design: The Forms of Postmodern Poetry* (Cornell University Press). I am used to being misunderstood, and would not bother with this if it were only a squabble between me and Joseph Conte. But Conte from the first raises the ante: my essay, he says, 'so thoroughly undervalues and misinterprets the intentions of the "Lake Superior" series that it seems … to be of some use; at the very least it teaches us *how not to read* Niedecker' (my italics). So if I seem at first to engage in in-fighting with Conte, it's on the understanding that more is at stake than his or my standing as commentators.

What sticks in Conte's gullet is my having found it useful to bring to bear on Niedecker's poem such other accounts of Wisconsin and the Lake Superior region as can be dug out of Francis Parkman's *France and England in North America* and Janet Lewis's *The Invasion*, among other sources. 'It should not have to be said', Conte contends with a flourish of metaphor, 'that he grinds the delicate pebbles of Niedecker's series to dust under the weight of such multivolume nonfiction mortars'. But I have more respect for Niedecker than he has: her poem is sturdier, and its constituent 'pebbles' less 'delicate', than Conte supposes. I called into evidence alternative versions like Parkman's and Janet Lewis's precisely so as to show that Niedecker's version survives the comparisons, if only by showing that from her point of view much of what the alternative versions make salient is irrelevant. If Parkman's version, and Janet Lewis's, had not been acknowledged, then Niedecker's version could not be seen as having outdistanced or outflanked its competitors. Conte says that my 'requirement that the full historical context be present in the poem displays either an ignorance of or aversion to an Objectivist poetics'. But on the one hand the historical context is, as I present it, by no means 'full', since it was limited by what I had to hand at the time I wrote my piece; secondly I do not at all represent such contextualizing as a *requirement*, but only as an instructive exercise, and ultimately as a demonstration that the poem, returned to a historical context defined by other documents, passes that test and survives as a poem.

Considering the treatment in Niedecker's poem of Pierre Esprit Radisson, Conte quotes me as saying that in Radisson 'we have a subject that cries out for heroic treatment', and that Niedecker has 'either missed the opportunity or else set her face against it'. 'Certainly', says Conte, 'the latter is the case'. And I agree, a sympathetic reading of my article will show that I agreed in the first place. But, says Conte, '"Heroic treatment" is a call for a rhetorical contextualization that invariably lies about the particular historical facts'. Invariably? I readily admit that Niedecker refuses the heroic perspective on Radisson, and had good aesthetic and philosophical reasons for doing so. But she does not thereby, as her admirer does, rule out the entire tradition of 'the heroic' as fraudulent. Homer? Virgil? Tasso? Milton? Dryden? All these apparently are ruled out of court by Conte's judgement that 'a heroic treatment' is one in which 'the whole context is a rhetorical forgery'. Certainly that takes care of Janet Lewis's modest and obscure hero, 'John Johnston, of Craige, County Antrim, Ireland'. And more certainly it takes care of Francis Parkman's *France and England in North America*, which presents, among a wealth of scrupulously researched documentation, a series of heroic portraits: La Salle, Henri de Tonty, Montcalm, Pontiac (among others). But is this really what Joseph Conte means to say: that not only in the Ancient World and in Europe, but in North America, the hero no longer has any status or any validity? It seems that this indeed is what he intends, for he asserts that what Niedecker rejects is 'a heroic treatment in which the whole context is a rhetorical forgery'. Not expecting to be challenged, I had described Parkman's multi-volume history as a 'masterpiece of American historiography'. But rather plainly I had not counted on Joseph Conte, his associates and his pupils; for them, I am forced to recognize, not only is Parkman's work far from being a masterpiece, but the whole enterprise called 'American historiography' is fraudulent. This is where postmodernism shows its teeth: anything from the day before yesterday is to be written off as deceiving, by that very token. I wanted to suggest that Niedecker's enterprise in 'Lake Superior' is continuous with those of Parkman and Janet Lewis, and nowhere more so than where she radically revises their versions of the history of the mid-West. But the postmodernist will settle for nothing less than a non-negotiable discontinuity between today and yesterday. It is the commentators who insist on this: Lorine Niedecker as I know her through her writings, and George Oppen as I knew him in person, had no such high-handed attitude towards the records of the American past. Moreover, Niedecker had her heroes; they were mostly naturalists.

The rest of Conte's objections to me, as he finds me moving to an account of 'Lake Superior' that doesn't differ essentially from his own, take the form of imputing motives. To these the only possible rejoinder is 'Prove it!' Davie 'describes the Objectivists' "approach to the real world" under the guise of a reproach' (prove it!); 'this treatment of materials which Davie disapproves is precisely that which Objectivists extol' (prove it, not their extolling but my disapproval!); Niedecker's allusion to Shakespeare in section six of her poem 'pleases Davie no end' (prove it!). I am not so easily categorized, nor are my responses so predictable, as Joseph Conte supposes. What he objects to is not that I come to a different understanding of Niedecker's poem from his, or a different valuation of it (for I don't), but that I arrive at that understanding and valuation by a route that he cannot approve. Francis Parkman and Janet Lewis are witnesses that must not be called, even though they testify in the defendant's favour. Not only must we agree with the court's verdict, but we must do so without calling to the stand any witnesses beyond those that the court has approved in advance.

Enough of the commentators. Hear the poem:

> Sea-roaring caverns –
> Chippewas threw deermeat
> to the savage maws
> '*Voyageurs* crossed themselves
> tossed a twist of tobacco in'

But here is the commentator, bright as a button. Does not the stilted diction of 'savage maws' put this item in a paratactic arrangement out of kilter with its fellows? Apparently not. 'It is the Chippewas who recognize a natural force for what it is and return to nature something of what it has given them; the *voyageurs* who sign themselves with the cross make an appeal to the supernatural for protection and then, ironically, vitiate their gesture of faith by tossing in a twist of tobacco.' The snatch of verses will support this interpretation; it will – cryptic and unpunctuated as it is – support several others. And anyhow, weren't we given to understand that postmodern verse had devised strategies so as not to be co-opted by any socio-political programme whatever? What else explains Joseph Conte's vehement denial that 'Lake Superior' could be enlisted in the service of an ideal that could be called 'heroic'? Ah but, it seems, Christian ideology is a special case; for that it is always open season. The *voyageurs* are, not by Norine Niedecker but by Joseph Conte, damned before they ever start crossing themselves or appeasing the waters with tobacco – which is of course what nature has given them, as much as is the Chippewas' deermeat.

Poems are not written (good ones aren't) so as to be considered in classrooms. So questions of pedagogical procedure concerning them are always gratuitous. Yet Joseph Conte, like virtually everyone who writes about 'postmodern' or any other poetry, holds a college teaching post. So it's natural to wonder how his pupils must comport themselves, to earn his commendation. Not only will they earn no good marks from him for consulting other authorities than Niedecker regarding the subject-matter that she offers to deal with; it seems they will be marked down for opening so much as an encyclopaedia. He might have noticed that my article was addressed in the first place to a British audience: that's to say, to readers who might not know (why should they?) where to place the state of Wisconsin on a map of the United States. Conte's students in Buffalo may be thought not to suffer this disadvantage, though my ten years of teaching in California, and ten more in Tennessee, have not persuaded me that ignorance is much less common among American students than among the British. For Joseph Conte however such ignorance is to be welcomed, and if it is wilful ignorance, so much the better; it is positively a *desideratum* if Niedecker's poem is to be preserved within the clinically created vacuum that alone, he seems to think, ensures its integrity. (As for the possibility that Niedecker's poem might be read by non-Americans, that he overlooks and perhaps even deplores; for him 'postmodern poetry' is exclusively an American product, and meant only for American consumption.) In the current tediously widespread climate of head-shaking and soul-searching about American higher education, it is worth noting that some American poets who deserve better are apparently promoted in a way that puts 'know-nothing-ism' at a premium.

However, Joseph Conte's attack on me (for that is what it is) seems to be an aberration. As a whole *Unending Design* is sensible, temperate and illuminating; it is also, unusually for books about postmodernism, well-written. Particularly momentous, I judge, is the firm distinction that Conte makes between 'sequence' and 'series' as modes of poetic composition. Rashly, in *Parnassus* (vol.124, no.1), I described the twelve units that make up 'Lake Superior' as a sequence. Conte persuades me I was wrong; the units are arranged not as a sequence, but as a series. The distinction is not pedantic: Conte's case for it is closely argued, and I shall not try to summarize it. What it amounts to is that the sequence is still conceived of, and practised, within the parameters of Coleridgean 'organic form', whereas the *series*, as practised by Niedecker and a few others, breaks free of that Coleridgean Romantic precedent. In so far as Conte represents that breaking free, that liberation, as distinctively postmodern, he makes a stronger and more plausible case for postmodernism in poetry than any other I have come across. Between one of the verse-units of 'Lake Superior' and the next, we should not look for either narrative or thematic continuity. That is true, I think; though in my original reading of the poem I was not seeking such continuities so insistently as he implies. Parkman supplies narrative continuity, and Janet Lewis gives, though in very relaxed fashion, thematic continuity; when I pointed out that Niedecker provides neither, I did not mean this as a mark against her.

On the other hand Samuel Johnson remarked of *Paradise Lost*: 'The want of human interest is always felt'. And the same must surely be felt of 'Lake Superior'. Niedecker's determination to work only in the cycles of geological time, or else in the shorter but still daunting perspectives of etymology, undoubtedly scants the experience of time as the human being suffers it between the cradle and the grave. Fortunately in other poems Niedecker more than compensates:

> My daughters left home.
> I was job-certified
> to rake leaves
> > in New Madrid.
>
> Now they tell me my girls
> Should support me again
> and they're not out of debt
> > from the last time they did.

We hardly need the title, 'Depression Years', to recognize in this – with its surprising and bitterly mordant rhyme – what we may call 'historicity'. (Certainly not 'historicism'.) And Niedecker, particularly in verses about her unfortunate parents, writes in this vein more often than anyone seems disposed to remember. To do so she did not have to surrender the principles she had learned from Zukofsky, which determined the writing of 'Lake Superior': the items she vouchsafes about her unfortunate and victimized father are still given to us in series, not in sequence; we are left to draw our own conclusions (as we can, without trouble). The evidence of Niedecker's short poems, good and less good, is that Niedecker wasn't in her life happy or fulfilled at all often; one looks in vain for that 'incredible zest and joy' that her executor, Cid Corman, assures us of. On the contrary the best of her short poems register with some indignation the imaginative and emotional sterility of the life that people like her parents were condemned to in that rural place, in that depressed time. Discerning this, do I show a hankering for a distressingly *linear* understanding of historical time, a sort of narrative or thematic continuity that postmodernism has declared decisively out-moded? In that case, so much the worse for postmodernism. For 'linear' is what time unavoidably is, when experienced between cradle and grave. And if poetry can't make sense of the sorrows endured in that passage, what use is it?

In the sixth section of 'Lake Superior' Niedecker alludes to Shakespeare:

> Beauty: impurities in the rock
> And at the blue ice superior spot
> priest-robed Marquette grazed
> azoic rock, hornblende granite
> basalt the common dark
> in all the Earth
>
> And his bones of such is coral
> raised up out of his grave
> were sunned and birch bark-floated
> to the straits

Conte says that the Shakespearean allusion – '"Of his bones are coral made" – pleases Davie no end'. He is sure of this because he has me typed as a New Critic, for whom 'only metaphor, allusion, or irony constitute figurative language – not metonymy'. (And yet it is he, not I who detected irony in the *voyageurs'* casting of tobacco on the waters.) As my essay makes clear, it is not the allusion as such that pleases me, nor is it any assurance I might find in having the securely canonical Shakespeare acknowledged. The allusion finds its place in a notable heightening of language that has already made near-puns on 'superior' and 'grazed'. I find an equal heightening two sections later, where there is no question of the canonical or of 'the Old World':

> Ruby of corundum
> lapis lazuli
> from changing limestone
> glow-apricot red-brown
> carnelian sard

And when I contrasted the sudden splendour of such diction to a previously established level of language that I called 'blank and blunt', 'stunned' and 'drab', I did not mean to object to the latter sort of language. On the contrary I meant to praise it as the carefully fashioned setting out of which more jewelled language, when it occurs, can shine with the more splendour. In Niedecker's other serial poems, 'Wintergreen Ridge' and the unhappily entitled 'Paean to Place', I do not find this placing or spacing of brilliant effects in a designedly less brilliant setting. And this is a pity; for these poems encompass *historicity* in a way that 'Lake Superior' could not find room for.

It cannot be denied that 'blank' and 'blunt', 'stunned' and 'drab', are epithets that will be applied to Niedecker's diction by readers who intend by them something more derogatory than I intended. Felicities and splendours of diction are, in Niedecker's poetry, quite hard to find. The Objectivists were, as a group, very puritanical in their attitude to language and linguistic art. The only one of the original brotherhood who escapes this category seems to be Carl Rakosi. For Niedecker who – there in rural Wisconsin! – was at the point of intersection between Zukofsky's Judaic puritanism and Bunting's Quaker frugality, the preference for the plain, at any cost in drabness, must have seemed an imperative. (On the other hand, her suppression of all punctuation but the sparsest was something that she learned from neither Zukofsky nor Bunting, and must figure in her work as a disabling affectation.) In consequence, her verse provides only *Spartan* pleasures; but then, it seems, every new generation of the literate throws up a larger minority of Spartans, as against Athenians.

Still, there she is. If, as seems to be assumed, the postmodernists in American poetry are the heirs of the Objectivists, Niedecker is one abundantly authenticated postmodernist poet whom it is possible to admire and to feel for without any grievous reservations. Undoubtedly this has something to do with her being a woman: the historicity in her short poems and some of her longer ones brings home, without her ever pressing it, how the cramped horizons of her upbringing restricted her particularly because of her sex. That was just one more of the disadvantages she had to battle with. Though the last thing she wanted was to dramatize her predicament, it's impossible not to remember:

> Grew riding the river
> Books
>   at home-pier
>   Shelley could steer
> as he read
>
> I was the solitary plover
> a pencil
>   for a wing-bone
> From the secret notes
> I must tilt
>
> upon the pressure
> execute and adjust
>   In us sea-air rhythm
> 'We live by the urgent wave
> of the verse'
>
> Seven-year molt
> for the solitary bird
>   and so young
> Seven years the one
> dress
>
> for town once a week
> One for home

                            faded blue-striped
            as she piped
            her cry.

That rhyme – of 'blue-striped' with 'piped' – is heart-breaking.

28 The Black Mountain Poets: Charles Olson and Edward Dorn

The name 'Black Mountain' as it is attached to the poets I am going to discuss, derives from Black Mountain College, an institution in North Carolina, now long defunct, where several of the most prominent members of the group first came together in the early 1950s. The history of Black Mountain College is itself of great interest, though it isn't my concern at this moment. Suffice to say that it was in most ways the earliest instance of something that is now much in the public eye, which is to say, 'the anti-university'. It was founded by disaffected teachers from an American university, who despaired of effecting what they understood as 'education' in the institutionalized places of higher learning in their country, smeared and distorted as those places were by the prevailing ideology of the national society. In the last years of its brief but eventful history, Black Mountain College was directed by Charles Olson, who at the age of forty-one came from a career in politics and government service to serve as rector of the college from 1951 to 1956. Olson, who did not publish his first poem until he was thirty-five, was at that time known in literary circles chiefly as the author of a monograph on Herman Melville's *Moby-Dick*, a book entitled *Call Me Ishmael* which first appeared in 1947 and is still the best introduction to his thought. But the exceptionally discerning reader of poetry might have noted also, published in a New York poetry magazine in 1950, Olson's essay-manifesto, *Projective Verse*, which has since been reprinted several times and is available most readily as a 'Statement on Poetics' in an appendix to D.M. Allen's anthology, *The New American Poetry 1945–1960*. Allen's sadly indiscriminate anthology, which came out in 1960, was the means by which the so-called Black Mountain group of poets came to be recognized as, for good or ill, a feature of the Anglo-American literary scene. And this delay in the group's establishing itself was no accident. For just as Black Mountain College repudiated the institutionalized organization of higher education in the USA (and so repudiated the normal, high-powered channels of publicity for itself), so the members of the group for many years shunned the normal channels of publication, the well-established and soundly-financed maga-zines, and the New York publishing houses. Their own magazines, shoddily produced in small printings and distributed privately, often for free, are now already collectors' items; as are their slender booklets and pamphlets, often produced on private printing presses. Even now, when in many cases the reputations can be said to be firmly established, the collections are brought out by small and sometimes fugitive publishing concerns; they are very seldom reviewed, and hardly ever in the expected places; and they are hard to come by except through a few booksellers, whether in New York, in San Francisco or in London.

This distinguishes the Black Mountain poets from a group which externally looks similar, with which they have had, and still maintain for the most part, friendly relations. I mean the so-called Beatnik poets centred on San Francisco in the late 1950s, of whom the most familiar names are doubtless Allen Ginsberg, Gregory Corso, Jack Kerouac, Lawrence Ferlinghetti. The Beatniks were always, and remain, very astute self-publicists, whereas the serious Black Mountaineers have shunned publicity very effectively.

So much for general information: now for the poetry. But at once I must warn you that there is a disappointment in store for you. I have chosen no specimen poems to dissect for your benefit. No, on consideration I have decided against this. For that procedure smacks altogether too strongly of precisely the milieu for poetry that the Beatniks and Black Mountaineers alike want to avoid: the graduate seminar class which spends a happy hour winkling out the symbols and the ambiguities from a dozen lines of Allen Tate or Robert Lowell or Ted Hughes. The poems of Charles Olson, of Ed Dorn and Robert Creeley, are not written for that sort of reading, any more than are the poems of Allen Ginsberg or Walt Whitman. As Olson's treatise makes clear, they are written very insistently for the speaking voice, and for the speaking voice of the poet himself; and they are composed so as to be performed, live, before a live audience by the poet in person. It need not be the bravura performance before massed microphones of an Allen Ginsberg; on the contrary, Creeley's poems in his way, and Dorn's in his (I haven't heard Olson read) are meant to be given a very soft-voiced performance, hesitant and deliberate, intimate and personal. And equally, it does not mean with Creeley and Dorn as it seems to do with Ginsberg that the text of the poem is a slack and colourless 'score', which comes to life only in the charismatic presence of the bard. The poems have much to give to the solitary and silent reader, as I hope to show. (And the scoring for the speaking verses is in some cases, notably Creeley's and Duncan's, extremely punctilious and exact.) But they are not meant to be mulled over excitedly, and tugged this way and that, in earnest discussion. And in fact, of course, we too seldom remember how few poems ever were written with that sort of reading in mind; how very special and peculiar is this sort of treatment of poems, which we tend to regard as normal.

But there is another reason why it isn't appropriate to approach the Black Mountain poets by close reading of selected specimens. Some of their poems can be submitted to that sort of inspection, and can survive it, as can the poems of Milton or Ezra Pound. But in Olson's case and Dorn's, as in Pound's case and Milton's, such an experiment is in any event wide of the mark. With these poets it is not the case that the poem in isolation, if only you scrutinize it closely enough, will reveal to you everything you need to understand it and enjoy it. Even of T.S. Eliot and Robert Lowell, Allen Tate and Ted Hughes, this is not true; for all these poets, like all poets there ever were, expect the reader to bring something to the poem – and something more than just receptivity, sympathy and alertness. The reader is expected to bring to the poem a certain body of information, and certain assumptions. In the cases of Olson and Dorn, Milton and Pound, this is more than usually important; for the stock of information, and the body of assumptions, which you are expected to bring to the poem are not those you would normally come by as part of the equipment of a normally well-educated person. Poets like the four I've named have followed a wayward and eccentric path through the records of human experience; they have read books that aren't on the normal curriculum, and they set more store by these than by some which *are* on the curriculum; as a result, when they do encounter a monument of the curriculum, an acknowledged 'classic' (Homer, for instance) they find their way into him as it were from an unexpected angle, they are interested in things about him that are not the things usually singled out for attention, they place the emphasis in places we do not expect and are not prepared for and which, often enough, we consequently fail to recognize. As a result, with poets like these, there is a lot of spadework for us to do before ever, as it were, we open their books. They are very learned poets, who write very learned poems; and they have come by their learning in out-of-the-way places. What's more, they are not interested in making their poems self-sufficient, sailing free like so many rockets from the learning that was accumulated only as it were to assist take-off; on the contrary the poems depend on the learning, they emerge from it only to burrow back into it again, the poems depend upon – and are themselves *part of* – the lifelong addiction of the poet to the business of educating himself, i.e. the business of understanding the world that he and we are living in. The poems differ in degree but not in kind from the excited letters that the poets write to each other and to their admirers, or from the reviews and articles they write for each other's magazines. And so the poems have, quite deliberately, the sort of untidiness and hastiness that we associate with lecture-notes and reading-lists.

This is very different indeed from the fastidious impersonality that T.S. Eliot sought for and attained in his poems, or Wallace Stevens in his. And in fact what gets in the way of most of us apart from the very young, when we attempt to approach these poets at the present day, is precisely our experience of Eliot's poetry and the way we have nearly all been conditioned, more than we realize, to regard Eliot's procedures in poetry, and Eliot's sort of poetry, as the norms for poetry in English in the present century. This is the point of insisting on the name of Pound. For Olson and his followers derive from that side of Ezra Pound on which Pound is most unlike his esteemed colleague and one-time protégé, T.S. Eliot. To put it more exactly, these poets, as Americans, use Pound so as to bypass Eliot, because only by bypassing Eliot can they re-establish contact with the great American poet of the last century, Walt Whitman. (The line of descent from Pound to Olson can be traced in more detail through two other American poets – William Carlos Williams and Louis Zukofsky.) Not only Eliot, but also the poets of the past whom Eliot taught several generations to esteem afresh (for instance John Donne and Andrew Marvell) are stumbling-blocks if we want to get into the world of Black Mountain poetry.

Far more useful, if as British readers we want a British name – far more helpful and worth remembering is the name of D.H. Lawrence, and not just Lawrence's poems either. Olson's most Lawrencian book is his *Mayan Letters*, written from Central America to Robert Creeley, when Olson was pursuing archaeological researches into the Maya civilization. And Dorn is at his most Lawrencian in *The Shoshoneans*, his prose book on the Amerindian peoples of the part of America he has made his own.

After what I have said, it will not surprise you that I think the best thing for me to do in the space that I have is to introduce you to some of the preoccupations that Dorn and Olson share. (For these are the two poets I'm really concerned with.) These preoccupations appear in – indeed, they are the substance of – many of the poems that these men write; but in order to recognize them when they appear in the poems, you need to be acquainted with them beforehand – in other words they are part of that stock of information and assumptions which you have to bring to the poems. The ones that I want to isolate turn around the notion of 'geography'. And as good a way as any of beginning to show how important this has been, and is, for Dorn and Olson, is by quoting from one of their acknowledged forerunners, William Carlos Williams, writing a manifesto in 1930: 'To what shall the mind turn for that with which to rehabilitate our thought and our lives? To the word, a meaning hardly distinguishable from that of place, in whose great virtuous and at present little realized potency we hereby manifest our belief.'

The portentousness of the phrasing here should not prevent us from recognizing that this is the sort of thing that has been said often before. The crucialness of a grasp on *locality*, the imaginative richness for poetry of a sense of *place* – this is no novel perception. We need go no further back than to the generation preceding that of Williams; to Yeats saying, 'And I, that my native scenery might find imaginary inhabitants half-planned a new method and a new culture.' And so it should not surprise us if *The Maximus Poems* of Charles Olson, the only poetic enterprise of the present day in English which appears to be planned on a scale to challenge comparison with Williams's *Paterson* and Pound's *Cantos,* should be geographical rather than historical in its focus. *The Maximus Poems* aspire to give in language a *map,* a map of one place, the town of Gloucester, Massachusetts. This town, Olson's home-town, is otherwise known to twentieth-century literature only by way of Rudyard Kipling's *Captains Courageous.* And the Portuguese-speaking fishermen of Gloucester, embodied by Spencer Tracy in the film that was made of Kipling's story, figure repeatedly in the poems that Olson has made about his home place. For the poems do not, by concentrating on the geography of Gloucester, thereby *ignore* its history. Quite the contrary. The great geographer Alexander von Humboldt remarked that 'In classical antiquity the earliest historians made little attempt to separate the description of lands from the narration of events the scene of which was in the areas described. For a long time physical geography and history appear attractively inter-mingled.' And of course this is true; the ancient Herodotus is the father of geography but also the father of history, and he fathers the one by virtue of fathering the other. Crucial terms from Herodotus, as well as the name of Alexander von Humboldt himself, figure in Pound's *Cantos.* Yet it was probably not in Pound that Olson found the grounds for the veneration of Herodotus which he repeatedly professed. A more likely source is an American geographer of the present day, Carl Ortwin Sauer, whose name figures in a pamphlet that Olson published some years ago, called *A Bibliography on America for Ed Dorn.*

(The slangy in-group flavour of that title, incidentally, as of much of the excited telegraphese prose which it introduces, is something that you may well find tiresome; but it is inevitable, given a movement which defines itself as all that organized society is not. Such a movement is an open conspiracy, which is only another word for a coterie, though an unusually ambitious and serious one. The same set of social circumstances produces the equally tiresome and not dissimilar telegraphese idiom of Ezra Pound's letters.)

At any rate Sauer's essay of 1925, 'The Morphology of Landscape', makes the same point about the ancient geography of Herodotus that we have just seen Alexander von Humboldt making: 'The *historia* of the Greeks, with its blurred feeling for time relations, had a somewhat superior appreciation of areal relations and represented a far from contemptible start in geography.' Dorn dutifully learned his lesson, from Olson's reading-list, and uses the very word 'areal', in the poem he has addressed to Olson, called 'From Gloucester Out':

To play areal as particulars, and out of the span
of Man, and as this man
does,

      he does, he
   walks
     by the sea
in my memory
and sees all things and to him
are presented at night
the whispers of the most flung shores
from Gloucester out.

The same emphasis – on the home-base, on the local terrain as needing to be securely grasped by the imagination before it can afford to look further abroad – is in Dorn's similarly entitled poem 'Idaho Out', in his third collection with the significant programmatic title, *Geography*. These poems by Dorn, like many of *The Maximus Poems* by Olson which they emulate, may be regarded as investigations of just what it means to have 'a standpoint' – the place on which you stand, the place which necessarily conditions everything which you see when you stand on that place and look from it.

Olson recommends the geographer Sauer's writings as a whole. But he specifies as particularly important an essay by Sauer called 'Environment and Culture during the Last Deglaciation'. And it's easy to see why Olson does this. For this particular essay by Sauer takes up, and applies to North America particularly, a thesis which Sauer argued in another paper called 'Agricultural Origins and Dispersals'. Both these essays argue that the culture-hearth of agricultural man, which is to say of Neolithic man, is not, as is still most generally supposed, in south-west Asia, but in south-east Asia; and this for the reason that (so Sauer maintains) the break-through to agriculture made by Neolithic man came from a fishing culture rather than a hunting culture. Only if this precarious and disputed thesis is true can Olson in his *Maximus Poems* use his chosen standpoint, Gloucester (which is primarily *a fishing* community), in the way he wants to do – as a vantage-point for surveying and understanding human society however various, and human mythology however archaic.

This, it may well be thought, is an instance of how poetry may become entangled with geography too much for its own good, an ambitious poetic enterprise perilously dependent upon a particular disputed geographer's thesis. But the point is important, because otherwise we might think that Olson chose to concentrate on Gloucester simply because it happened to be the poet's home-town, out of some familiar Romantic notion of mystical properties available for a man in his native origin, his 'roots'. This is not the case; Olson *chose* to make Gloucester his standpoint, there was no mystical compulsion upon him to do so. This is where it's instructive to remember his essay on Melville, with its title 'Call Me Ishmael'. Ishmael – the archetypal nomad and wanderer. And in fact Olson's argument about Melville's *Moby Dick* shows once again with what desperate seriousness he takes the matter of geographical location; for his argument is that the greatest character in Melville's great and strange romance is the Pacific Ocean, that the book as a whole celebrates the imaginative discovery and appropriation by Western man, specifically by American man, of that great waste of waters in the West, the Pacific – one more territory which the pioneers could light out into when they had crossed the entire continent and found themselves faced by the sea. The standpoint which Olson, and more consistently Dorn, are concerned to investigate is not characteristically a fixed point, the place where roots are sunk; it is a moving point, the continually changing standpoint of a man who is on the move across continents and oceans. Thom Gunn exhorts us to be 'on the move', but Dorn's poem 'Idaho Out' gives us this man moving, and moving by automobile, from Idaho into Montana and back again, his standpoint changing as he moves, yet conditioned by the terrain it moves through and over, as much as by the consciousness which occupies the moving point. One might compare the novels of a prose-writer, Douglas Woolf, who has published in the same magazines with Olson and Dorn; in particular his wittily entitled *Wall to Wall*, the fictional narrative of a trans-continental journey by car from the Pacific Ocean to the Atlantic.

But one could compare equally a much earlier poem by a quite different kind of poet, Yvor Winters's 'The Journey', which is like Dorn's poem in nothing except in being a very Western poem about the experience of moving over the vast distances of the American West. The America of these poems has nothing whatever in common with the Atlantic seaboard America of Robert Lowell, or indeed Charles Olson. (For Olson's slim little volume, *West*, is an exception for him, and to my mind not distinguished.)

Edward Dorn and Yvor Winters, neither of them Westerners by birth, choose to live in the West and to celebrate it in their poems, not at all because they had chosen to sink their roots there (as Wordsworth chose to root himself in the English Lake District), but because the history of the Western States – both the brief recorded history, and the much longer unrecorded history of the indigenous Indian peoples – is a history of human *movement*; and the still largely empty landscapes of those territories are images of nomadic life, an arena for human life to which the imaginative response is still (as it always has been) to *move*, to *keep moving*. Moreover, because the human history of those territories is so short and scant, and because they are still so empty, the spectacle of them – like the spectacle of the oceans when one travels on them – teases the imagination into conceiving that human migrations across these spaces are only the last chapter of a history of non-human migrations, a history which is read out of geology and climatology. This is what Olson says in a recent poem:

in successive waves basically NW
as in fact the earth's crust once – and mantle or at least
the depth of the asthenosphere broke
apart and went
    itself mid-
                              north north West
    150,000,000 years ago to that,
definitely now established by
J. Tuzo Wilson as well as other
oceanographers and geographers who have paid
                           attention to the
fit of the Earth's continental shelfs
   on either shore of each
ocean – including runs right down the middle
                     such as when
India ground a path for herself traveling
  from an original place as African about where
                    Mozambique
and sometime about 150,000,000 years ago
went off to where she now is, attaching herself to
Eurasia – as if Tethys went under Ocean to
  maka the love with him
    a love with
               near Crete
   on the water's
     surface at or about
Gortyna
        migrations
   turn out to be
 as large as
bodies of earth and of
  stories
        and primaries
of order which later is taken for granted are
such as the Atlantic migration which filled America[1]

And this same area of human learning – where geography and geology, oceanography and climatology, anthropology and archaeology and pre-

---

1   'An Essay on Queen Tiy', *Wivenhow Park Review* 2 (1967).

history meet – is the area which Dorn's imagination explores; not didactically like Olson (who in this respect is much nearer to Pound), but more freely and provisionally, as a sort of serious make-believe. Dorn is not committed to this field for imaginative speculation, as Olson is. On the dustjacket of his latest collection, he says for instance: '(In my latest poems) I have tried to locate another hemisphere. And I want this collection to be the last necessity to work out such locations.'

That is to say, his explorations of geographical space are now over; as he says elsewhere in the same blurb: 'That non-special dimension, intensity, is one of the few singular things which interest me now.'

The element of make-believe, of merely *provisional* belief in the primacy of geography, shows up in Dorn's humour, which is much more in evidence and also more various and shifting than in Olson. Olson's jokes (like 'maka the love with him') are hearty, but bluff and simple-minded. Dorn's humour is much harder to pin down, and also much harder to take – particularly in *The North Atlantic Turbine*, the latest collection where it seems to be often raucous and sick, a sort of snarl. This is particularly hard for the British reader to take, because *The North Atlantic Turbine*, Dorn's fourth collection, consists of the poems he has written in England since he came here, to the University of Essex, in 1965; and the image he gives of England, often in this languid snarling tone, is decidedly unflattering. He is no more flattering to his own country, the United States. But then ... he refuses to take nation-states (the UK vs. the US) seriously. That indeed is the meaning of his title. His subject is the North Atlantic, as Herman Melville's (so Olson argued) is the Pacific. The tide of human migration long ago crossed the North Atlantic, and left it behind; and so the only movement left in it is rotation, a 'bind' or circular swirl; it is now to all intents and purposes a landlocked ocean, and the swirl around it (imaged as the pulse from a dynamo at its centre) locks together and makes virtually identical, in one pointless round of activity, all countries that have a North Atlantic seaboard – the UK, the US, Canada, France, Spain.

The North Atlantic Turbine contains a long poem in six parts on 'Oxford'. The most immediately accessible and engaging of these is Part II, in which we see Oxford through an eye which refuses to be daunted by the historical patina on that or any other city of the Old World, insisting instead on 'locating' it for the imagination in a way which is natural for territories like Idaho, Montana or the Dakotas – by way, that is, of the geological structure of the land mass which supports it:

> The sands of the Cotswolds
> line the streets, the stone portals
> a light of light brown brilliance
> when the suns of May

cast a black swatch
by Radcliffe Camera
solitary as
any Baptistry encrusted
or a product
of the sea.
However the streams of thin
elegance come down past the town
it is the linear strip
of the beautiful Jurassic lias
running from Flixborough in Lincolnshire
hanging from there
this liana falls, lier
as the most springing joint
of England
to Bristol

But more challenging, and less palatable, is for instance 'Oxford Part V':

England beware
the cliff of 1945
turns a natural insularity
into a late, and out of joint
naturalism of inbred
industrial indecision. The hesitation
to hard sell small arms
to backward countries and
'if we must, can't the man
be more civilized' of a man
who only knows his business
be it selling washing machines
or machine guns: un 'produit
de l'industrie moderne'.
White Sunday,
the day of the Big White Sale.
We speak of payments as
balanced
Oxford, the dull if sometimes
remote
façade
is balanced in limestone, the
Bodleian has as a copyright
every book,
Lincoln College
has high on the wall

in the first court
a small bust of John Wesley, fellow
there is in Merton an Elizabethan
stretch of building and beyond
that, under a passage
the treed lawn where only fellows
and there is the garden where Hopkins
as at Cambridge the tower
where Byron's Bear near
the rooms of Coleridge
or Shelley's notebook in the
case at the Bodleian, the Lock
of His Hair, his glove, in a case.
not two gloves as he must
have had two hands to cover
but that hip thing
one glove you can do something
with
in terms of those and these brown spectacular
times, two
of course are a boring reminder
we are the animals we are
a lovely glove admittedly
but not so lovely as Shelley.

I walked back from Merton
with two lads who spoke of the police
and their perilous adventures
in Oxford's streets of explanations
'I shall climb up a drain pipe –
'But won't that disturb the authorities?
'it shall disturb them more
'if you wake them to report me
and thus we walked along –
there were more great names
than you'd care to hear
But at one point one of them said
it's impossible to write of it
every substantive fit
to name and celebrate has been spoken
and named. Then there was
a turning, we entered another street which
I'm more used to a grid,
swore to myself I'd never reenter,

but once I loved the idea of such narrow places.
And the easy talk of obscure things
I must admit I envied
            those children
because I love the dazzle of learning
and I am only concerned
when I think the strings
have gone loose.
      if I weren't an intelligent man
I'd share the attitude
      of my president
'Education is a wonderful thing.'

                  But I said *everything*?
has been talked about
around Oxford. I was assured
it had been. I didn't *say* while walking
but I thought well then make up!
something! Because baby if you don't
they's gonna take all your wine away
they's gonna turn you into a state
institootion and you'll all be working
for the state just like in America
and you'll have to *prove*
you're useful, the most *useless*
sort of proof you'll ever have to make
....
                  Thus those children
could start by naming themselves and the rocks
in a larger than
national way and then more intimately,
if only for a more hopeful world
say what hope this 'rock
from which the language springs'
can be in the world. Can't
you tell yourselves it is time
Oxford stopped having a place
in English life as sanctuary,
World War II was *not* ended
in Europe because you failed
to take up the language
– not *the* language
oh you still have *that*, you
are stuck with that, that's

> *all* you have,
> because you so desired
> to be the English Race
> you so much wanted the courses
> o come in their proper order
> 'where's the fish' you said
> you were so impatient
> and now
> all you have is a few people you consider
> problems anyway who won't even bother to speak
> your language
> and all they want to do is beat
> your unemployment schemes, the best
> of them have gone off
> to Katmandu, the best of them
> aren't even interested, except Tom
>   Pickard
>   who still makes his own sense
>   in Newcastle, but he's a northerner.
>   and will steal and resell
>   every book Calder and Boyars prints
>   God bless him.

Part IV is introduced by 'An Epistolary Comment: knowing none of it accurately, the world can be surveyed'. And this ought to tell us the sort of poem we are dealing with: a poem in which concern for locality and for 'locating', so far from leading to localism or regionalism, lends itself on the contrary to vast and rapid panoramas. This poetry sets up the tourist as hero, and would persuade us that the only trustworthy eye is the travelling eye, casual and disengaged. In this *The North Atlantic Turbine* is like eighteenth-century poems such as Goldsmith's *The Traveller*, or Thomas Gray's *Education and Government*, or the prose-poetry of Burke's speech 'On Conciliation with the Colonies'. For those eighteenth-century works were similarly inspired by geography, indeed by a geographer – the French thinker, Montesquieu. The difference is that Montesquieu's bird's-eye view nourished a buoyant sense of diversity and plenitude. He argued that differences of climate and terrain made for different national temperaments, and hence that the form of government evolved by one people would not be appropriate for another differently located. Some of this buoyancy and eagerness appears in Olson. But Edward Dorn's space-capsule eye reports on the contrary that none of the differences matters, that one 'turbine', pumping out trade-cycles of production and consumption, governs and defines us all – the Communist East set on the same objectives as the Capitalist West, the Negro American indeed different from the white American in (alas) no more than the pigment of his skin. The only valid and total alternative is the *Red* American.

POSTSCRIPT

In his latest work, *Gunslinger*, Dorn has reached the 'spiritual address' which he announced he was setting out for after *The North Atlantic Turbine*. Departing from geography and moving across 'that non-special dimension, intensity' (its colouring that of the American southwest, but not literally located anywhere), Dorn has beautifully recovered his good humour. Of the verbal horse-play which carries the surreal narrative on a steady ripple of comedy ('horseplay' is exact – a talking horse occasions much of it), a broad and therefore quotable example is when in Book II we notice, as do the more-than-human travellers in the poem, that the first person has disappeared from the narration. Lil, archetypal madam of a western brothel (but of much else – she practised two thousand years ago in Smyrna) is first to notice: 'What happened to I she asked/his eyes dont seem right.' The Poet, another of the company, reports, 'I is dead', and is reproved: 'That aint grammatical, Poet'. Lil responds:

> Oh. Well I'll be …
> We never knew anything much
> about him did we. I
> was the name he answered to,
> and that was what he had
> wanderin around inside him
> askin so many questions
> his eyes had already answered …

Gunslinger himself, archetypal westerner but also Greek, sun-worshipper and solar deity like Alexander the Great, explains:

> Life and Death
> are attributes of the soul
> not of things. The Ego
> is costumed as the road manager
> of the soul, every time
> the soul plays a date in another town
> I goes ahead to set up
> the bleechers, or book the hall
> as they now have it,
> the phenomenon is reported by the phrase
> I got there ahead of myself
> I got there ahead of my I
> is the fact
> which not a few anxious mortals
> misread as intuition …

Since among the areas of language drawn upon for ambiguities is the dialect of drug-takers ('acid', for instance, and 'grass'), this questioning of personal identity is serious and comical at the same time. At once comic and profound, narrative and piercingly lyrical, the form and idiom of *Gunslinger* transcend completely the programmes of Black Mountain, just as they transcend (dare one say?) any programme so far promulgated or put into practice in Anglo-American poetry of the present century.

'The Black Mountain Poets', *The Survival of Poetry*, ed. Martin Dodsworth (Faber and Faber, 1970). Reprinted in *The Poet in the Imaginary Museum*.

29 Edward Dorn and the Treasures of Comedy

What will get least attention in Dorn's *Gunslinger* is just what first strikes and beguiles any halfway competent reader – the fact that it is a jokey poem, high-spirited and good-tempered, carried forward on a steadily inventive play of puns and pleasantries. For centuries now English-speakers have not known what to do with comedy, in verse or out of it. We have been quite at a loss before the classical conviction that comedy is one of the great canonical modes in which the imagination exerts itself; that the comic vision is as inclusive, as rigorous, ultimately as grave, as the tragic vision which it complements. 'But is he serious?' we say anxiously, quite as if Molière and Aristophanes, or for that matter Chaucer and Shakespeare, had never lived. Satire! there is the lifeline that we leap for. All our comedians have to be made into satirists; either that, or else flip entertainers. Between satire on the one side and 'light verse' on the other, comic poetry gets no showing at all. So *Gunslinger,* I predict, will be applauded as satire or else damned as frivolity; and it is neither. That is what one means by calling it good-tempered or, better still, good-humoured; it has no illusions about a figure like Howard Hughes, and what he signifies in present-day America, but it delights in him, in his absurdity and the absurdity of his career and his life-style. It quite conspicuously lacks the indignant anger of satire. There are passages in Dorn's earlier books, particularly *The North Atlantic Turbine,* which show him working up to this; working out, not that the comic vision is truer than the satirical, but that it is more honourable. It is more honourable because now, when indignant disgust with America has been taken over as a reach-me-down uniform by successive generations (and by the journalists who aim to please them), satire and invective and lampoon are for the moment devalued and discredited forms of writing. They come into a buyer's market; readers tune into them too promptly, too unthinkingly. And *Gunslinger,* like any good poem, wants to jolt its readers into reorienta-tions. Dorn is a poet too ambitious and too honest to play for prepared and predictable responses.

For thirty years there has been a poet in America saying things like this, and writing confessedly comic poems that are not light verse nor yet satire.

This is W.H. Auden. And Auden deserves more credit than we usually give him, for having sustained and implemented the claims of poetry, and for insisting in the face of various kinds of portentousness that at the heart of imaginative activity there is an element of play, even of playfulness, of free-wheeling improvisation and caprice, such as we find abundantly in *Gunslinger*. However, in this respect Auden is still the British poet that he used to be. And the British, as every one knows, pride themselves on having a sense of humour. But British humour though it is genuine enough, shows up in British stories and poems in one or both of two ways: in the first place it is *social* – British comedy is the comedy of manners (even, for instance, in William Blake, who incidentally is not far off-stage in some of the later sections of *Gunslinger*) and secondly, British humour is characteristically *reflexive*, that is to say, self-mocking, deprecating. And most of Auden's comedy is British in these ways, like that of his friend John Betjeman or the rather more saturnine comedy of Philip Larkin. American humour can take this form too: without going into the light verse of such as Ogden Nash, one can find pleasant self-mockery in W.D. Snodgrass, in Reed Whittemore, even Gregory Corso. What's more, American Jewish humour is very like British; deprecating comedy of manners is a Jewish-American specialty.

What should be plain is that Dorn's comedy is radically different. It isn't in the least reflexive, if only because there is no character in *Gunslinger* who can be taken as in any way a stand-in for the author. (The possibility is ruled out early in Book 2, when jokes are made about the disappearance of the figure that in Book 1 was called 'I'.) And the comedy isn't social, because the characters in it aren't recognizably people at all, still less people with any social status or social function. (They consist of two groups, one in a stage-coach moving towards and across the Southwest, another in a luxury train travelling south and west from Boston; it seems the two groups are to meet ultimately in the place, which can be found on the map, called Four Corners.) Names like Parmenides and Levy-Strauss, together with a lot of the jokes that are made out of etymologies, show that Dorn's comedy on the contrary is metaphysical, or epistemological. It is playing with – that is to say, it is *exploring* – such matters as Being and Becoming, and Identity and Difference, and the One and the Many. And to my mind this takes it out of the range of characteristically British or Jewish comedy. If we look for precedents, leaving out of account the possibility of finding them in American writing, I suggest that they might well be Irish. One name in particular comes to mind: Swift, in the first two books of *Gulliver's Travels*, a book that Swift's closest friends treated as an exuberant joke, high-spirited comedy, whereas for two hundred years we have (characteristically) told ourselves that it is satire, and of a specially savage kind. How to be a laughing philosopher, how to be a comedian without being either irresponsible or heartless –

these are secrets that it seems we lost the key to, two centuries ago. (And of course the Irish tradition has been travestied too, by the stage Oirishman doing his act 'with a smile and a tear'.) If Dorn has found the key, and can wean us from the portentous 'concern' on which we congratulate ourselves, there are treasures he might unlock for us – treasures not just of enjoyment, but of bracing good sense.

30 Steep Trajectories

I have been enthusiastic about Ed Dorn's writing ever since I was introduced by the Englishman J. H. Prynne to Dorn's first collection of poems, *The Newly Fallen* (1961). I have followed him since through *Hands Up!* (1964) and *The North Atlantic Turbine* (1967 – Dorn's 'European' book); also through the prose books *The Rites of Passage* (1965), *The Shoshoneans* (1966), and *Some Business Recently Transacted in the White World* (1971). A book which stands rather apart from all these, but very valuable, is *Recollections of Gran Apacheria* (1974). As for Dorn's most ambitious undertaking to date, which occupied him from 1967 to 1974, the comic and visionary narrative poem *Gunslinger* (called *Slinger* when it came out from Berkeley in 1975), I did my best to keep abreast of it as its four books appeared one by one over those years, but it's a difficult work and I've never yet given myself the opportunity to take it in as a whole.

My enthusiasm for this body of writing is one that I've been able to share with very few of my friends, whether British or American. And I understand why. Dorn's latest collection, *Hello, La Jolla*, for instance, will move most of my friends to exasperation, and some to apoplexy. What are they to make (I hear them snarl) of misspellings like 'exhuberant', 'who's' for 'whose', 'eminent' (for, apparently, 'immanent'), 'queezy', 'idealogical', 'footbol', 'catagorize', 'practise' (for 'practice'), 'feignt' (for 'feint'), 'permenantum' (for, apparently, 'permanentum'), 'oecological', 'thorobred', 'nickleplated', 'emmigrate', 'excitment'? Are these misspellings deliberate? (Some are; others I think aren't.) Are they misprints? (Again, some are, some aren't.) Wasn't there a poet (Eliot) who said that poetry must be 'at least as well written as good prose'? And haven't poets from as far back as Dante forward through Ben Jonson taken as one of their responsibilities the provision of a model of propriety and serviceable correctness to all other users of language? Where then but in California (I hear my friends splutter) would one find, elegantly printed on good paper, the misspellings listed above, or a complete poem like Dorn's 'A Sense of Place'?

> I'd live on the Moon
> if the commute were
> a little less.

What is this but the new barbarism, Walt Whitman's 'barbaric yawp' updated and even more raucous, an impudent fraud on a reading public either too uneducated to notice it is being conned, or else too cowed and disoriented to protest?

I sympathize with these friends of mine. Indeed, so far as they are British, I agree with them. Dorn's practice is indeed, and cannot help being, an affront to the British tradition in writing – and this despite the fact that Dorn has lived in England, has been happy there, has collaborated with an Englishman on translating from the Spanish, and has indeed a British-educated wife. It's just because Dorn knows England well, and is at ease among the English, that he defines his own tradition, and indeed his own language, as firmly distinct from theirs – as *American*. It's as an American addressing a fellow American that he says to his interviewer:

> Our articulation is quite different from other people's; we arrive at understanding and meaning through massive assaults on the language, so no particular word is apt to be final. It's rapidly rerun all the time. And I think that can be healthy usage. On the other hand, there's so much of it that it gets the reputation for being loose. A lot of it in fact is.

And this means that if my American friends, for instance Tennesseans, are affronted by Dorn's way of writing, they are in a more awkward situation than the Englishmen. Is Dorn just wrong about American speech habits? Is he mistaking Californian usage for American usage? Hardly; *Hello, La Jolla* is emphatically a Californian book, but Dorn himself isn't Californian; he is as much at home in Chicago, Idaho, Colorado, New Mexico (all of them places he has lived in). Besides, there are Californians – notably those influenced by the late Yvor Winters – who will be as affronted by this book as any Tennessean could be. And finally, if I may turn the knife in the wound, a poem out of Tennessee like Robert Penn Warren's 'Pursuit' ('The hunchback on the corner, with gum and shoe-laces') seems to my English ear, though it rhymes and so on, and despite its incidental splendours, demonstrably 'loose' in the way that Dorn tolerantly describes.

How Dorn can tolerate such looseness – metrical, grammatical, lexical – in his own work and the work of others comes clear from other passages in the interview, for instance where he says, 'My attitude toward writing is that I handle the language every day like a material, and I keep it in *interesting* repair. I don't really care about *good* repair.' This of course leaves it open for someone to retort that in American poetry as in any other, while some writers may go to work as Dorn does, there have to be others who perform the Jonsonian function of keeping the language in *good* repair. (Dorn himself might agree.) And when Dorn makes the same point again, saying 'I'm always roadtesting the language for a particular form of speech', another retort is possible: Why 'speech'? Isn't American English a written, as well as a spoken, language? And why should the spoken language have an automatic priority for the poet, over the written? Dorn might even concede this point too, but reluctantly I think; for he's convinced of the unexploited possibilities in American speech, and eloquent about it, as when he explains the ironic or sarcastic inflection of much of his *Gunslinger*: 'It seems to me that our speech is not nearly as flexible as it ought to be, that its potential hasn't been realized, and I would seek in that poem to elevate it from its eternally Flat Trajectories.'

At any rate, 'interesting repair' is what Dorn claims to do for the spoken American that is his chosen language in this book. And I think he is as good as his word. Jokes and puns, bizarre collocations overheard and imagined – these are his stock in trade; and they are more than 'interesting'. They are entertaining and also instructive, so long as we recognize that 'correctness' isn't the point (we are listening to American speech as it is, not as conceivably it *should be*), and so long as we remember also how comedy can be a way of discussing seriously very serious matters (like transplant surgery, which is the subject of several poems here).

It must also be said that Dorn is not, like other poets who seem to be on a similar tack, in any way an aggressive know-nothing who wants to deride and reject the English and European inheritance. *Hello, La Jolla* reveals that he has been reading Edward Gibbon and William Cobbett. And he *does* sometimes use the written rather than the spoken language. It is probably my British and literary conditioning that makes me like him best when he does so, as in these lines from a poem about the current opening up of Alaska:

> The creatures of ice feignt and advance
> with a consciousness a great deal more
> pervasive then the rise and fall of wages.
> The tremendous pitch of their crystal stacks
> the vast smell of their lunar coldness
> the mammoth draft of their freezing humidity
> the highminded groan of their polar turns ...

The misspelling 'feignt' is one that is undoubtedly deliberate, and justifiable: in a way that has nothing to do with speech and everything to do with writing, it packs two meanings into the one word, just as (to take another example) 'pitch' in line four is the pitch of a ship but also (and more) the pitch of a roof.

The book will do harm if it gets into the wrong hands? No doubt of it. But who ever thought that poetry is a safe commodity? The stuff is dynamite!

This review first appeared in 1978 in the Vanderbilt Campus magazine, *Maxie's Journal,* edited by Craig Chambers. Reprinted in *Trying to Explain.*

31 Tortoiseshell
(for Ed Dorn)

Nothing but rules of thumb,
Ever! I perceive
The need for a rule more golden
Beginning: 'Poetry is ...'
But I was never at home
With generalities.

And going by rules of thumb,
Which ought to be humble, seems
Oracular rather, a voice
uttering *arcanum;*
Presumptuous, as if one
Boasted a golden thumb.

Artificer, not artist,
Pretends to the golden thumb;
The English carver, enacting
The new Perpendicular Style
Greeted it, I suspect, with
A crooked treacherous smile.

Does his every exactly rendered
Cusp not grudge the enormous
Access of confidence in
His architect? I go
Resentfully along with
Your self-possession, so;

As it might be an ancient tortoise,
Because his grandsire's quaint
Slouch-hatted or pie-crust shell
Supplied the sounding frame
Behind Apollo's string,
Should think his was the fame.

The American Scholar, Winter 1981/2.

32 Voices Modern and Postmodern

The Harvard Guide to Contemporary American Writing, ed. Daniel Hoffman
   (Harvard University Press, 1979)
Jerome Mazzaro, *Postmodern American Poetry* (University of Illinois Press,
   1980)
William H. Pritchard, *Lives of the Modern Poets* (Oxford University Press,
   1980)
Helen Vendler, *Part of Nature, Part of Us: Modern American Poets* (Harvard
   University Press, 1980)

One of these critics has reviewed one of the others. William Pritchard, in
an enthusiastic notice of Helen Vendler, mourned that he could not say
of himself what she strikingly says of herself – that, for her, poetry is 'the
one form of writing that is ... the most immediate, natural and accessible'.
From her this carries complete conviction; and her being so 'at home' in
poetry is what gives a quite distinct, perhaps unique, flavour and weight
to this bulky collection of reviews and essays, a volume which has accordingly, as has been generally realized, a significance much greater than most
such rag-bag books, even when they come from distinguished hands. It
means in fact that her book isn't a rag-bag at all. But William Pritchard
was inclined to feel guilty that he couldn't, despite his passion for poetry,
declare himself quite so much at home with it as Helen Vendler is; and I
don't think Pritchard should feel guilty. For how would it be if we
proposed that poetry quite properly is not something on a level with the
rest of our lives, that it lifts us above that level, that accordingly it is and
should be something reserved for special hours, a medium not for
expressing the steady run of experience through our days but on the
contrary for certain experiences that are usually concentrated or even, we
may dare to say, unusually elevated? This is certainly, as Helen Vendler
recognizes, how most readers regard poetry – to the point indeed where
many of them decide that such a special experience is something that they
can, regretfully or not, do without; and many poets we admire, perhaps
most of them, have spoken of it in the same way – as the product and the
record of visitations, rather rare ones, and/or of exertions that they only
intermittently rise to. Helen Vendler, I think, has foreseen this objection
(if that is what it is) and has defiantly refused to accept it. So, at least, I

understand the title she has chosen, which comes from some lines of Stevens:

> As part of nature he is part of us,
> His rarities are ours: may they be fit,
> And reconcile us to ourselves in those
> True reconcilings, dark, pacific words.

In these verses, thus isolated as an epigraph, 'he' can only mean 'the poet'; and so the implication is that, however many readers think otherwise, the poet – even the most arcane and austere sort of poet – is on a level with his readers, and can be encountered by them without their having to make special exertions or put themselves in a special frame of mind. This is in one sense true, and cannot be said too often – as all of us know who daily meet people (for instance, students) who suppose that poetry is a legendary beast to be approached with caution and skirted whenever possible. It is obviously true that poetry is eminently natural, since the impulse to make it and enjoy it appears to be a constant in human nature, through the ages and in every society we have records of. And yet … isn't it a constant only in the sense of a constant *potentiality*, a potentiality that in many ages and societies, notably in our own, most people do not actualize? And again, would it not make as much sense to say of the poet: 'as part of *nurture* he is part of us', or even 'as part of *culture*'? For 'nurture' and 'culture' are words for those agencies which release human nature into actualizing certain potencies which otherwise might not be actualized at all. And may not poetry be one of these?

These are unpopular thoughts because they go against the democratic grain. Helen Vendler's implicit invitation – 'Come one, come all' – is by contrast frank, expansive and buoyant. Yet there is a longer tradition behind thinking of poetry in the opposite way – as something that will at any time be practiced only by an elite, a semisecret society of initiates, and by them only on special occasions, perhaps ritually prepared for but through recent centuries rather more often seen as unpredictable. And by 'practice' I have in mind at this point the practice of writing poetry, rather than the reading of it. For we all know that in modern American society, whereas the practice of reading poetry (as distinct from *studying* it) seems far from wide-spread, yet the practice of writing it, producing it, seems to expand explosively with each year that passes. Though the reading of poetry seems not to be a democratic activity, the writing of it abundantly is. Turn a stone, and start a poet. Were there so many poets, ever, as there seem to be through these last years in the United States? Even that tiny proportion of them that in one way or another get published constitute a throng so numerous that no one can begin to keep track or take stock of it. And isn't that, when we think about it, just what we might expect from the programme 'Part of nature, part of us'? Come one, come all – but it is poets who come, not readers. Helen Vendler has done her part in 'winnowing', in 'taking stock' – as in two poetry-chronicles, one of eight poets, one of ten, reprinted here from the *Yale Review*; and she's not such a democrat that she isn't properly severe on inflated reputations, and on writers who have rushed into print before they have learned their trade. And yet it is down here in the underbrush that I sometimes find myself at a loss to know what value she expects me to put on the poetry she discusses. From one poet for instance, C.K. Williams, whom she reproves sharply enough for some faults, she quotes the indeed charming line: 'A whole section of the city I live in has been urban renewed.' And she remarks: 'A man who could write that line can get all of our speech down, if he wants to. Williams is a speech poet, riding on the inflections of American voices, refusing epigram, conclusion, and distillation in favour of narrative, digressions, interpolations, and above all, a buttonholing assertion of the interest of the whole hectic organism which his poems see as life.' I can see what she means from the quotations she gives, and I am interested and entertained. Nor do I mind that she doesn't trade off plus against minus so as to assign this poet, as it were, a grade. What I'm not clear about, however, is what value I'm to put on 'getting all of our speech down'. This has some value to be sure; but is it enough to compensate for the lack of 'epigram, conclusion, and distillation'?

I don't know the answer to this, nor perhaps does C.K. Williams, nor Helen Vendler herself. Indeed I suspect that the question would stump most poets writing in America today, and most of their readers – that's why it seems worth insisting on. There are those among us who have an answer, however. Most of the readers of the *Southern Review*, and most of the poets who appear there, would surely answer: 'No, getting American speech down is *not* something for which I'll trade distillation and conciseness.' On the other hand, admirers of Ginsberg and Frank O'Hara, even of Whitman (the three names Mrs Vendler invokes in relation to C.K. Williams), would surely tend to reply: 'Yes, the bargain is a good one – what's so great about the epigrammatic anyhow?' And it is surely these latter, those who would strike the bargain, whose voices are heard most often. Their confidence in declaring their option is one result of a revolution in taste and theory, now more than twenty years old, which Jerome Mazzaro painstakingly documents in what would have been a very useful book if only Mazzaro wrote better English. This is the revolution from 'modernism', still a going concern for the late Allen Tate, to what Mazzaro calls, reasonably enough, 'postmodernism'. This last, though it appears to be a peculiarly (perhaps parochially) American phenomenon, originates – so Mazzaro interestingly argues – with Auden, and oddly enough with Auden while he was still living in Britain, not after he'd become a New Yorker. More precisely, postmodernism originates not with the youthful Auden himself, but with what American readers made of that British poet after they'd been reading him for some years. And no one of those American readers was more important than Randall Jarrell. Helen Vendler says, unkindly I think (and she's not usually unkind), that Jarrell 'put his genius into his criticism and his talent into his poetry'. But certainly Jarrell's criticism has been, and still is, vastly more influential than his poems; and he was influential not just through print but in his lifetime through conversation – notably on his friend Robert Lowell. This was very important because it meant that postmodernism was then espoused not just by the O'Haras and Ginsbergs, those whom Helen Vendler calls 'speech poets' (among whom I wish she could have brought herself to consider Ed Dorn), but also by those more formal and even academic poets whom Mazzaro considers: Roethke and Ignatow, Berryman and Plath and Elizabeth Bishop. The attention to American speech-habits indeed is only one, and not the most important, characteristic of postmodernism. As Mazzaro says:

> In conceiving of language as a fall from unity, modernism seeks to restore the original state often by proposing silence or the destruction of language; postmodernism accepts the division and uses language and self-definition … as the basis of identity. Modernism tends, as a consequence, to be more mystical in the traditional senses of that word whereas postmodernism, for all its seeming mysticism, is irrevocably worldly and social. Rather than T.S. Eliot's belief that poetry 'is not the expression of personality, but an escape from personality,' postmodernists propose the opposite.

This explains, in a literary world dominated by postmodernists, not only why we have more poets than we know how to deal with but why each of those poets writes too much. More precisely postmodernist poets and readers inhabit a world of poetry where the very idea of 'too much' no longer has any meaning. We have seen this already in the way that we are required no longer to ask or look for terseness, the epigrammatic, the *distilled*. But it goes further than that: if, as Mazzaro says, postmodernism 'uses language … as the basis of identity', then the overriding injunction for the postmodernist poet is *to keep writing*; for he loses his identity as soon as he stops hammering language onto his typewriter. Is this not the explanation of Lowell's and Berryman's determination – surely monstrous from one point of view, though perversely heroic from another – to keep on pounding out their poems day by day, though their lives were falling into chaos around them? In postmodernist poetics the distinction between a long poem and a short one has collapsed, not to speak of those nicer distinctions that were possible while the doctrine of *genres* still had a sort of posthumous and phantasmal life among us. The one and only poetic form, for postmodernism, is the diary – as Lowell recognized when he published *Notebook*; the diary entry is a short poem, though open at both ends, and the diary is not just a long poem but interminable, by definition inconclusive and inconcludable. Did Lowell or Berryman write and publish too many poems? The question is meaningless. And silence, that effect which Mallarmé at the start of modernism treasured above all else as the unuttered, hovering on the white paper between two blocs of utterance, now in postmodernist poetics is the void, self-annihilation, to be avoided at all costs. Hence ... too many poets, and also too many poems. And in the process, since great swatches of poetry are going dirt-cheap all around us, and more is pouring off the conveyor-belt every second (Mazzaro is surely right to see the postmodern aesthetic as 'industrial'), how can poetry not be devalued? Everyone has some, can get or can make as much as he wants; poetry not only mirrors, but *is part of,* what Mrs Vendler calls 'the whole hectic organism' of us living together as we do. We cannot get back (nor should any one want to) to the position of thinking that some themes and some intentions are beneath the dignity of poetry. But might we not set up a hierarchy of ends for poetry to aim at? And in such a hierarchy might not the keeping of verse-diaries and the notation on paper of American speech, rank low?

These questions do not arise for William Pritchard, concerned as he is with the poets of that now-distant era we call 'modernism'; Yeats and Frost, Pound and Eliot, Stevens and Crane (though also Robinson and Hardy, also W.C. Williams). Of those many pages of the *Cantos* where Pound garrulously ruminates, or pencil in hand excitedly underlines and excerpts the book he is reading, Pritchard has no qualms about deciding 'This will never do' – faithfully though Uncle Ez has captured American speech-rhythms, and integral though his annotated reading was to the diary of his life. Conversely both 'elevation' and 'silence' (he explicitly uses the first concept, and could well have used the second) serve Pritchard well in what is I think the finest of these essays, the one on Frost. He has been chided for presumptuously challenging comparison, by his title, with Dr Johnson's *Lives of the Poets*; and it is true that Johnson's position *vis-à-vis* his culture (not that he was its 'spokesman' – emphatically he was not) is so different from Pritchard's *vis-à-vis his* culture, that we are made, more than Pritchard intends, aware of the great disparity between his enterprise and Johnson's. Indeed Johnson's evenhanded enumeration of points for and points against is more like Helen Vendler's procedure than it is like Pritchard's, so concerned as he is – quite explicitly by the end – in setting up a hierarchy among the poets and the poetic achievements that he considers. All the same I think I see, and I honour, the reason why Pritchard wanted to evoke the Johnsonian model: he wanted to reassert the validity and the necessity of the critic's role as not just interpretative but *judicial.* He wanted, that is, to adumbrate precisely that hierarchy of poetic ends which postmodern poetry, and postmodern criticism like Helen Vendler's, either does not want or else can smuggle in only as a sort of contraband. On his final scoresheet, for those who are interested, it is Yeats and Frost, Eliot and Stevens, who come out tops. But these final rankings are less worth attending to, and quibbling about, than the challenging assumption that for a reader who really cares a scoresheet, a ranking, a hierarchy there has to be. That, but also the explicit admission that love is something else again. Thus, among the four modernist masters whom Pritchard most respects, there are two whom he loves. They are Eliot and Frost – a surprising conjunction, and one that will not recommend itself to Helen Vendler, who can be seen in her comments on Eliot to be struggling, not always successfully, against a temperamental antipathy to Eliot and a more conscious antipathy to institutional Christianity. Pritchard, I think, has to struggle with a similar temperamental antipathy to Stevens. But just this, surely, is the noblest spectacle that the critical activity affords us: the struggle between love and justice; the determination to do justice to a man or a woman whom we unreflectingly dislike; and, conversely, the determination not to weigh the scales in favour of the poet we are in love with. This drama, it is evident, is possible only when the critic does not refuse the judicial function.

Any critic in some degree abdicates this function when he is party to anything like *The Harvard Guide to Contemporary American Writing*. Yet smuggling is still possible; and only a very naïve reader will fail to notice the contraband that Daniel Hoffman smuggles into the three essays which he, besides masterminding the whole encyclopaedic enterprise, writes on American poetry since 1945. It's not hard to discern for instance that Hoffman vehemently disapproves of both Charles Olson and John Ashbery, whereas he strongly approves of Anthony Hecht (whose absence from Mrs Vendler's purview is striking and may be significant). What one questions is why anybody at Harvard University Press thought this an enterprise worth undertaking, and why Daniel Hoffman undertook the commission. To the first question I'm at a loss for an answer; to the second, Hoffman's participation, I suspect the answer may be that Hoffman thought, by immolating himself on this treadmill, to halt, if not to reverse or heal, the ravages of postmodernism. 'If you can't beat 'em, join 'em' is advice as good for literary as for any other kind of politics; and Hoffman, by attempting the impossible, has highlighted how impossible it is not just to judge but even to categorize American poetry in the age of postmodernism. For reasons that we have glanced at, the sheer bulk of what offers itself as American poetry through recent decades defeats any attempt at discrimination. And so of course Daniel Hoffman fails – as he had to; one poet who rates an essay from Mrs Vendler, Louise Glück, gets from Hoffman no notice at all, nor does David Ignatow, who gets a chapter from Jerome Mazzaro; and Ed Dorn, who is named by Hoffman, is named and that's all. When Donald Hall told London (*TLS*, 5 September 1980) that 'this Harvard Guide is an unrivalled map to slovenly academic America', he was being just but also uncharitable. In the age of the postmodern, discrimination is out of the question; when poetry becomes democratically available to everyone as a mode of expression, then it becomes as amorphous as democracy is.

And so, when one envisages the treadmill that Daniel Hoffman has laboured upon, the sheer *slog* involved in at least looking at so many of what offer themselves as volumes of verse, the mind boggles. Helen Vendler after all, not to speak of William Pritchard, harnessed herself to something much less exacting. She and Pritchard too advance as their principle of discrimination something that they call 'voice' – a remarkably capacious and therefore serviceable notion. Mrs Vendler says: 'A poem by Ammons does not sound like a poem by Merrill, and neither sounds like a poem by Lowell. It is given to only a handful of people in each century, in any language, to invent a written voice that sounds like no one else's. All other poets of the century become part of a common music, but the voices of genius live vividly in their oddness and their intensity.' Well, yes, one reflects uncomfortably, but so do the voices of *cranks*. Does 'genius' in our time mean the same as, or at least overlap with, 'crank'? It would not be strange if this were so; for in an industrial aesthetic, such as postmodernism is, the cranky unmistakable 'signature' corresponds to the brand name. Yet have there not been poets of past centuries of whom we need to say, whether or not we endorse the modernist's high valuation of 'Impersonality', that their distinction and their achievement was in fashioning a voice that was precisely not *theirs* but rather the voice of their age and of their culture? Both Vendler and Pritchard, I believe, are the poorer for not envisaging how this might be so, or else for not bringing to bear on the poetry of our own time this perception that they undoubtedly have, from their study of periods earlier than our own. Lorine Niedecker for instance is a poet whose name appears in none of these books – doubtless because the extremely clipped and succinct style that she perfected precludes any display of a distinctive 'voice'.

The Sewanee Review LXXXIX: 1 (Winter 1981).

33 The British and American Experiences of Poetry

About three weeks ago I received a letter from a publishing house with an address in the United Nations Plaza, New York City. It read, in part:

> Recently a large number of very talented poets have come to our attention whose subject matter, though contemporary, is reminiscent of Dickenson (*sic*) Emerson and Thoreau and other transcendentalist writers. These poets might be called the 'new transcendentalists.'
>
> We have in mind such younger or less well-known poets as ... (XY, YZ, ZX, AZ) ... whose work seems to be following the paths marked out by Thomas Merton, Gary Snyder and Alan (*sic*) Ginsberg in that they turn away from the earlier nihilist tendencies of twentieth century literature and toward a positive view of life based on their knowledge of Eastern thought. It seems to us that the 1960s drug culture, growing into 1970s interest in Zen, Yoga and meditation and other spiritual and quasi-spiritual activities has given birth to a genuine literary movement with deep roots in popular culture ...

Elsewhere in the letter they told me, 'We are interested in forming relationships with respected teachers and researchers in literature who might edit and review collections, write criticism and sample reviews and use some of these editions as text books in their classrooms.' And they put to me the straight question: 'Are we right in thinking that this is a valid new movement in English literature with a potentially broad base of readers? ...'

My answer, I am afraid, was intemperate. I replied that their guess at 'a potentially broad base of readers' for this rubbish was alas all too probably well-founded, but I vehemently denied that what they described was 'a valid new movement in English literature'. I pontificated that the USA was a Western society, necessarily heir to all the guilts as well as the glories of Western European culture since the Ancient Greeks; and that it was childish to think this divided inheritance could be shucked off or bypassed by recourse to the necessarily exotic cultures of the Orient. And I said that, so far from being new, what they called 'the new transcendentalists' represented one of the hoariest recurrent nuisances in American culture – to be found, as they pointed out, in some of the weaker and less considered writings of Emerson and Thoreau, to whom they might add Walt Whitman but certainly not Miss Emily Dickinson of Amherst. I reminded them that W.B. Yeats, sixty years ago – the Irish poet who had taken instruction directly from an Indian Swami – had said that Indian thought as refracted through the sensibilities of New England already in his day failed to hold the attention of responsible thinkers because (he said) it *denied the existence of evil.* I hinted broadly that because he took for granted the reality and the real existence of evil W.B. Yeats doubtless figured for them as representing 'the earlier nihilist tendencies of twentieth century literature'; and I suggested that for 'nihilist' we read 'unillusioned'. Finally, since they had obligingly sent me samples of the work of three of the poets whom they named, I gave it as my opinion that what they wrote was not poetry if by 'poetry' we mean what was written by Ben Jonson or Emily Dickinson or W.B. Yeats.

Well, I enjoyed writing that letter. But I tell you about it in the first place so as to warn you that the matter I have chosen to speak on is one about which people can very easily get hot under the collar, intemperate, rude and acrimonious – so much so indeed that I'm not at all sure it is appropriate for the attentions of what is after all a learned society. I have two good friends – one a British poet, one an American, both of them civilized and educated, even *courtly* people – who for some months now have been conducting in various journals a desultory quarrel about the friendship, during and before the First World War, of the American poet Robert Frost and the Anglo-Welsh poet Edward Thomas; my British friend suavely hinting that the Englishman was just as good a poet as the American, my American friend maintaining that Edward Thomas was a pint-size version of Frost, a sort of 'clone'. I am almost ashamed to reveal that discussions of this kind can be so petty, can so patently muddy the waters of the Pierian spring with considerations of national status and *amour-propre*. Almost … I am *almost* ashamed. And yet when we come right down to it I am not ashamed at all; for to poets nationality *matters*, deeply and intensely and quite properly. The earnest and ambitious poet conceives of himself as called on to *utter*, to give utterance to, the otherwise inarticulate values and desires of his people, his nation. Consider only, in this connection, the heroic martyrdoms invited and endured by Russian poets of this century – by Pasternak and Mandelstam, Akhmatova and Tsvetaeva – in the service of this vocation. A lot is at stake, for the poets on both sides, in these civil or not so civil altercations about the American and the British experiences of poetry – to which we might add, were there world enough and time, the Australian experience, the Canadian and the Caribbean experiences, and others.

What makes the Anglo-American, the Anglo-Australian, Anglo-Caribbean confrontations so hard to deal with is a phrase in that letter from

New York publishers that I didn't bother to quarrel with, though I might have. They asked me, you remember: 'Are we right in thinking that this is a valid new movement in English literature ...?' In *English* literature, you note, not American – though all the writers they seek to promote, and all the precedents they quote, are in fact American. If we ask ourselves what 'English' can mean in that expression 'English Literature' as they use it, we can only suppose that it means Anglophone, 'in the English language'. We are invited to suppose, therefore, that there is a homogeneous literature produced variously in Birmingham, England; in Edmonton, Canada; in Kingston, Jamaica; in Adelaide, South Australia; and elsewhere – though overwhelmingly or predominantly, so we are to understand, within a radius of a few hundred miles from United Nations Plaza, New York. Guilelessly, and without meaning any harm, my correspondents from United Nations Plaza (the address seems steadily more appropriate and significant) suppose that there is an Anglophone culture world-wide, of which the natural and inevitable metropolitan centre is not many yards from where they sit, writing to me. (And they write to me in Nashville, Tennessee – did it not occur to them that in doing so they were crossing a cultural frontier, even within the continental United States? Apparently it did not.) In assuming thus, and writing thus, they were – though I'm sure they were unaware of it – paying out the British for many decades of similar, not altogether unintentional, condescension; until well into the present century – and indeed even at the present day instances may be cited – the British assumed that London was the cultural metropolis of the Anglophone world, the seat of normal usage by reference to which all other usages were to be judged as 'provincial' or 'colonial'. Now that cultural metropolis is no longer Fleet Street, London; but United Nations Plaza, New York. Tit for tat! But there is no wonder if such a momentous shift of cultural authority provokes a certain querulousness, a certain acrimony.

It is time to confront the central issue. Though it must be true that the hegemony of a certain language – English, with its resources and also its limitations – imposes a certain homogeneity on all the cultures which use that language; yet the post-colonialist condition of a Caribbean poet, even of an American poet, must mean that his cultural stance cannot be homogeneous with that of an Englishman, representative of the erstwhile colonizing power. And so for my part (for these are matters that *I live with*) I long ago decided to agree with T.S. Eliot, that native American naturalized Briton, that what we have is two and potentially many more literatures inside one language. (Eliot remarked that he thought this situation was unprecedented.) Only if we thus firmly recognize our distinctness, Briton against American, can we move forward from the twilight in which at the moment we grapple and collide haphazard. What Eliot proposes to us is that, however the American and the British literary traditions may have been intertwined in the past, now they must be recognized as essentially *distinct*. And only if we proceed on this assumption, can we establish comparisons between them that shall not be *invidious* comparisons, of the nature of 'Which comes off better? Which shapes up worse?' This is what I tell myself repeatedly, though sometimes in vain, as I try to make sense of the situation that I have chosen for myself – of being a British, indeed an English poet, living and working most of the time in the US, having (I am glad to know) American readers on the one hand, British readers on the other. I cannot fail to recognize, and in practice to allow for, notable differences in the expectations and assumptions which these two sets of readers bring to the reading of poetry, including of course (and very urgently from my point of view) the poems that I write myself.

The first such difference that I am constantly aware of is one that many of you will have arrived at for yourselves. It is implicit in that letter which I have already made such play with; but I can sharpen the point of it by referring to a modest book lately published in England, called *An Introduction to 50 American Poets*. Although the author of this book is an Englishman, he has surprisingly and admirably (so far as I can see) no axe to grind and no post-imperialist resentments to satisfy. And it's instructive to see how, chronologically, he shares out the fifty poets that he has to play with – in his scheme eleven American poets, no more, take us from 1620 to 1900; and there remain thirty-nine poets, no less, to represent the last eighty years. It is my impression that an American writing such a book would not allocate his poets very differently. And if I were to undertake such a commission, I wouldn't distribute my poets very differently. And yet to a British reader – even if, like me, he thinks that the present century has seen a prodigious flowering of American poetry – such a disproportion between the present and the past, or between the immediate and the more remote past, is inherently implausible. Eleven poets to represent 280 years of your history, and thirty-nine to represent the last eighty years – does it seem likely that this is a just estimate? And in fact the chronological time-span can be scrutinized to yield even more startling disproportions. Thus, the first 200 years of the white man in North America provide just two names – Anne Bradstreet and Edward Taylor; whereas forty-eight poets are taken from America since 1820. Similarly, in an anthology published in New York a few years ago, a book which advertises itself with justice as 'A New Reading of American Poetry from Pre-Columbian Times to the Present', we are offered, out of more than 300 items, just six that were written in English in North America before 1800. Six, out of more than 300! Does that seem plausible? To be sure, there are demographic and other circumstances that might explain some of these disproportions; and a British reader will almost certainly give less weight to these than he should. But all the same, his incredulity is surely not misplaced. And his incredulity may properly prompt suspicions and disquiets that are far-reaching. May he not legitimately see the intrusion here, in these disproportions, of an assumption of PROGRESS, of this year's 'improved model' conclusively replacing last year's? And may he not legitimately protest that, however built-in obsolescence may be a feature of industrial production, in artistic production it has no place? That in the art of poetry 'Progress' has no meaning at all? That no one has ever *improved on* Homer or Ovid, Catullus or Dante? However that may be, he is surely right to be alarmed at the foreshortening of historical perspective that presents as 'the antique', as 'an ancient master', a figure no more remote from us in historical time than Ralph Waldo Emerson. For the British reader it is at any rate possible, though it is no doubt foolish, to rule out the entire nineteenth century as an unfortunate aberration in the history of poetry – after all a hundred years is very little in the history of poetry since Hesiod or even Catullus. But for an American reader such a response is much more difficult, perhaps impossible.

To be sure, Chaucer and Shakespeare, Spenser and Milton, Dryden and Pope and Oliver Goldsmith are as much yours as they are mine – if you want them; and that means that your historical perspective, as Americans, could be or should be just as long as mine, the Englishman's. But – and from here on I must admit to proceeding by impressions – my impression is that by and large you *don't* want them, these great poets; that for you they belong in the pre-history of your poetry, not in its history as perpetually and inexhaustibly relevant to you in the here and now. By and large through recent decades American scholarship has served these great poets of our common past better than British scholarship has – and the British are not so ashamed of that as they ought to be; but I'm afraid there is another side to the coin – a poet may be available to scholarship precisely because, and at the point when, he is no longer a living presence in the poetry that we write and read for ourselves, here and now.

I am rather keenly conscious of just where I am, as I make these remarks. I am standing in a place where, fifty or sixty years ago, a group of young poets and scholars certainly proceeded on the assumption that John Milton and Alexander Pope, Virgil and the author of the *Pervigilium Veneris*, were as pertinent to them as Americans, and to their American readers, as they were to their British contemporaries. In this those Vanderbilt Fugitives may have been wrong. Certainly communications from New York and New Haven, such as the letter that was sent to me, suggest that they were wrong; as do (I am forced to say) certain attitudes that I encounter quite often among Vanderbilt students today, both undergraduate and graduate. But if those men were wrong, they were gallantly wrong; and it's not surprising if I look back wistfully to their writings as testimony to a state of affairs in which there was not, or might not have been, such a gulf fixed as there now is between the American and the British experiences of poetry. I long ago learned, from experiences in the West as well as here in the South, that American culture is not so homogeneous as my correspondents from United Nations Plaza seem to assume, and that the true metropolis of that culture is not necessarily in their vicinity. But their blithe disregard of that possibility – is it not what we expect of people who live with such foreshortened perspectives, who think that they can junk the entire cultural inheritance of the West by way of a whimsical turning instead towards Zen and Yoga? For them the history even of their own nation cannot be other than what Henry Ford called it – 'bunk'. And our common language, which registers in etymology and semantic change every phase of that history (American and behind that, British) – how can that language fare at their doubtless well-meaning hands? And yet that language, nothing else, is the medium out of which we carve our poems, whether we are American or British.

What I have been suggesting, as the first and perhaps pre-eminent difference between the British and the American experiences of poetry at the present day, is this: that the British poet and his British reader are conscious of contributing to a venture continuous since at least Geoffrey Chaucer, whereas the American poet and his American reader are likely to think that the enterprise he is engaged in dates back, for practical purposes, no further than Emerson. (This emphatically does *not* mean, incidentally, that the British reader has fuller and more exact *information* about Chaucer than the American has.) From this discrepancy arise certain consequences. And one of them irritates me a good deal – because the British reader is aware, however nebulously, of how many poets there have been writing English in how many historical generations, he is a great deal cooler, more guarded and more captious about contemporary writing than the American is. And so it is my American, not my British, readers who supply me with heart-warmingly enthusiastic responses, which are necessary to me and for which I am grateful. It was the British poet, W.H. Auden, who said that 'poetry makes nothing happen' – and the British stomach that hard saying sooner than Americans do. Indeed my compatriots stomach it so readily and so complacently that I am often moved to protest: 'Making things happen isn't the only honourable objective for human beings to aim at.' Secondly (and this is no doubt a profound difference between the two cultures, one that shows up in many spheres besides poetry) the American typically regards the past as something to be surpassed, the British as something to be preserved and at best equalled, certainly not transcended. The American regards the past as something to be improved on; the Englishman (and of course I mean the responsible Englishman, for we produce as many raucous vulgarians as any other nation) sees the past as something to be *not too shamefully fallen away from*.

I will return one more time to the letter that reached me from United Nations Plaza. I have received letters just as foolish from England, and often enough indeed serving the same foolish manifestation – 'the 1960s

drug culture, growing into the 1970s interest in Zen, Yoga and meditation and other spiritual and quasi-spiritual activities ...' What I have not
found in them, nor would expect to find, is any appeal to nineteenth-
century authorities – to Emerson and Thoreau, or to their British
contemporaries, as it might be Thomas Carlyle or Lord Tennyson. But
what I might very well find, though conveyed in a somewhat more
muffled or circumspect vocabulary, is the appeal to 'a positive view of life'.
This is part of the common legacy of what the late General de Gaulle used
to call 'Anglo-Saxondom'; a persistent assumption on the part of both our
peoples that the poet should be a moralist and sage, an educator, one who
teaches us how to *live* better, 'more positively'. Whether or not this is in
fact an 'Anglo-Saxon' characteristic (for I seem to detect a moralistic strain
just as vehement in other ethnic strains in America besides the Anglo-
Saxon), I am Anglo-Saxon enough myself not to be ashamed of it. Yes, I
believe that the poet *is* in some sense moralist and sage and educator. But
I think it may well be true that we all, British and American alike, have a
strikingly naïve and old-fashioned idea of the way in which the poet takes
on these additional roles. The challenge to our preconceptions on this
matter comes, as General de Gaulle would have been happy to admit,
from the French; from certain French poets of the last century who have
a better title than any one else to be thought the fathers of Anglo-
American modernism in poetry. There *is* an important sense in which the
Baudelaire who wrote *Les Fleurs du mal* is a great moralist as well as a great
poet; and it's significant that T.S. Eliot devoted an important essay to
teasing out in just what way that might be true. It certainly isn't true in
any way that can be provided for by my correspondents' distinction
between 'the nihilist' and 'the positive'. And one remembers the anecdote
that W.B. Yeats records with such relish – of Paul Verlaine reading *In
Memoriam*, and commenting in disappointment that he had expected the
English poet to be heart-broken, whereas instead he had had noble senti-
ments. Poetic vision and moral vision are, I am sure, interconnected; but
those interconnections are far more devious and subtle than has ever been
recognized either by the British (for whom morality is mostly social and
quasi-Marxist) or by the American (for whom it is mostly individualistic
and quasi-Freudian). At this point I am as much at one with my American
poet-friends as with my British ones: we each and all of us write for publics
which are defiantly and complacently *monoglot*, and the more so with each
year that passes. And in both nations there are poets who in one way or
another appeal to, and sustain, the linguistic and therefore cultural insularity of their readers; for which of course they duly receive their rewards
in popular acclaim. But the necessarily few good and responsible poets in
each nation know that not all the valuable perceptions have so far been
recorded in English; and accordingly that the enterprise they are enrolled
in transcends national and linguistic boundaries. And this, it should be

clear, in no way belies what I insisted on earlier – the seriousness with which poets take nationality.

So far in this matter I have been able to proceed with some confidence, and you I think have been able to decide whether my contentions are persuasive. But I cannot conclude without reminding you that poetry is a mysterious affair, and that we may well have advanced only to the frontier of an obscure and largely uncharted region wherein, it may well be, there lie hidden those differences between us that are most radical and intractable. I mean that vast region of our experience which we gesture at, for the most part helplessly, under the name of *rhythm*. There is not much we can say of this, though we know that we ought to say a great deal. One thing we can say, surely: we are talking about the speech-habits of our two peoples, and the difference between them. You are experiencing this as you listen to me, as you *hear* me. Though you know how speech-habits vary from one section to another of this country, still you know, hearing me, that you are not hearing an American voice. Where this difference lies, who can say? In pace, tempo, pitch, enunciation – in all these things, and more. Tongue, larynx, teeth and lips are doing things in my mouth that they do not do in yours and *vice versa*. The difference goes as deep as that – as deep as if the difference were physiological. And what you hear from me is only one variant of British speech, which varies from section to section of the British Isles, indeed from region to region merely of England, as widely as American speech varies between Maine and Mississippi. Confronted with this bewildering array of variables and imponderables we throw up our hands and recognize a mystery. We do so too easily; there have been – and obscurely there still are – phoneticians on the one hand, and prosodists on the other, who have let some beams of light into the murk, and we rather scandalously fail to attend to them and to what they have to tell us. But all the same they would be the first to acknowledge that they are operating only on the skirts and fringes of what will remain, and probably ought to remain, a mystery. Somewhere inside that mystery, inside what we recognize as the different *musics* of our two sorts of speech, dwells, I am sure, the profoundest and never-to-be-elucidated difference between the British and American experiences of poetry.

Cumberland Poetry Review Vol. I No. 1 (Winter 1981).

Index of names